From Ghetto to Ghetto

Ernest H. Adams

From Ghetto to Ghetto

An African American Journey to Judaism

By Ernest H. Adams

Grace Edwards, Editor

iUniverse, Inc.
New York Bloomington

From Ghetto to Ghetto: An African American Journey to Judiasm

Grace Edwards, Editor

iUniverse books may be ordered through booksellers or by contacting:

iUniverse
1663 Liberty Drive
Bloomington, IN 47403
www.iuniverse.com
1-800-Authors (1-800-288-4677)

ISBN: 978-1-4401-2085-5 (pbk)
ISBN: 978-1-4401-2086-2 (ebk)

Printed in the United States of America

iUniverse rev. date: 2/18/2009

Little in human history is inevitable…

David Brion Davis

If you are willing to go to the light, you have to be willing to face the darkness.

Marcia Landau, 1994 (NYT)

CONTENTS

Prologue

The Soul Has No Color

Rabbi Simon Jacobson

He [William James] is a man for our age in his belief that we are all of us afflicted with a certain blindness 'in regard to the feelings of creatures and people different from ourselves.' He understood, and he said repeatedly, how hard it is to really see things, to see anything, from another's point of view.

Robert D. Richardson

Today is Saturday, January 15, 2000, but Saturday is no longer Saturday and tomorrow begins when the sun goes down: it is Shabbat, and the day of my Bar Mitzvah. Also, it is the birthday of Martin Luther King Jr. I lay in bed, in the dark, wondering about all I have to do in a few hours: leyne (chant) the Torah and the Haftorah, and give a dvar Torah, a sermon. As sleep leaves and the dawn rises, I muse about how I had arrived to this day.

According to Jewish Law I was a Jew when I emerged from the mikvah and answered the inquiries posed by the beit din (Jewish court). Though joyously embracing Jews and Judaism, I felt incomplete: possessed with a burgeoning need to feel like a "real" Jew. My drive to become a "real" Jew was not rooted in any experience I suffered in the Jewish community. The meta-rationale was driven by a gnawing desire to know the sages better, to know Hebrew, to study Torah, to understand the complexity and confusion of God not always clear to me: to be as close to understanding God to the best of my human capability.

The heart of the modern ritual that I found the most intriguing and the most daunting was the writing of a dvar Torah. What could I say that was worthy of people listening and learning? Could I be a teacher of God's word and spirit and impart a moral lesson that was worthy of consideration? It had to be a teaching that was dynamic and original. I wondered aloud if I could produce a teaching that was as worthy as all the many dvrei Torah I had not merely heard, but experienced.

The reason I chose January 15 was that the Torah portion had a biblical vibrancy with the story of the Exodus—many say the defining event of the Jewish people—Pharaoh, the plagues, and freewill. My self-doubts were transparent as Rabbi Marcelo Bronstein nodded his head ever so slowly, reassuring me, "I will help you." I found comfort in his offer of support. "Ernie, Roly and I are not speaking that day, it is all on you," Rabbi Bronstein said.

"Rabbi for a day!" I chuckled silently as my heart picked up speed. Black Junebug, ghetto boy from 129th Street, was going to be a rabbi for a day. It doesn't get anymore surreal than that.

I knew I was going to apply my rendering of the Torah based on my sojourn as a Negro colored boy growing up in Harlem, young Black man coming of age, African American man maturing with age, an African American Jewish man be-coming of age and, the last stop, a Jewish man.

In full mental operation was the notion that black people have to perform at above average levels to be recognized as merely competent, the ubiquitous double standard every black person recognizes. Though I felt reassured by Rabbi Bronstein's offer of support, I was also sure of one thing: I needed to do it alone, without anyone's help; Black Ernest had to do his Jewish thing alone. I needed to prove to myself that I could develop a moral teaching and modern lesson from the ancient stories in the Torah, with a universal lesson derived from my ghetto experiences, with a Jewish credibility and God's imprimatur.

The prototypical question from many synagogue mates, "What are you going to say?" In the initial stages of my thinking I only had vague responses and the typical retorts were, "Who is working with you," said with a presumption my dvar Torah would be fatal if done by me without assistance.

Or so it sounded to me.

Another popular question, "How are you going to deal with God taking away Pharaoh's free-will yet holding him responsible for the Israelite enslavement?"

"I am going to argue that God did not take away Pharaoh's freewill," I said hesitantly, not wanting to discuss ideas not fully developed.

"That's going to be hard to prove, the commentators say…" I tuned out, since it was being said as if it was impossible to prove.

That was how I heard it. I was annoyed at being challenged in that manner. Very annoyed.

"The rabbis will help you," said sympathetically, but, as if I was intellectually challenged.

So it sounded to me.

"Fuck you, fuck the rabbis, and the motherfucking horse you rode in on," I thought with black fury, as I was being ever so amiable while placing a fork full of Shabbat lunch in my mouth at the home of a good friend. My black baggage was spilling over.

I am not saying that all such inquiries had racial motives. Why take anyone's comments as racially tinged? After all, Socratic inquiry is part of the Jewish tradition. Rabbi Bronstein's offer of help I took as rabbinic support supplied to all Bar Mitzvahs. Why not see my shul mates as being supportive like the rabbi? One person gave me notes (that I did not use) from a class she had taken to help give me some ideas. Sometimes I wondered, even as some spoke, "Are they responding to me this way because I am black?" It is a constant measuring stick, a survival shtick.

What is important here is the chronic bleeding, chronic hurt, from the chronic wounds dispensed by the chronic racist ecology, and the result you witness is the torture of me trying to figure out, "Is it safe?" May I let down my guard, relax, turn off the sensor, have it fade from red to black, and use my God given senses? "Hell No!"

This "stuff" is part of my instinct, character, thought processes and emotional make up; it influences how I learn, and how I teach. And so all of my stuff: the good, the bad, the beautiful, the ugly, the confusion, the racial, went into creating and the giving of my dvar Torah.

With no specific idea about what I wanted to say I delved into the Torah and began rummaging around. Ideas did not flow readily, and a story was not emerging. Rabbi Finkelstein said when he prays he speaks to God, but when he reads Torah, God speaks to him. I was witness to a silence from God.

But I kept re-reading the Torah portion looking for a "new" story, but little was forthcoming. Then, when re-reading for the umpteenth time, I experienced a dynamic encounter with the text. "The same day Pharaoh charged the taskmasters and foreman of the people saying, 'you shall no longer provide the people with straw for bricks as heretofore; let them go and gather straw for themselves. But impose upon them the same quota of bricks as they have been making heretofore; do not reduce it, for they are shirkers; that is why they cry, 'Let us go and sacrifice to our God!'" (Exodus 5: 6-8) The fingers of the text touched me, slowly gripped me, and as it held firmly, a new meaning began to galvanize forthwith and would lie at the core of my dvar Torah.

The cruel demands orchestrated by Pharaoh were an ancient biblical tale of exploitation and degradation. Across millennium and disparate historical context and conditions, thoughts and ideas were rocket-propelled, sans hesitation, from the ancient Israelite experience to the modern American experience. They crashed through my learning process like a meteorite. When the intellectual dust settled, new thoughts had landed with an abrupt thump, but with excitement and my understanding as the welcome committee: "This is the African American experience, this is the same standard to which black people are held today," I said out loud. Since slavery, white Americans have used the pharaonic standard to judge black Americans.

Rabbi Finkelstein was right. God began to speak to me.

Growing up in Harlem, the distance between Negroes and Jews grew as I grew up and I knew little of commonality. Every piece of information I heard, even from loved ones without a racial edge and a healthy respect for Jews, pointed out the obvious differences. My Uncle Charlie, of blessed memory, in describing how Jews were able to be successful and black folk could not, said, "The difference between a black man and a Jew, you don't know if he is a Jew until he is right up on you, but a nigger, you can see a mile away."

However, there was convergence between some Jewish and black friends, albeit for different reasons, around my perceived politically incorrect and gleeful state and statement that, "I'm going to be a Bar Mitzvah *boy*." The fact that I was an adult performing an adolescent rite was emphasized by two rabbis, who invariably centered on the language as inadequate given my age, "You are a man," "You are not a boy," each said, annoyed. "Ben Mitzvah" or "Ben Torah" (Ben means son) was their suggested alternatives. Amused that they took offense, I explained that my black manhood did not feel threatened. They remained unconvinced. B'nai Jeshurun officially dubbed me Bar Torah. (Bar means son)

When I chortled exuberantly to a group of black friends that I was to be a Bar Mitzvah boy, comments streamed in: "How do you call yourself 'boy' as a black man?"

"You are disrespecting yourself."

"Can't the rabbis make you a Bar Mitzvah man?"

Laughing, I explained that I still was very much a man, a black man; that it was my choice to use boy, in the term Bar Mitzvah boy, which offered faint solace to my black friends.

Two days before my Bar Mitzvah I was visiting Stanley Futterman, a dear friend of twenty-eight years, lawyer and fellow Jew, in his oak wood panel office. Stanley loves me and was a staunch advocate for my conversion. As we schmoozed, he was leaning back in the comfort of his cushioned leather swivel chair with his feet hanging off, bobbing slowly from left to right. Unable to contain his curiosity he thought out loud, "What are you going to say on Saturday?"

"I will give you and you only just a snippet," I teased. "The heart of it is the notion that God's rescue of the Jews was the first tikkun olam—repair of the world—the first example of Affirmative Action. In its essence, Affirmative Action was designed to help out disenfranchised people."

His chair stopped moving, he sat up, his feet touched the floor, and he gripped the chair handles with his elbows out and his shoulders hunched up to his ears, he looked straight at me and in exasperation said, "Is that what you are going to do to *us*?"

Us, the first person plural, reverberated in my head. *Us,* sounded like every white Jew and, *Not Me*. I felt excluded from the tribe. *Us* resounded throughout my being and my collective ancestral memory echoed: *Us Blacks* versus *them Whites*.

I flashed to the Sixties Black Power radical Rap Brown's description of American justice: "*Just-us, just-us white folks*."

* * *

The increasing daylight in my apartment interferes with my musing, and it reorients me to today's agenda: chant the Torah and Haftorah and give a dvar Torah. I learned to chant the Torah by learning the Torah trop, wordless melodies indicated by seemingly random scribble that pass for "notes." Having to chant from the Torah scroll in Hebrew with its absence of vowels, I nervously weigh the likelihood that I will forget how to pronounce the words. I am also afraid that I will mix the Torah trop with the Haftorah trop—the same notes but different melody—when I read the Haftorah from the printed text with vowels. "My dvar, I cannot forget," I say in absolute terror of the possibility I could leave it at home, and end up standing before the congregation trying to remember every word and every sentence with my mind going blank. I recall the Bat Mitzvah girl who recently failed to bring her dvar Torah and stood valiantly naked before the synagogue, stumbling to piece together her words of Torah—she broke down in tears of shame at the conclusion of services.

As I rise from bed, I scold myself not to forget my dvar Torah. Then I remember that I gave Barbara a copy to bring. "But suppose we both forget?" I ask myself. Holding the pages in my hand, I reiterate, "Don't forget the dvar." I wash up. Then I read and reread my Torah portions with the yad—a pointer. Although I have it memorized, confidence eludes me. I keep looking at the clock and the minutes seem shorter this morning. To make sure I am chanting the trop correctly, I practice the melodies one last time, then again, then again. I read the Haftorah and feel okay. I read my dvar Torah again—what will they think? I still have no idea—then place it with my Haftorah text in front of the door so I cannot forget to bring them. I look at the clock, and time tells me it is time to go.

I take a washcloth and lightly wipe the tension that has accumulated doing my final rehearsal. I dress in a dark blue pinstripe custom-made suit, white shirt, and as I tie the knot in my Brioni tie in the mirror, I tell myself to be calm so that I don't sweat too much and stink with body odor. The knot is just right. I say out loud, "Damn, you look good brother. If you do fail you gon' be the best lookin' failur' in history." I smile at my humor. Momentarily relieved, I put on Armani socks, Crockett and Jones shoes, Bergdof Goodman overcoat, and new black hat from Stetson's. My armor is complete.

Still, I feel the pressure to give a dvar Torah that is an enduring and timeless contribution, knowing that I will be held to a higher standard as an adult, an even higher standard as a black man, and even higher self-imposed standard: that I have to "represent" African Americans—my parents, grandparents, ancestors, all black people, and me. I pick up my dvar Torah, yad, Haftorah text, Diagnostic and Statistical Manual for Mental Disorders, and leave for my chosen destiny: to be a Bar Mitzvah boy, at age fifty-three, so I can feel like a real Jew.

I arrive at B'nai Jeshurun and there are the regulars who show up early every week. I look at the bema, and it seems to beam back at me, beckoning for my presence. A shot of nervous energy streaks through my body. I suppress the thought of what it will be like on the bema. I don't want to become any more nervous than I otherwise would be. I take a deep breath. I'd chosen this Shabbat specifically because it coincided with Martin Luther King Jr.'s birthday, so I could honor him, and honor me. He was the best that black people had to offer, he was the best that white people had to offer, the best, that humanity had to offer. On my arrival as a real Jew, there was no better person to accompany me.

I become anxious about how my black guests will fit in, knowing most will feel uncomfortable in a synagogue, and, not so deep-down-inside, most, would not want me to be a Jew. I muse for a moment. It remains somewhat perplexing that such a beloved, admired, and universally respected leader of the African American people failed to bring the majority of us—myself surely included—to the same level of principled commitment to the Jewish people and the state of Israel that he preached and practiced. I can only wonder if Martin Luther King Jr. had lived and written a "dream" speech and marched against the black hardened hearts antagonistic to Jews, Judaism, and Israel, if the African American Weltanschauung would have been altered?

More people stream in and as I greet my black guests, I feel the sadness and disappointment of William Haden's absence. A good friend since college, William Haden failed to respond to my written invitation and follow-up phone calls. I asked his wife Jennifer, "Is William coming to my Bar Mitzvah?" An involuntary sigh came out of her mouth.

Jennifer said she was not coming either, "I'm leaving Saturday morning to see my father," who was sick. She and I had already discussed how significant the Bar Mitzvah was for me, so I did not ask her to postpone, for a few hours, her drive to Pittsburgh, Pennsylvania. Jennifer Haden did not speak to me for nine months, and William Haden did not speak to me for two years.

I see Robert Jekyll, a friend for over thirty years, sitting with his son and nephew. Even though Robert told me he was coming, it was a pleasant surprise because he once baldly asserted, "I will never come to your synagogue, never, but if you invite me to your home and your Jewish friends are there I will come." I go to greet them, and there is an absence of tradition: none wore a yarmulke. An usher, Paula Dubrow, spots the unadorned Afros and enters the conversation uninvited, holding out three yarmulkes in a stiffened arm salute, silently bidding them a traditional response.

Sitting poised and dignified, Robert gently states, "We don't wear *them*."

Unfazed by his polite rudeness, Paula retorts, "It is traditional to wear one in the synagogue."

Rising gracefully out of his seat until he reaches his 6'3" height, Robert looks down at 4'11" Paula and insists with gentle defiance, "We just don't want to wear them."

"Ernie," Paula beseeched. A distressing call for help and all three black faces turn to me.

My first thought was, "My God, what messages are these children receiving from their father and uncle, a learned, respected, active community member?" Both young men appear anxious and their facial expressions suggest they have no idea why their father and uncle chose to throw down the gauntlet now. This is one of the biggest days of my life, and I am feeling tremendous pressure to perform and have things go smoothly. Robert knows this because we discussed on several occasions my concerns about making a credible presentation. I had watched other black friends come in and put on yarmulkes without a prompt precisely because they showed the proper respect for the Jewish tradition. What galled me the most: Robert knew what to expect because his deceased sister was a Jew!

Now I am pissed off. Trying to broker my own anger and disappointment I choose the path of least resistance and say, “It is tradition, but if they don’t-”

Paula cut me off. Armed with the history of blood-stained pogroms and three thousand years of Jewish survival, Paula, compelled to truth, spoke with profound conviction. She looked straight up into Robert’s dark eyes, “It is the *Jewish Tradition*.”

Under the weight of Paula’s uncompromising tone, Robert’s defiance dissolves. He literally slumps back into his seat. He places his right arm on top of the pew, slouches in his seat, face crumbling in sullen silence. He takes the yarmulkes from Paula’s hand, puts one on his head and passes the others to his son and nephew who follow his example. Now, their Afros look respectful, traditional.

Robert is not always overtly hostile and narrow-minded. He has a close relationship with a white Jewish friend, Michael, but said, “He is not really a Jewish Jew, because he thinks practicing pure Judaism is a waste. He combines eastern religion with a little Jewish stuff.”

Robert once told me he attended a professional educational seminar and was the only African American, all the others were white and many were Jews. “There were some bona fide racists in the room.”

“How did you know?”

“I just knew.”

“What was said that was racist?”

“I heard one of them mention something about blacks and Latinos. Could tell they were against *us*, the way they said it.”

“But what did they say?”

“I told you they talked about blacks and Latinos, and I could hear the way they said it they were racist.”

“How did they say it?”

“Like they were racist.”

“But can you be specific?”

“Look, man.” He was annoyed and feeling trapped. “I was there. You know how *they* are, their racist shit can be real subtle, you know that.”

“Yeah, it can be, but be specific, what was said that upset you?”

“I just know they were racist.” He became frustrated and walked away in a huff.

At one time Robert openly dated white women, then went underground. He even dated Jewish women, one as recently as a few years ago. He seemed to be accepting of his sister's conversion but blurted out, "The Jews stole my sister."

With that unholy brushfire extinguished, I go and sit down. Sitting next to me are Liza and Daniel Goldstein, the grandchildren of Rabbi Baruch Goldstein. He is unable to attend because his wife Riva is ill. Sitting in the same row is Rabbi Noah Golinkin, wife Dotty, and their son Abe, a cantor. Now it is time for the service to begin.

* * *

Sitting in the first row as Rabbi Roly Matalon begins the service, all I could think about is my time to ascend the bema. My usual concentration while praying is absent, and five minutes before my turn to go up, I rush to the bathroom to satisfy my lingering fear I would have to go while speaking. I return and feel relieved for one moment. I ascend the bema. Quite off key and quite nervous, I lead the Torah service. My voice is melodiously dysfunctional. Holding the Torah as I walk around the synagogue, I flash back onto the first time I held the Torah, the honor of holding the Torah.

The Torah reading begins, and I listen but do not hear the words being chanted. When I am called to the Torah, my heart is pounding like a boxer's fist against a punching bag. I ascend the bema and look out at the congregation and see a sea of faces. I do not make an effort to distinguish them. I place the yad at the beginning of the sentence and start to chant. My voice is steady and true and melodiously acceptable, even as my heart continues to thump rapidly. The yad and I are moving in tandem and my neshama (soul) and ruach (spirit) pass through the yad into the Torah scroll, and I ride the words of Torah and hear God chanting to and through all of me, as the neshama and ruach of the Torah pass through the yad and enter my soul. God's spirit is kindled. I listen and hear God's "voice" draw me closer to the Awe as waves of vibrations verify my soul.

"An angel of God appeared to him in a blaze of fire from amid the bush. He saw and behold! The bush was burning in the fire, but the bush was not consumed." Exodus 3:2

Now I comprehend that it was Moses who was aflame at the burning bush when made aware of God's presence. God's presence divinely heightened and expanded the neshama and ruach of Moses, and an internal glow sprouted, only to be manifested externally when both Moses and the people had matured. My love of Torah reading is consummated; an internal "glow" has settled in and become an internal "organ." I read the Haftorah and then begin my dvar Torah.

From my jacket, I nervously pull two hand written notes from Shoshana Avner and Stephen Rudin wishing me well, expressing their love and admiration for me. I hold them up for the congregation to see, acknowledge my anxiety, and announce that the two notes will serve as emotional flak jackets, as I place them back inside my jacket. My fears are allayed.

I scan the unusual scene of large numbers of black folk in B'nai Jeshurun, many in the seats I reserved. They look as if they are praying in the designated COLORED SECTION of an 18th century white church; other black folk add splashes of color throughout the synagogue. I continue my visual survey and notice the balcony is several rows deep. It is almost a full house, primarily because there are two baby-naming ceremonies scheduled. I begin to distinguish faces, see family, friends, and mentally acknowledge their presence. I speak slowly and humbly:

In today's parasha we find the usual cast of characters, the usual suspects and themes: God, Pharaoh, Moses, Aaron, Israelites, Egyptians; sex, violence, power, wealth, exploitation, good, evil, redemption. We get action, a chariot chase, special effects, the plagues, Sea of Reeds. There is life, death, winners and losers. Sounds so modern doesn't it? It is Thee classic story, or event that puts God on the map, so to speak, the story that indelibly links God and man forever, sears God into the human consciousness.

I feel a palpable, slow, infusion of energy; like when my mouth is parched, and cool water wets and is absorbed by the dryness.

In all fairness to Pharaoh, who perceived himself as a deity, if I am he and two representatives of the slaves showed up at my door and said they had been hired by the voice of God and was instructed to order me to release the Israelite slaves, I would not be convinced right away. And neither was Pharaoh.

While studying the Torah, I realized that Pharaoh met a psychological profile and I pull out the Diagnostic and Statistical Manual for Mental Disorders IV. The numerous mental health professionals in the congregation recognize the red cover and laugh. I diagnose Pharaoh. I read all nine indices, and only five are needed for diagnosis. Pharaoh's behavior met the criteria for all nine indices. The diagnostic name: Narcissistic Personality Disorder.

Narcissistic personalities are hurt very easily when criticized or experience a defeat. Listen to what the DSM IV says: "They react with distain, rage, or defiant counterattack." In biblical language their hearts harden, stiffen. So when God said He would harden Pharaoh's heart God only meant He would challenge Pharaoh's perception of himself as deity or god of Egypt, and God knew Pharaoh would not relent. This helps to explain why Pharaoh went into a rage and became vindictive with the Israelites when Moses and Aaron initially approached him.

In a palpable natural rhythm, the dvar Torah begins to take on a life and energy of its own as the words and emotions come together, form a sacred union, synthesize and harmonize. Each word that I utter, I feel individually; each comes from a place deep inside of me and connects to a much deeper place outside of me. I am living my dvar Torah. When I speak of the Exodus, dreams I had as a seven year old of having lived in Egypt form a parallel image above the words. The dreams were so frequent and intense I had gone to my mom and asked, "Ma, have I been to Egypt before?"

"Why you askin', Junior?"

"Because I been dreamin' almos' every night, for a long time, and it seems so real, like I've been there before."

"Boy, you ain't never been in no Egypt, you just havin' foolish dreams," she said with a voice full of humor.

"But Ma, it feels so real."

And it did, and now it feels even more so as I am speaking.

To date, God has made only one personal appearance in human history, to free the Israelites and grant a land of milk and honey...God heard the cry of the Israelites and God voluntarily responded to their anguish. I believe God wanted to show this nascent nation how to respond to oppression and injustice for all time to come. Thus God served as a role model demonstrating the prototypical Tikkun Olam, repair of the world, one of Judaism's leitmotifs... Faith had to be established as the people had to be convinced as Moses and Aaron were, that one Supreme Being existed. Just as Pharaoh had doubts, so did the Israelites. Even Moses had doubts on one occasion about God's sole Supreme Power...and faith could not be developed in the abstract, God had to do. There had to be a veritable sense of justice, fairness, this is a just God, a fair God, this is a God of action. A God of Affirmative Action. Yes, you heard me correctly, a God of Affirmative Action. I am suggesting that the Israelites were the initial recipients of Affirmative Action. This makes me an Affirmative Action Jew, and this is an Affirmative Action dvar Torah.

The congregation is goaded and stirs palpably in visceral motion. I continue:

When the American Civil War ended, black people were free, but there was no milk, no land, no honey. America reneged on its promise of forty acres and a mule. Shortly thereafter, there was the rise of the Ku Klux Klan and a vicious suppression of black people was reinvigorated. Black skin was tantamount to a yellow star. And during this same period Jews fled pogroms in the late 19th century and 20th century, and came to America, land of the free, home of the brave. Black people had no place to flee to save lives, develop dignity, develop talents. Nowhere to run. Nowhere to hide.

The congregation is captivated. I feel and hear the attention of everyone as the silence magnifies every word that leaves my lips.

The prophetic words from Rabbi Abraham Joshua Heschel provides the coda:

"You cannot find redemption until you see the flaws in your own soul, and try to efface them. Nor can a people be redeemed until it sees the flaws in its soul and tries to efface them. But whether it be an individual or a people, whoever shuts out the realization of his or her flaws is shutting out redemption. We can be redeemed only to the extent to which we see ourselves."

I pause and conclude, "Shabbat Shalom."

Thunderous applause erupts, before I could blink. Everyone is standing and clapping vigorously. The claps rise joyously to the vaulted ceiling like soaring birds filling the sky, clap birds flying and flirting with the air and rays of the stained-glass sun, filling the cavernous airspace until only claps could be breathed and the congregation is in rapturous delight. From the last row of the balcony to the first row in the orchestra, black and white, Christians and Jews, all in unison, for an all too brief moment.

Caught in the headlight glare of applause, I'm momentarily paralyzed at the thunderous intensity. All the well-defined faces suddenly become white and black squiggles as I try to penetrate the glare and regain the clarity of purpose I just lost. Trembling ever so slightly, I feel like a prizefighter holding on. I look to the right and see my mother, sisters, and childhood friends vigorously clapping. I involuntarily look for my dad, too feeble to attend, hoping for a miracle, and my heart aches.

I begin marching the Torah around the synagogue and feel the Torah marching around in me. People line both sides of the aisle, smiling joyously, kissing the Torah, kissing me, with looks of adulation and words of praise that lick my spirit, my love of God, Judaism and all Jews, imperfections and all. I am being exalted in "God's kingdom." Shoshana Avner says, "*You, you, are* the Torah." Placing his face close to me, Jeff Segall says, "I never heard anything like that before in my life, it was great." A frisson of disbelief occurs when I see Uncle Charlie's grinning face and hear, "Hey Adamswich, you did us all proud." As my eyes blink the apparition away his granddaughter Nichelle, smiling, touches my arm and says, "Granddad would have been proud."

When the service concludes, throngs of well-wishers queue up to offer congratulatory remarks. I feel like a celebrity as I give verbal autographs and promise delivery to untold numbers of people who ask for a copy of my dvar Torah. The line keeps growing and I tell all those still waiting to descend downstairs so that we can all eat, that I would speak to them during the Kiddush. As I turn to leave, I see Stanley Futterman, walking quickly toward me with tears streaming from his eyes: "Ernest, I had *no idea*; *no idea*; my imagination was too small to grasp the possibility of what you were going to say, and the magnitude of what you said."

Once downstairs, I did not think about food, though I was beginning to run on fumes, until Meyer spotted me "indulging your fans." I treasured the respectful way people reacted to me. I grew tired and could no longer concentrate, and manufactured a stare that looked right at people, but that really looked through them. I continued to listen when I could no longer hear. My smile was tired; my jaw muscles felt heavy, ready to collapse.

Gifts are handed to me and as they begin to mount up Meyer found a place for them. Winston McGill, my childhood friend from 129th street, thrust a gift-wrapped package in my face and insists, "Open it now."

Tired but curious, I open the small box and I am sentimentally impressed with a Star of David and gold chain. Before I can express my appreciation, Winston gives me two other gifts, but this time he insists I open them at home.

"Why?" I want to know.

"You will understand when you are home," he says smiling.

When I opened the packages at home I fell into convulsive laughter. Though Winston McGill is both a mechanical engineer and urologist, he has always been more clever at humor. The first package was a CD of Sammy Davis Jr. songs, the second contained a black eye patch.

Elliot Burgess, a friend since eighth grade, gives me a Kiddush cup and anecdote that go together. He entered a Jewish store in Baltimore and browsed for an extended period getting frustrated because, "I just did not know what to get Junebug." So he went over to the saleswoman, explained his situation, and she recommended a Kiddush cup. "But I did not trust that white lady, so I went over to a black man in the store and asked his advice and he said, 'Kiddush cup,' the same as the white lady," he says laughing at himself.

My mom and sister Florita are inundated with greetings and congratulations from a lot of my synagogue mates. Some with smugness asked, "How do you feel about Ernest's conversion?"

"He is my son. *He will always be my son* and I love him. That is why I am here," Mom said, slightly annoyed.

Florita added, "My brother is an adult and he can make whatever choice that pleases him. He is still my brother and always will be."

I have no idea who made such impertinent inquiries of my family, but I can only wonder if the love of their parents and siblings could withstand such a challenge.

A B'nai Jeshurun acquaintance said exuberantly, "I felt like cheering." He went off into the crowd and returned fifteen minutes later and was on edge. "Ernie, I went over to your mother and congratulated her, chatted some, and I said, "I know you are proud of Ernest, he spoke so well, so outstanding, it must have been *quite a surprise* for you?"

Mom looked at him through the eyes of eighty-two years of dealing with unwittingly discourteous white people, and with a polite edge said, "Thank you. Yes, I'm proud of Ernest, but, I'm not surprised. *My* son has *always* been a good public speaker."

After recounting this to me, I say, "Yep, that's right, I have always been a good public speaker."

Mom did not explain that I had been giving "talks" at the Kingdom hall of Jehovah's Witnesses since I was nine years old, and that she used to have me rehearse with the broomstick as a microphone.

The comments and reactions continued for a long time after the Bar Mitzvah. The next day, Dr. Michael Teitelman called, "I heard you gave a great dvar. I was not feeling well yesterday so I gave myself a break. I am so sorry I missed it. I want a copy."

Bruce Rosen called: "I heard you gave the dvar of dvar's, the dvar of all time! Can you mail me a copy?"

I tried to react in a normal manner, but I did not know what normal was in this situation. I was flattered that people I admired as learned were calling me because other people had called them. But all the comments received were not well placed.

Lisa Schachner, a B'nai Jeshurun member said, "Some people were surprised at how well you spoke, that you had a commanding presence."

"What did they expect?" The words bolted out of my mouth. "Did they expect me to dribble a basketball?"

Lisa's head dropped and she looked down at the floor in embarrassment.

As I was walking the Torah around the synagogue, Robert Jekyll said he and his girlfriend Carol, perceived with certainty, "You left your family, you are no longer part of them. We saw it. We looked and noticed it at the same time." Carol vigorously nodded in assent.

At a Shabbat lunch the following week Miriam, a Jewish Theological Seminary rabbinical student, slowly nodded as Mandy, a Jewish Theological Seminary cantorial student gave me high praise for my dvar Torah, "You were really really good, genuinely good, *unbelievably* good."

"Unbelievable?" I thought, looking politely in their eyes. Defined in the dictionary as "too improbable for belief." Then Miriam cautiously asked, "When you gave your dvar Torah were you present? Were you aware and conscious while giving it? I know that sometimes people can 'blank out' and talk and not be 'conscious' as they speak."

Despite the praise Miriam and Mandy heaped on me, I felt preyed upon. In conversational tone I said, "No, I was there, I made a promise to myself to be there for myself and enjoy the experience." *But I was really thinking, "Damn, can't black people, even black Jews perform well without scrutiny and second guessing? Why are you trying to understand what does not need to be understood? Even if I had not been "present" what difference would it make now? Let alone when I gave my dvar Torah? Would a mental footnote have been made: "Great dvar Torah, intellectually rigorous, original insights, great command on the bema, but he was not really present. He blanked out. Not bad for a black Jew, though."*

Not one black person questioned my presence and all expressed high praise with words like "awesome…brilliant…."

Except for Florita who typed the manuscript, all the black folks that day were surprised by the bluntness of my ideas and teachings. "Ernest, when you said Jews were the first recipients of Affirmative Action, I looked around to see their reactions. Nobody left. I said to myself, 'Oh my God, go Ernest,'" said a delighted friend.

Another person said, "Ernest, I could not believe you said that, and you weren't excommunicated? But it was something they sure needed to hear. But Jews don't support us, and I still don't understand how you do it, how you can stand to be around them." I knew she was just warming up. "This is the core, at the vortex of their racism. I don't understand you, how you deal with their racism, you were bold enough to admit you are an Affirmative Action baby, actually it was more brave than bold, maybe more stupid than anything, because you know they don't support Affirmative Action which means they don't support you, brother. I know they don't support me, and I don't try to pretend."

"I was trying to teach a lesson through the values in the Torah."

My friend cut me off. "But as *you see them* not as *they* see them. They don't really respect you, you have to go along with them or you are out brother. They are white. What do you have to do to yourself to stay a Jew? I don't know how you do it?"

"I was explaining the black experience through the universal truth of the Torah, to the original subscribers to God's word and law. No one is going to change overnight, some never, and many have no intimate contact with black people. When you speak through the Torah with the language of truth, Jews will listen."

She cut me off again. "The *truth,* Ernest, the *truth*, Ernest, is that they are white and listen with white ears from a white experience and see with white eyes only. Jew or Jewish has absolutely nothing to do with whether they listen. They don't support Affirmative Action because they are white."

"I think you have to look at the Jewish historical experience to understand the-" With razor edge sharpness I was cut off again.

"History! That is bullshit. I don't believe that! You don't believe that!" Said with acid edged alienation as she turned away.

"Look..." Cut off again.

"Look yourself, look at the reality, that is, reality with a capital R." She took a deep breath, "racism, it is their reality, it is their racism. Where is your reality testing, Dr. Adams? Master psychologist." She was soaking with sarcasm and rage. Raw anger was swirling around inside and outside both of us, causing us to pause, then stop in mutual frustration.

I used to feel the same way.

I had some sense of why black folks gave me a standing ovation, but was unsure why members of the congregation did. A few weeks later I asked Rabbi Matalon, "I don't get why I received a standing ovation. I was trying to be thought provoking and critically honest. I really don't understand."

"Ernie, first it was a great dvar, it stood alone as great words of Torah," Rabbi Matalon said affectionately. "The second thing, you took us to a place only you could have taken us. That is why people were clapping. You took the synagogue to another level."

Then there was the indelible impression I left on myself. I felt proud and was comforted by being able to feel and function like a real Jew: reading Torah, the greatest achievement of them all; reading Haftorah, the greatest achievement of them all; creating a dvar Torah out of the still pristine words of Torah, struggling to comprehend, making sense of, finding meaning, listening for and hearing the voice of God, the greatest achievement of them all.

But of all the compliments I received, the one I remember most, "You are three words from being a rabbi," said Debby Lissaur.

"And what are those three words?"

"Jewish Theological Seminary," was all she said, and, Debby said it all.

* * *

The road I traveled on my journey from Harlem to Halacha—Jewish Law and ritual—was filled with potholes, ditches, detours, intersections, tolls, tunnels, bridges with many signs and symbols often not clear. The trauma and uncertainty during my travels taught me no white person was ever to be truly trusted: that the singular and insular composition of "whiteness" and its thoroughly insidious impact produced the ghetto I was born into and that was born in me and borne by me. My stereotypical notions predominated: Jews were those people who came in varieties of, stingy, stingier, and stingiest; people with black hats, long black coats, and long black beards.

Self-rejection and self-hate were the only motivations my African American community could imagine my becoming a Jew: a repudiation of my blackness and black people. White Christian friends while less vexed were equally perplexed. The inquiry of merit I attempt to address: How did I challenge my reality-based fears of whites and fears of Jews as white? How did I come to trust Jews as Jews as white people? How did I come to trust my trust of Jews?

The world is a very narrow bridge but the main thing is not to fear at all.

Still in battle, still struggling, I remain uncertain as to *why* I became a Jew. After such a dramatic shift, I can't fully explain why a Christian Negro boy, who turned into a godless cynic and unforgiving black man, then returned to God as true believer, but as a Jew. I have been asked so many times I am engaged to the question, and this book will be the consummation of our odd relationship.

I would be privileged, proud, honored and more than delighted if you joined me in my voyage of self-discovery of how I arrived to be on this bema and beyond. I will attempt to anticipate and honestly answer many of your questions, especially the tough ones, the politically incorrect ones, about my journey. I will let the truth—embedded in my thinking, choices, priorities, propensities and behavior—take wing and travel as only the truth should.

This is a quintessential American story, more than half-century in the making, about an African American man and how I found Judaism and how Judaism found me; how I now walk with a Jewish pep in my step. It is less a tour de force than it is a complex, complicated and sometimes confusing story about the human condition: love, hate, race, racism, anti-Semitism, class, religion, faith and belief, or lack thereof, and God. It is about the attempt to transfer and use the best of what I learned growing up, and attempt to transcend the worst I incorporated into my daily life, especially the panoply of race, cynicism, paranoia, anxiety, pessimism, fear and doubt that was emblazoned in my consciousness. Finally, it is a story about the strength and conviction to challenge myself, and others, and to cross boundaries that have imprisoned better persons than myself.

The Basement: Signs and Windows

"It's a burden…but AIDS isn't the heaviest burden I have had to bear……you're not going to believe this…but being black is the greatest burden I've had to bear…having to live as a minority in America. Even now it continues to feel like an extra weight tied around me."

Arthur Ashe

A Light Born in Darkness Can Never Go Out

Rabbi Simon Jacobson

Jewish Perspective: You have to go down in order to go up
African American Perspective: Been down so long seems like up

I was born in 1946, eighty-one years after American slavery ended, but the vestigial stench of slavery was billowing with bold-faced restrictive signs and restrictive covenants. Segregation was practiced with righteous white pride. For the Negro, the fear of being lynched was pungent, and permeated everything.

Born on a warm August morning in Harlem, in New York, I greeted the world crying, a natural phenomenon, that first gasping sound of life

But I soon came to learn not to be so obvious with my emotions.

Had I known where I was going to live I would have cried louder, longer and in complete despair. My home for the next eighteen years of my life, was an apartment at 419 West 129th Street, where I would be shaped and molded was the next stop: The Basement.

Truly, the gift of life was and is a blessing but coming to live in the Basement was a curse. I hated living in the Basement, hated it hated it just hated it. This was my Birthright. This was my Birthwrong.

Pipes ran throughout the apartment and there was always a leak, always a leak. My maternal Uncle Charlie sent a picture postcard of a room that had many pipes with many leaks and basins were placed to catch the water, and a family, looking bewildered, saying, "Damn leaks everywhere." Except for the white faces it was an accurate snapshot of my plight. Despite its mocking, my parents did not destroy it. They displayed it on the refrigerator like a religious icon!

When Uncle Charlie came for a visit he gleefully pointed to the postcard proudly pasted to our refrigerator and roared with guileless infectious laughter. Absorbing his humor, my parents joined in, and the three of them laughed heartily and happily. Excluded from their generational humor, I became the proverbial outsider looking in, as the smile on my face served to hide my shame and confusion. I went unnoticed, but took note that their unabashed good feelings were genuine as they celebrated my shame.

The white American Basement was Harlem, capital of the Negro "nation," and I lived in its Basement; living in the Basement of the Negro Basement, literally at rock-bottom, was excruciating. The apartment was always clean and had quality furniture but it offered no mitigation because the smells of the Basement were the smells of any Basement that had garbage, putrid and dank, and I became inured. Everyone in the building emptying garbage had to come past my home and pick one of several garbage cans lined up, waiting to be filled with wastes that turned to rotting smells.

The garbage attracted cats; they lived on it, settled down, and raised families. Seeing cats get under the lids of garbage cans looking for food seemed to be one of nature's phenomenons. While walking through the Basement to my apartment with Ronnie, a neighborhood friend who was street wise and gang tough, he heard rustling in a garbage can and saw the garbage can top shaking mysteriously. He suddenly stopped, riveted, scared, and startled when out popped a cat, "I thought that was a rat," he said, the fear in his voice dissipating as the cat ran away. Absent any concern on my face he queried, "Aren't you scared?"

"No," I responded nonchalantly, "We don't have rats, what's there to be afraid of?"

This was my territory, my jungle, and I was quite at home. What he did not know was that I used to sometimes play with the cats to liven up some of the boring moments or chase them endlessly when my energy was excessively abundant. I once brought a favorite kitten home to keep; I had the pick of the litter, but Mom would not allow it. It was fun watching the kitten chase the shadow of the long cord to the kitchen ceiling light as I pushed it back and forth. Besides, the cat could chase the mice away. One night while trying to sleep I heard the mousetrap shut with a loud snap. I got up to investigate, met my mom as she walked into the kitchen and turned on the light to reveal a successfully mangled mouse.

The roaches were another story. While they never overran us, it seemed to me we had more than the average New York ghetto share. One evening during dinner, I was drinking a glass of fresh squeezed lemonade that was sweet and delicious, childhood pleasure ran through me until Mom caught my attention and pointed at my glass, "Look."

I lowered the glass and discovered a dark brown dead roach floating like it belonged there in the lemon pulp, poised to become part of my dinner.

My childhood pleasure disappeared. Gloom enveloped me. I emptied my glass, unable to empty my demoralized feelings. I felt bound and trapped. How did I miss a roach in my glass? We had plenty of roach spray, but they kept coming, no matter what. Nothing *ever* went my way. Ever. Nothing. I wanted out. I wanted to be someplace, no place, anyplace, everyplace, where I could simply enjoy a clean sweet glass of lemonade with my fried chicken.

At about age seven, I began to dream that I had some doo-doo on me; circumstances varied, but the one constant was my trying to wipe it off, trying to cleanse myself. Instead of going away, it only became softer and spread, the more I cleaned the more it spread, yet, I still tried to cleanse myself. Inevitably, despite my best efforts, it spread out of control. Unable to cleanse myself, I felt deeply depressed in my dreams, hopeless that I could not effect anything that could clean me up and make me presentable. This specific dream recurred for years, and the ache in my heart began to grow out of desperation. This psychic pain was torturous and I tried to escape by waking up to the real world. Temporary relief usually followed. Then one day, I woke to feel the deepening ache in my heart, and it felt the same as in the dream. It became my constant companion, present wherever I went, and participating in whatever I did.

One day I heard a knock at the door and opened it to find an eighth grade classmate with a perfect smile, happy to see me, Sylvia Barnes. I was instantly frozen in monumental embarrassment. She had stopped by uninvited. I did not tell her I lived in the Basement but she found me anyway.

She lived above ground in a spacious apartment in the LaSalle Street Co-Ops on 123rd Street and Amsterdam Avenue. Her father was a professional and her mother spoke with a black middle-class accent. I was being invited to a movie and dinner as part of Sylvia's birthday party. My first and last such invitation as a child. Sylvia was middle-class, which I desperately wanted to be, but I was more humiliated by her visit to the Basement.

When I took Juanita Bryant, later to become my wife, to her high school prom, my mom wanted to see her that night, and I most assuredly did not oblige. Juanita lived one block away and she never saw the Basement. Mom asked with the answer lingering in her tone, "Are you ashamed of where you live?"

I looked at her in disbelief. She really had no clue about how I felt, how much disdain I had for my home, how I had been humiliated so many times, so many fucking times, sometimes intentionally, sometimes not.

I became good friends with Richard Jefferson in ninth grade and liked his buddy Frank Murphy. I was loath to bring new friends home who lived outside the immediate neighborhood, but I brought my two newest chums home for lunch to feed them in the Adams' tradition.

As we descended to the Basement, I felt self-conscious, and before I could get my key out of my pocket, Frank reacted to the silver piece of sheet metal covering the front door as if it was intrinsic stimuli, "This looks like we're in sheet metal shop," he chuckled. His words were like sizzling coals placed in the grip of my trust. Richard, aware of my embarrassment, gently chastised him, "Hey man, don't crack on him like that, he's inviting you to his home for lunch."

Sheepishly, Frank nodded his assent.

Pat was a girl who lived in the next building who had what I perceived as a nasal condition and speech impediment, and I used to launch my sizzling coals zeroing in on her without mercy. I sounded on her one time too many, possibly made her cry, and her mother stopped me in the backyard of our adjoining buildings. "I want you to stop teasing Patricia," she said politely but firmly.

I spoke with my mom about it and she explained, "Junior, you don't tease people. Some people have something wrong with them, but you don't tease them. You should not be making fun of people. Just thank the lord you got ten toes and ten fingers. Don't take it for granted."

I listened but felt no remorse.

When I ran into Pat many years later, I immediately reconnected to the guilt I should have felt for my childhood ruthlessness. She greeted me like we were old neighborhood friends, which we were. She was happy to see me, there was no trace of anger, and proudly told me that her daughter was a student at Howard University. Pat was an intelligent articulate woman that I could never, as a child, imagined her to be. She sounded like her mother.

Richard Jefferson lived in the Grant Projects. His apartment had plenty of sun that painted the walls and floors with waves of light; it provided rays of energy that I eagerly absorbed, making laughter more fun and less cathartic. The view was spectacular. High above, in the glory, I basked. I looked down and saw the elevated Broadway subway line, the traffic of cars, people walking about, going in and out of stores, and children playing. I saw black tar rooftops and took note of the detailed architecture of buildings. Off in the distance the Hudson River flowed. New Jersey and the George Washington Bridge reflected the sun. Richard's window was a luxury: there was no garbage, no stink, no cats, no shadows, and no darkness. It was so, Un-Basement. When friends came by and shouted for me from the street, I would lift up the window, bend over, strain my neck up and shout up a response. I jealously wished I lived in the projects, above it all.

My paternal grandmother, Adams, dearly beloved by me, lived in a beautiful spacious apartment in Washington Heights. Winston McGill, my best friend in the neighborhood, lived on the second floor in 419, and both he and his sister Carol had their own big rooms. Why couldn't I live above ground and have my own room?

What made it more galling, my mom did not like living in the Basement, and her behavior implied she did not like the neighborhood. She would gather her children and begin to march us up to light and when I asked our destination, "Anyplace but here," she answered sharply. We rode the number three-bus downtown on Fifth Avenue.

"Why?" I asked.

"So you can see something different, Junior, to see something different from Harlem," she said. If we were lucky we caught a light green double-decker bus and rode up top. Climbing the steps up the double-decker bus was an anticipatory delight, and watching all the people below with the air massaging my face, was delicious—life was good. Mom never mentioned "white" and did not have to. I had heard enough stories as warnings to know that the Negro people were treated very differently by white people; white people were dangerous, not to be trusted, but interaction was unavoidable.

When the bus turned onto Fifth Avenue to make its way downtown, the majestic architecture imposed its grandeur. In grand buildings I saw black men in uniform standing in the doorways deferentially opening them for fancily dressed white ladies. The commerce of people was scant, they were in motion, in route to somewhere, or hidden behind the grace of the architecture. There was no gathering of people communing in front of buildings or adolescents on street corners or children playing tag, hide and go seek, loadies, jumping rope, or playing stickball, common activities on Harlem streets.

"Ma, do children live here?" I asked.

"Sure, Junior."

"I don't see them. Where do they play?"

There was a long pause.

"Maaa," I whined waiting for an answer.

Her head turned right and so did mine. "They must play over there in Central Park," she answered logically.

After the half-hour bus ride downtown we would walk the streets, observing and being observed. We browsed store windows and sometimes we went inside. Following mom's cue, I observed and absorbed how she made her way, boldly, yet gracefully poised, as if she belonged without actually being accepted. She shopped downtown as often as possible and shopped on 125th Street as little as possible. Mom always said, "I was not a Hearn's or Alexander's shopper. They did not have the quality I wanted." And her frequent refrain, "There is more to life than meets the eye," began to develop contours.

Though the bus rides were fun and captivating, I only wanted to move to the first floor. Mom explained that she asked for an apartment above ground but none was available. Had she asked only once? Did she really ask at all? My parents made the choice to remain in the Basement when they could have moved to another apartment in the building or above ground to another ghetto location. Most poignantly, my parents wallowed in the Basement for eighteen years, which was, sadly, their choice.

True, my parents were not able to move wherever they could afford due to segregation, but most everyone else in the building and community were black or Latino and there were clearly no social hurdles to jump. Clearly no white man or tangible racial oppression tethered my parents to the Basement. They did not always have a choice of where to live, but always it was their choice on how to live. I later wondered: how much of an impact, if any, should be assigned to race and racism on their judgment?

I shared a bedroom with my two sisters for eighteen years. Florita, six years my senior, slept on the top bunk of a bunk bed and Audrey, eighteen months my junior, slept on the bottom. I slept in my own bed and frequently daydreamed about having my own room. Despondently, I begged my mom to let me sleep in the room next to ours that was used for storage.

She looked at me, disappointed with herself for not being able to accommodate me, "Junior, it's too damp in there. It's not made for you or anybody to sleep in. You would get sick."

I would lie in bed at night imagining bricks surrounding me, enclosing me off in a desperate need for privacy: space to think, to imagine, to create, to dream at my leisure about who and what I wanted to be and become, my window to the world. Since that never occurred in the external world, I retreated to inside my head to find space, solace, and freedom—where I was free to be.

I built an internal defensive structure with emotional bricks that allowed me to withdraw and survive, but not necessarily thrive. Today, over a half-century later, the structure is so entrenched that at times I still respond as if I am in the Basement and fighting for my psychological space, solace, and survival. This is one reason why I don't mind spending time alone, why I can be self-sufficient but not quite efficient as I can be, need be, or would like to be.

Not an overtly angry boy but pissed off at my life circumstances, I expressed my futility by pissing in my bed. With disappointment, anger, and frustration, my father said, only once, "If you pee in that bed again, I am goin' to punish you and beat you." The next day he checked, and I had peed a larger puddle that rolled off the brown rubber mat under my sheet onto the mattress, adding new stains. When it dried, the soaked mattress and sheets stank to high heaven. I looked at my father in shame and confusion and he looked back at me, lost in ignorant anger. Defeated, he walked away and never said another word about my bed-wetting.

But there was one thing I really loved about the Basement, the storytelling of Edgar Clark, a master storyteller and Basement neighbor. A bunch of us kids used to gather in his home with his children and we sat in a circle around him, sometimes in a darkened bedroom, and he would weave a tale that was either funny or scary.

He would alter his voice, from hissing whispers to baritone moans, gesticulate, contort his face as he pressed it close to ours, the crescendo approached the denouement, and at that intuitive propitious moment he would jump up and chase us, and as I did my utter best not to get away he would grab me—when I was the most lucky—while belting out his official name for everyone, "Crumb bums, you crumb bums you, come here you crumb bum, I got you"

As he whirled me about in the bosom of his tickling humor, my soul filled with joy, until tears of pain became pain-joy, joy-pain, pure joy, ran down my face smoothing over the lumps of hurt. I was in a place where I felt no pain. No pain felt so good. The Basement became a Temple of Fun. It felt like Hope. It felt like Life. This was my Birthright.

Edgar Clark served as antidote even though he lived in the same Basement and was an alcoholic as was my father. Yet, Clark's sometimes stale whiskey breath did not detract from or spoil his life enhancing effervescence. He helped me to do more than just merely survive the Basement; how much so, I don't know and know less how to measure. Edgar Clark went to his grave not knowing, I would think, that he made a significant impact on my life. How would he know? He was a master storyteller who merely told stories to groups of neighbor's children. He took no special interest in me. I was among the chocolate bouquet with green fern wrapped in heavy need of laughter.

I was unaware of the powerful impact of Clark's storytelling until I was at his funeral in 1985 when I walked by his casket and stared deeply into the painless moments of times past and I touched him, placed my hand over his heart, the way he had touched me. And still, I did not make the connection how he had provided the medicinal spoonfuls of laughter that bloomed into the rays of light that had obliterated the pain of my circumstances—until I began to muse about my life and write my story in the twenty-first century. For however brief or extended, it sponsored renewal, joy, strength and quality years to my life.

Lives intersect in ways unplanned, unimagined, not knowable, and the mundane exchanges we may encounter by circumstance make us all potential heroes and diminish our flaws. That is, in the narrative of our imperfections we may inadvertently touch others with the best of who we are and what we possess. Plainly said, the same way we unintentionally hurt others, we may help others with that very same blindness.

Earl, one of Clark's three sons, observed that I touched his father and was especially taken aback, when I acknowledged my affection. After the service, Earl and his brother Bruce, praised my parents hospitality and told me that they found life sustaining good times and memories in their many meals and visits to my home.

Clark's infusion of laughter had been a critical adjunct, but the fertile crescent of my tenacious strength, and ever tenacious reserve strength, I absorbed from within my much-hated pipe-leaking apartment. My immediate association is to the kitchen and the kitchen table, which was the hub of good times. I made hamburgers, French fries, and ice cream sodas on Friday nights, the night Mom took off from the kitchen and we cooked our meal of choice; friends, including Basement neighbors Earl and Bruce Clark, and from the adjoining building the Johnson girls, Eloise, Lorraine and Alvis, came by to simulate a party, week in and week out. My home in the Basement was the gathering place for all our neighborhood friends, and we always had lots of other people's children around. I don't know of one friend who visited and did not have a meal. One day I looked around and saw all those sons and daughters of neighbors and neighborhood kids and asked my mom how she could stand all the noise, inevitable mess, and additional food expense, and she gently said, "Junior, as long as I know they are in my home, I know they are safe."

My parents entertained often and they had no obvious hesitation about inviting anybody and everybody to the Basement. The many guests, included family and friends of my parents who seemed not to mind being below ground. The anticipation of a party pumped up my excitement and a certain gaiety filled our home as we prepared for the arrivals.

The guests arrived and my parents greeted them as if we lived in a Beverly Hills mansion; stylishly dressed, conversation and laughter flowing, the people were happy to be there, imploring us children, including friends of Audrey and me, to show them the latest dances. They enjoyed a banquet of food and drinks: the Basement was transformed into a Palace.

Sunday morning breakfast with the scent and flavor of pork sausage, eggs, and bacon, warm biscuits with butter, jelly and homemade pear preserves from my grandfather's farm was satiation personified. Mom's scrambled eggs with cheese made me think I was in heaven. "Ma, please make the cheese-egg," I used to beg some mornings when waffles were on the menu and I loved waffles.

My father liked fried eggs and he would first eat the whites, then maneuver the remaining two to three yolks whole on his fork, open his mouth wide in exaggerated fashion, then slowly lower the fork into his mouth, then we would call him "greedy gut" and groan with wide-eyed laughter in delirious amazement.

Sunday dinner was always special with the possibility of ham, Cornish hens, lamb chops, lasagna or steak on the menu. Fabulous desserts were a treat we all anticipated from German chocolate cake to fresh baked pies. These sumptuous meals were the perfect way to end the week fortified. But of all the delicious food Mom prepared, my personal comfort food was peanut butter and jelly on Tasty bread, and when dipped in chocolate milk, this ambrosia helped me through many a bad moment and many bad periods.

Playing five hundred rummy with my father, sometimes for small change, was pure fun as we engaged in braggadocio and unfettered competition. And sitting in my high school cafeteria I received a secondary gain when enthusiastically and quite naturally, I would tell and retell my classmates, some who did not have fathers at home, how my father and I discovered unrestrained joy in a prosaic card game.

Also, the first and only time I saw my parents embrace with warm affection was in the kitchen. I watched in awe as my father turned on his charm and turned my mom's brooding eyes into sparkling light.

My paternal grandmother Adams, very much loved by me, was a child of Abraham Lincoln's Republican Party. Sitting at the kitchen table with Florita eating lunch on a hot summer afternoon, she told me, "When Adams was in the army they thought she was white."

"Get outta here, nobody thought she was white." I said vehemently denying the possibility.

"Yes she did pass for white I saw…" I interrupted her unbelievable story.

"Get outta here." I dismissed my sister six years my elder for talking nonsense.

"I saw it on her papers from the army. I saw the army papers," Florita said with irrefutable truth. Then Florita got up, went into my parents' room and produced the army documents and there it was, in black and white, my black grandmother was checked off as "white." How could white people be so dumb and stupid! My grandmother had nurtured and took care of me. To help defray the costs of three children when my father was in the army and Mom was on welfare, my grandmother decided to dote on me. She took me shopping for clothes, gave me lovely birthday gifts, and I loved it when we dined over a hotdog or hamburger. She often let me keep the change when she sent me to the store; other times she slipped a few coins in my pocket. Periodically she would take the entire family to dinner in restaurants in downtown white New York or Westchester County.

When Adams joined the Army in 1940 the white officer filling out the admission papers looked up at her and checked off "white" next to race. "I did not say a thing, I let him think what he wanted," she confirmed when I asked. Maybe they figured it out, maybe not, because she only socialized with other Negroes. I always proudly showed my friends a picture of Joe Louis and my grandmother when they were stationed at the same location. I had *never* noticed that my grandmother looked white: and still, she did not look white. How *my* grandma could be mistaken for white I had no idea. None.

My first conscious memory of a white person entering my home was the Fuller Brush salesman who sold Mom many household items. He initially sold brushes, combs, mops and the like, then he expanded and "had some of everything," Mom recalled. "He got you good quality, like that nice chrome kitchen set and we kept it until we moved to the Bronx, then I gave it away. Good quality, Junior, it may cost a little more, but good quality lasts a long time," she said self-assured and more than satisfied.

When the Fuller Brush salesman was at the entrance to the Basement, he immediately began to call loudly, "Adums, Adums, Adums." The rising volume let us know he was approaching for landing. When I heard his voice I knew it was white, foreign, but friendly. I would open the door and wait the final few steps for him to appear from around the corner.

He was tall, pale, with wire rim glasses, black suit, black shoes, white shirt, white socks, always with a smile and friendly greeting. The white man in a white world was afraid every time he came to my home, afraid of the Basement. I now can hear the rumbling fear in his European voice, as he began to shout out, "Adums, Adums, Adums," as soon as he stepped onto the Basement floor and the door slammed shut behind him, like our family name was an incantation that could and would rescue him, if need be, from whatever lurked within. Maybe it was the precipitous decrease of light, the plunge into the underground of shadows with no windows and where the pipes overhead had stoked his demons.

Mom, in our family tradition, always offered him something to eat, but he always pleasantly declined, but on many occasions he accepted a refreshing glass of lemonade to quench his fear. An adept salesman, Mr. Weingarten sold his products throughout the neighborhood and permitted people to purchase products on credit. He would stand at the 125th street subway station on payday to wait for those persons who owed him money. Mom always paid on time so there was no need for street corner negotiation, or embarrassment, depending on your point of view.

I have no memory of when I became aware that Mr. Weingarten was Jewish, as I have none for the pejorative names for Jews that became part of my active vocabulary. My parents did not bandy about such words, but my friends and I referred to some of the local Jewish merchants derogatorily. Bela and Charlie owned a grocery store on Convent Avenue, and I recall us children, some as young as five years old, repeatedly, mercilessly, referring to them as "Cheap Charlie," to their faces, without fear. Yet, just across the street, I have no memory of anyone making derogatory remarks about Eddie the butcher, a white Catholic, though Miller, the Jewish owner of a grocery store next door, was referred to as "stingy and cheap." Also, I have no recollection of inculcating the notion of black inferiority and white superiority.

Despite the many good times and because of the trying-times, I wanted to live anyplace but the Basement. Anyplace, with one exception: The South.

* * *

During many a summer vacation I visited my maternal grandfather, Henry Charles DeLaine, known as H.C., on his one hundred acre farm in Johnston County outside Clayton, North Carolina where he used mules to plow the fields. He grew fruits, vegetables, cotton and raised hogs, chickens and cows.

I walked to the disquieting smell of the outhouse and fleetingly stared down into the mounting plop of human dung, swirling abyss of flies and stink, sat on an abrasive wooden toilet seat, now turned grayish by the elements, hoping not to get a splinter, hopelessly unable to relax while trying not to choke on the reeking wastes. Still, the farm was a welcome oasis and haven in the desert of the inhumanity of white Southern hospitality.

H.C. never did understand how people in the city could live in apartments, "How you live in boxes on top of each other, I don't know."

Running barefoot and looking as far as the forest of trees and wild green grass and wild shrubbery allowed me to see, I was mesmerized by the pristine nature of it all. The surround sound of open spaces and quiet; the many flies and various insects, acres of grass with cows nonchalantly chewing chunks of cud, monotonous rows of endless plowed fields of corn, cantaloupe, watermelon, cotton, green beans, and I now understood the need for the wet of rain, the sweltering heat of July as the sun baked me a richer darker chocolate. From my imagined reality of the American classic: "Oh beautiful for spacious skies with amber waves of grain," leapt forth nature's reality. Now I understood H.C.

Helping Uncle J bale hay as he filled the stalls of the cows, I stepped in a sizable turd of cow dung, disgusted and embarrassed as only a city boy could be. Uncle J merely produced a hefty smile that notified me that this was life in the barn, life on the farm. The cow dung signaled by flies was avoidable, that which was camouflaged by hay unavoidable—life in the barn proved to have parallels in life off the farm—and, well, I became "country," I became part of the human landscape that dotted the farm and nature.

I made credible attempts at milking cows, bringing the cows in at dusk, slopping hogs and feeding baby chicks. I learned to keep the door shut to keep predators out and the proper temperature in, while learning to capture, kill, and enjoy eating them once grown. Uncle J brought to my attention that when asked, I readily went to the field to work or harvest the edibles like watermelons or tomatoes, which we would sometimes eat directly off the vine, but never said yes to picking cotton which I found harsh, distasteful and boring under a blazing sun.

Uncle J lived on and off the farm with his family, and I grew to love and respect him. I had some of the best times and most fun of my entire life with him, as he taught me about life on and off the farm. Traversing the streets of the South also presented great teachers.

I loved hamburgers and as Uncle J pulled into a gas station I saw what I thought was a White Castle restaurant and jumped out of the car, and Uncle J who was always kidding around tried to grab me and said, "Junebug," but I was lightening quick and slipped under his grasp racing as fast as my ten year old legs could carry me, to order a delicious hamburger, French fries and a shake. I had not had a hamburger, fries and shake since leaving New York three weeks prior. It felt like forever, and I was determined not to be deprived any longer. As I ran, my taste buds rumbled with delicious memory and anticipation.

As I got closer I could see the people eating their goodies and watching me through a large plate glass window as I raced toward hamburger heaven. There was a sign that brought me to a staggering halt. I stared and stood, stood and stared. Immobile. The sign and I exchanged meaning, grafting itself into my consciousness, as it seeped uncomfortably into my unconscious: "Whites Only."

Was this a historic sign, horrific sign, warning sign, signal, command, signature, direction, identification, greeting? It was all of the above, and more. And above all, it provided more than an immediate and irrevocable hurt, a cruel disappointment, and a crushing burden that latched onto my soul.

This moment was a lifetime; there was no going back.

I live in this moment and this moment lives in me.

I am not a Negro boy nor are *they* white. I am hamburger-less boy; *they* have hamburger.

Hamburger heaven was now hell in North Carolina. America the beautiful, with its open skies and spacious land and unprecedented freedom in the land born of freedom, greeted me in my first independent foray with an unwelcoming welcome mat. Welcome, Negro Junebug.

In that moment I was re-routed from anticipated ecstasy to the reality of unanticipated shock, confusion, bewilderment, with no understanding why I could not have a simple burger, fries and shake. The mood swing was humongous, traumatic, and I was devastated as the people in the window suddenly turned white. They looked at me nonchalantly, and I met their eyes in equal curiosity. Their body language was their "sign" language. I did not notice they were white until they treated me as Negro.

Their white skin remained pale with no registration of any overt change, they were not interested in my plight and continued to eat, chewing their food slowly, carrying-on per the usual and stared at me as if I was an animal to be curbed, stared with blind 20/20 vision right through my Negroness, unable to see me. I was Ralph Ellison's first born, the invisible child.

Uncle Charlie told me when he was stationed in the Philippines during World War II, the indigenous people thought he had a tail based on the stories told to them by white Americans. Initially, I assumed he was kidding as both my uncles were wont to do. But he described with intense detail how a few men actually turned him around searching for his tail. The sense of truth was pervasive, and I believed he was speaking from an actual experience.

All those involved in denying me a hamburger were co-conspirators in the continuous crime of damaging the developing hopes, aspirations, expectations, confidence, and trust of a ten-year-old child. Included are the person who wrote the sign and the person who placed the sign in the window. They were co-conspirators and guilty, as were the people eating in the window whose stares and inaction passively displayed a complicit belief, active support and behavior, that I had a tail.

Sitting in such composed manner, civil, without frothing anger or apparent racial malevolence, this is the modern American model, to discreetly practice racial animus, and infect the Negro victim's purview. Those persons in the window became the sign that I packed and now carry with me, wherever I go or come, forever.

It was my first direct stab wound to the heart, my first face-to-face confrontation with racism in the raw and the accompanying sense of powerlessness, but not my last. With shoulders slumped, head bowed in stunned disappointment, my spirit at its lowest, I returned to the car newly baptized by the true American freedom. Uncle J mournfully said, "Junebug, I tried to warn you."

Lynched emotionally, I came to later understand there could never be enough warnings, that life as I experienced in those moments was the veritable text and context of the American moral norm. That at any time, anywhere in the American corridor I was subject to be denied any need, goal, or heart-felt ambition and certainly subject to the stares and sentiments exhibited by the people turned white, simply because, yet not so simply, I was Negro.

On another mundane occasion I craved an ice cream cone and my Uncle J's guidance. I told him I wanted to go into the local luncheonette that boasted of no "White Only" sign. He looked down at me and gently said, "Junebug, come with me." He walked me to the back of the store, pointed to the words in green background and bold white letters: "COLORED ENTRANCE."

"Do you still want to go inside," he asked with the logical answer in his sarcastic, gentle, yet angry tone.

"No," I shot back with a modicum of defiance, but more with deep-seated hurt because I was not welcome to step through the front door like any other human child to have the pleasure of all anticipated pleasures, a double scoop of chocolate and vanilla ice cream.

Then there is the tale of two brothers, my Uncles Charlie and J. Uncle Charlie lived in the Bronx, drove me "down South," and on this day drove me to Sears and Roebuck. It was a typical hot North Carolina day and I began drinking from a water fountain when I felt the sting of someone's hand across my butt. I turned around and there was Uncle Charlie glaring at me.

"What did you do that for? I ain't done nothin'," I said angrily.

He urgently jabbed his finger past the water fountain as if I had missed some obvious and menacing threat to my life. Perplexed, I turned and discovered a sign that read "White" pasted above the water fountain.

I was thirsty and could not drink white water.

Confusion and rage coursed through my body, touching every part of me, tainting me, tainting my soul. I got hit because I drank water.

The finger kept jabbing into the air, Parkinson disease like, as if out of control, pointing in the opposite direction as if I was lost and needed urgent direction to get back on course. There it was, ten feet away, an identical water fountain labeled, "Colored."

My thirst had not been sated but I refused to drink the colored water. Hamburgers, French fries, shake, ice cream and now water, just what was my crime to be so deserving of such cruel and unusual punishment? Where was God? My sin, that is how it felt, was to be born with wooly hair, thick lips, broad nose and Negro skin.

I am reminded of a story my mom told me. She was a young child standing with her mother on family property when a white man came riding across in his horse and wagon. Upon reaching the gate to exit he greeted my grandmother with a wry smile and she greeted him with a loaded gun pointed at his head and stated, "I tol' you not t'be trespassin' on my land."

With bulging eyes focused on the gun that was focused on him, she continued, "Now I ain't tellin' you no mo' don't be ridin' cross my land."

In obvious distress, he rode on and was never known to pass through the DeLaine property again.

The need for recognition, respect, and some semblance of control—three essential characteristics of freedom—over one's environment and destiny is how I currently think about my grandmother's brazen and brave assertion.

Uncle J was angry that Uncle Charlie stopped me from drinking the water. "If I was there you would have drank the water, and I would have dared anyone to say anythin' to you." Naturally I aligned with Uncle J because he did not subscribe to the notion that I was wrong. I was a child who had not learned his "place" in the Southern hierarchy.

Uncle Charlie had grown up in North Carolina, knew his place. Now he lived in the North and was "teaching" me what he thought was the best way to survive, perhaps. Uncle J was alive and well in North Carolina in 1956. Obviously he had learned and practiced the rules of Southern "etiquette." If not, he would have been dead at the hands of Southern hospitality. So what was he trying to teach me?

I believe he looked at me and saw innocence—mine and his own before it was snuffed out—the intrinsic presumption of a child who had a right not to worry about getting a drink of water on a hot day in a public place. I believe Uncle J did not want to etch into my soul, any sooner than it had to be, a presumptive doubt about at least one aspect of my human value: I was worthy of a drink of water, at any fountain. Uncle J's attitude and behavior was refreshing and restorative, while Uncle Charlie's well-meaning intervention was wrong, that my angry response and natural feeling that I had been wronged unnecessarily was right. Today, I realize that both were right, that in order to survive in America I needed to develop awareness and survival skills, in each and every facet of American life, and also maintain a sense of dignity and preserve my intrinsic sense of self-worth. Both were lessons in how to survive without really dying, when one cannot fully live.

* * *

When the brusque cold and the whistling wind of December stiffens our relaxed autumn bodies, walking becomes an aerobic chore.

The early descent of darkness dampens our motivation and spirit, so the anticipation of the sunshine of Christmas exhilarates: This meant listening to Christmas lore, visiting Santa Claus at Macy's, then waiting for Santa to appear at home, the forever spectacular tree at Rockefeller Center, bubbling conversations with friends, spurred on by thoughts of little fingers tearing open presents oblivious to the beautiful wrapping paper and the artistry of its presentation, buying an ugly pine needle tree and transforming it into a festive national symbol.

Mom always preached Christmas was all year round for us. She very much disliked the idea of parents spending exorbitant sums of money to buy their children clothes and toys during a single season, while doing without during the rest of the year. Her reasoning made sense and we received fewer gifts, but I accepted it because we received toys and clothing all year round.

But watching Roy Rogers and his palomino horse, Trigger, Dale Evans and her horse Buttercup on an eleven inch black and white television helped to create a bursting desire for a horse that I envisioned tied up to the glass-paneled door in our bedroom. Having been a good boy, meeting all of Santa's requirements for a wish of my choice, I deserved a horse. Of course, when I asked Mom, she said, "No."

But with all the sincerity only an eight year old can muster, I beseeched her, "Why can't I have a horse? I'll take care of it."

With a smile and eyes glistening with love, my Mom looked at me. "Where you goin' to put a horse, boy?" No need to tell you that I did not get a horse even though I made the exact same request on Santa's knee at Macy's. But alone with my mom in front of the Christmas tree with all the splendor of its bright lights and decorations and presents, she announced: "This will be your last Christmas, Junior."

Last Christmas! Everything was spinning and spun out of control. Was the world coming to an end? In palpitating disbelief I inquired why, and was told she was becoming a Jehovah's Witness and they did not celebrate Christmas.

Gee Wiz, Ma!

What kind of religion does not celebrate Christmas? What God doesn't celebrate Christmas? It must be some strange religion and I wanted no part of it, and could not understand why she would join if there was no Christmas. It was crazy. I mean, what kid in their right mind would join a religion with no Christmas?

"But what about the decorations, Ma?"

"I will give them away, Junior." Indeed she did, to our next-door neighbors, the Clarks. You can give away Christmas ornaments, but you can't just give away Christmas. It was a season of awe, reindeers flying, presents magically appearing, a time when the sole purpose was for children to be listened to and heard; to please children, grant their wishes, brighten their spirits, and make merry merrier. To top it off, no school for more than a week, this always made it a "white" Christmas.

No Christmas. Ouch. But truth be told, in due time I came not to miss Christmas

The most vexing was being the only one in my class who did not celebrate Christmas, the different one, every year. Moreover, everyday I felt different, awkward, a reluctant outsider, since Jehovah's Witnesses do not salute the flag because it is considered a manmade symbol not to be worshipped. Sure there were other kids in the same predicament, but we only made up a small handful. But Mom did not mind at all; in fact, she thrived and put her heart and soul into her new religion. My father's life style and behavior suggested there was no God, so we kids followed Mom to the Kingdom Hall and belief in Jehovah God where she became "Sister Adams." I used to attempt to proselytize by selling the religious magazines of Jehovah's Witnesses, Watchtower and Awake, door to door and on the street, and gave "talks" (reading scripture and giving commentary) at the Kingdom Hall.

Having learned that God was All-Powerful, listened to, and answered prayers, I began to pray for solutions to my personal issues and concerns. Cringing fear clung to me while trying to decipher why an All-Powerful God allowed Emmett Till to be killed. I prayed for relief with genuine belief for a truck bike from the Sears & Roebuck catalogue that had glued itself to my fantasy, to move out of the Basement, and to stop white people from being so mean to Negroes. When nothing changed, I sought Mom's guidance and was told, "Junior, God does not respond to worldly needs, only spiritual needs."

I was ten and lived in the real world with worldly needs, and if they had been met, my spirit and spiritual needs would have been just fine, thank you. At that very moment, my waning belief in God died, appalled that God was not an active participant in my life for what I needed and wanted, therefore, God could not exist. I understood that I only had myself to rely on and placed exclusive trust and faith in myself. I became a surreptitious atheist and only went through the motions of religious practice to both please and get along with my mom.

After Mom's conversion to Jehovah's army, I of course wanted to be part of the winning side, and be prepared for Armageddon and the world to come, where lions would lie down with the lambs and not eat them for dinner. Though I did wonder what they would eat instead, Mom said, "Grass," when I asked. The idea was palatable and desirous, and I was seduced by the pictures of idyllic Garden of Eden scenes, with lions and lambs sitting peacefully next to each other with no primal or instinctive tension to suggest differently.

Damn right, I believed Armageddon was coming, that God would destroy the world again, sometimes too literally. With the memory of those who did not get a ticket to ride in Noah's Ark, fear was prominent that God could and would destroy me if I did not lead a holy enough life style.

But a funny thing happened on the way to Armageddon. Confined to Harlem, handcuffed to the Basement, unable to drink white water, eat ice cream, hamburgers and French fries when I wanted, and watched Negro lambs be intimidated and killed by zealous white lions was enough evidence that God did not exist. I lived in an Armageddon where the wicked were alive and well and very legitimate. A thick mist of cynicism descended upon my Santa Claus-like belief in God, as clouds of anger gathered.

I bought hook, line, and sinker, the notion that if good, the good would be rewarded; that I would be rewarded with resurrection and heaven on earth. I tried, I tried hard, really I did, and at first I was successful in meeting God's holy standards for children. I even asked to be baptized as a Jehovah's Witness, but was told by Mom that at ten years of age to wait and make the decision when older. I was surprised at her response, but she said it was a serious decision and there was no going back. I gradually succumbed to the angry impulses that slowly rooted and grew in me like malignant tumors

Mom repeatedly taught: "Junior, people cuss and carry on because they don't have other words to say what they mean." She did not allow cursing under her roof and everyone adhered to her uncompromising law, including my streetwise and profane mouth father. So I knew very well it was wrong to use profanity, and I had a perfect track record until one evening while taking a bath, without warning, "Shit, damn," leapt from my mouth, leaving a sinful taste. Jolted, I had no damn idea I harbored the profane.

Surprisingly, I was fluent in the scatological, and vowed that this would be my last and only time using those inferior and unholy words. I had to take a bath every night and each time I returned to the tub the curse words kept coming, involuntarily they found a way into my larynx and out my mouth. I tried to stop myself from sinning and allay guilt by bargaining with myself. "Look, it's okay to say them here but no where else."

During the day there were no sullying words in my thoughts, but as the daylight grew dim and the moon rose through the thick black night so did my anxiety, and when mom inevitably said, "Junior, it's time for your bath," the terror of meeting the demons lurking within was near and numbing. Returning to the bathtub every night, the terror grew progressively worse. Afraid of being heard, I whispered a litany of profane diarrhea, "Shit, fuck, motherfucker, goddamn."

This went on night after night for what seemed like forever and forever. Right before stepping into the tub, I felt helpless before the cleansing power of the water about to transform me to evil. It was further disheartening because I lost the only place I could have my secrets, find alone time, peace of mind and space to be.

In an attempt at control, I set a quota of no more than five bad words said only once, "Fuck, shit, damn, motherfucker, bitch." And yes, I frequently exceeded my quota. Feeling increasingly comfortable, still, I felt out of control, so I would stretch out in the bathtub on my stomach and prayed to God to help me stop.

When God failed to intercede and the urge became uncontrollable, I placed my face close to the water, the wetness touching my lips, and spoke into the water as if my curses and sins would be immersed and baptized. "Shit goddamn motherfucker fuck shit bitch." When all else failed I placed my head under water but could not stop the verbal gargle crusade as the profane bubbling attested, "Shiiiit, mothuuufuker, biccch, dmmanit, fugggrrgk."

Reluctantly, at first, I began to enjoy my unholy sprees and found relief and satisfaction. I kept my secret secret until I slowly began to introduce curses into my daytime vocabulary, and eventually my daytime and nighttime personalities merged into a new identity, and I became fluent but never quite guilt free.

At age sixteen I could no longer tolerate wearing the mask of my disingenuous praxis of religion, because it did not come from a place of genuine acceptance and belief. I felt coerced and burdened. It was never *my* religion. Then one day Mom called me from work and reminded me to prepare my scheduled talk, which was the norm, for the Kingdom Hall that evening. I prepared and appeared, gave my talk, then promptly left before the service was completed, which was the norm.

Feeling unusually weighted down, I called my father and told him in agitated desperation I no longer wanted to do this, and to stop my mom from exercising her parental prerogative. What he said to her I don't know and still don't care, I was now free to exercise my belief or more accurately my disbelief in God, Armageddon, and resurrection as the necessary windows to eternal life. I exited the religious half-life with a solid unmovable disbelief in God, knowing I would never return to a house of worship, but I did promise my mom if I ever returned to religion I would return as a Jehovah's Witness.

* * *

Because of my urgent and desperate need of an emotional laxative, I began my saga with the Basement. It was the most distressing and unrelenting part of my childhood existence, for sure the most tangible. It was in plain sight and lived in every freaking minute, of every freaking hour, of every freaking day. Whereas racism was like the brusque battering whistling wind of December, it impeded your progress, left you cold and out of breath, unable to relax, but never "seen."

The Basement, as distressing as it was and is, was and is not simply location, location, location nor simply race, race, race, therefore I am. Even my indelible and informing Southern educational experiences were not pure race, race, race. The differential responses of my uncles are to what I allude.

Likewise my parents, who complete the tripod of influential factors on my early growth, their individual and collective personalities and family stewardship are a kinetic part of the complex equation of my early years and subsequent development. Finding myself in a very disturbing world, I turned to them for answers. The narrow point expressed is that the role of my parents parenting had a significant influence on me and cannot be obviated by default due to racism in the telling of my story, but must be looked at in the context of the complexity of race and other contributing cultural factors. Those who fail to take such account of their childhood development omit germane information that may provide insights otherwise unattainable and not explainable by race, racism, social, economic, and political conditions, or perhaps made clearer.

The story of Ernest Henry Adams Junior began before the life of Ernest Henry Adams Junior. To better understand the routes I have traveled you must know the roots from which I sprang. Both of my parents were born and raised in the American South, a mere fifty-two years after slavery formally ended, but not the American slave mentality. The "lynch law" was in active and terrifying use; white racial attitudes and behavior blunt and violent, discrimination was practiced with pride, and opportunity thin, craggy, malnourished. These were limited times, trying times and dangerous times for the Negro American.

Paradoxically, it was the deeper structure of the United States Constitution and Government, which in its origins was a sanctuary for slavery and excluded the Negro as citizen. It was and is this very same constitution and government, while very flawed, that provided and provides an even deeper guiding, sometimes treacherous process, that harbors choices, progress, limited and imperfect, for Negroes in the whole body market of American racial life to make decisions about their lives.

Despite being on the penumbra, free will means no individual or institution may control the values one may adopt and adapt despite being harshly oppressed and exploited. I am only acknowledging the possibility of some semblance of control in Negro life, recognizing how fractiously tiny it was, and is now larger, with the potential for growing greater redounding to the black American community.

My father was born in the Deep South, in the red clay hills of Georgia in 1920, in the Common Era when hanging Negroes was a family and community event. His brother John, born in 1915, when their mother was fifteen, had a different father. Georgie Adams, came to New York shortly after giving birth to my father. She worked as a domestic, leaving both children with her sister. Both boys reunited with her in New York when my father was twelve years old.

Sitting on the floor of the living room while my father sat comfortably on the couch reading the Daily News—I relished being in his presence—a perfectly logical question for a nine year old popped out, "What was your father's name?"

I could hear my father stop reading, and the newspaper became a momentary shelter from my lacerating inquiry. So unexpected was my question, he was unable to parry it with his ever-quick wit. Slowly, he looked up, wondering and hoping he did not hear correctly; his stoic face hardened, inadvertently highlighting his distress.

His lips reacted slowly, "Tom."

Heavy silence followed. I waited for more knowledge about my father's would-be father. Peering from behind the silence, my father was lost, and lost as to what to say about my would-be grandfather. Continuing in childhood Ernest I wanted to know who he was: What did he look like? What kind of work did he do? What he was like? Where did he come from? Where did he live?

He put a brake on my unrelenting curiosity, "I didn't know my father."

He spoke from the sad eyes of a boy suffering and struggling with wretched deprivation, never sure of who he was, his still apparent need larger than my curiosity, a never ending sense of never having been his father's son, never having known his voice, his guidance, his laughter, his touch. This deep cleft savagely brokered his spirit and floated in him like a rudderless ship at the mercy of an impersonal, storm-wavering sea. I never again revisited that bottomless pit of absolute doubt within my father.

So I went to my mom and made further inquiry. My grandmother Adams never broached the subject with her even though she lived with my parents in her later years. Mom apprised me that my father never discussed in depth what he knew or felt. My Mom unintentionally added another perplexing sting, "That is part of your father's problem, he never knew his father."

Mom described him as staunchly defensive of his personal boundary, and when he felt the pressure of intrusive inquiries that even brushed against it, he prevailed with a prickly smile and retort, "I'm going to mind my business and let yours alone."

This became one of his oft-repeated mantras. One day he showed me a daguerreotype photo of his grandmother—he looked like her—and he smiled with fierce gratitude, "She did not let nobody bother me." He sounded as if she was the sole source of trust and protection.

My father possessed a lining of anger that could flair when provoked, but he was not grounded in racial animosity; he was angry, but not bitter. Nor was he judgmental. The other mantra he lived by and never stopped repeating: "Live and let live."

He had an amazing capacity to be open to other people, their values, their choices, and a sense of humor prevailed. The story of his going hungry during the Great Depression, he recounted in exaggerated remonstrance. He described, with serious countenance, having only grits on his plate for breakfast and too poor to have lunch. By dinnertime he was starving and another plate of grits was placed before him. Now the contours of his face slowly reshaped as an unexpected impish grin settled in. With mischievous affect he proclaimed, "I was starvin', starvin' starvin' and the grits were put on the plate, put down in front of me. I looked down at those grits, I stared at those grits, stared down at those grits, stared long at those grits, and I filled right up, wasn't hungry no mo'."

Now my father was holding back the rambunctious laughter about to escape, his eyes darted toward my sisters and me. He had our attention and we readily joined in laughing at whatever his pain was.

Shortly after I was born my father complained to my mom that I was getting all the attention and that she no longer had time for him. She did not grasp the import nor the depth and magnitude of his need, and reacted to his expression as irrational criticism of her role as mother. He became different and she did not know why. Mom described him as moody and sometimes measured his mood when she came home, "…by throwing my hat into the room, if it stayed, I went in, but if it came back out, I didn't go in."

Inconsistent he was, and to smooth out the deep fluctuations in mood, he used alcohol to float and steady his pain. He became a not very discreet womanizer, spending too much time outside his home.

I always knew my father would protect me from anything or any person in the physical environment. Only 5'8" inches tall, he was street wise and street tough. He had an edge, fearless thick edge—that he could call upon when needed—that allowed him to cajole or defend as needed. He carried a razor for protection and when I remarked that it was against the law, he retorted, "It's against my law to be caught in the street by those hoodlums without it."

However, there was a depth to my father, multiple layers not easily recognized. At age twelve I was on punishment, Ernest came home and inquired if I had completed all my chores and errands. I lied like an experienced son, wanting to get outside again with friends, and was caught in my untruth by a more experienced Ernest who said, "I knew you had not done what you were supposed to do before I asked. I just wanted to see what you were goin' to do. You lied to me. You looked me straight in the eye and lied to me."

But he was surprisingly calm and my fears of further punishment began to slip away. In general, Ernest exhibited a greater spirit of mercy and leniency than did my mom. I preferred to be disciplined by Ernest because he was less likely to use the rod and more likely to use punishment. I would call him on the job and more often than not he would grant clemency. "Anything you do or even think about doin', I already done it, and more. I'm goin' to punish you some more, not because you didn't do what you were told, but because you lied to me and did not take responsibility."

All I could hear was that more punishment was on the way and I was going to be stuck at home.

"You have to learn to take responsibility for what you do, that is what a man is supposed to do."

"But I'm not a man yet I'm only twelve," I quipped.

He smiled at my lame attempt.

"I promise, promise, really promise, I won't do it again."

Then he gave me that look. "I don't want to say it again, I've tried and done everythin' you can think of and things you ain't thought of. In life you have to learn to take responsibility for what you do." He was repeating himself so I knew he was serious and punishment was on the way. "You have to learn to be a man about what you do in life, lyin' about it ain't goin' to do you no good, it will not fix things. You only goin' to make people mad."

Both my parents always stressed how they hated liars. He grounded me and went off to work with an unfamiliar refrain, "And don't call me on the job." At that moment I did not like Ernest, not very much, because there was no nuclear threat due to my point blank lies, and more importantly, he cut off the appeal process.

I got involved in a childhood dispute and it escalated. My friends and I started throwing things at the boys we argued with. I threw a rounded metal object about half inch thick and half inch long that shattered a window in a first floor apartment and everyone scattered, except me. Nervous within, I calmly walked across Convent Avenue, and the woman whose window I broke asked who did it, and I claimed responsibility. Fuming, she asked where I lived and I told her "across the street." She growled the standard boilerplate about my recklessness and the harm I could have caused. Thanks to my dad, during my life, I have scattered less from accepting responsibility than I otherwise would have.

I felt compelled to attend Automotive Trades high school to become an automobile mechanic though I had no intrinsic interest even as all my friends, except Richard Jefferson, were about to enter academic high schools. Mrs. Mangum, my sixth grade teacher, appalled to hear I was going to attend a vocational high school, said to my father, "Your son could breeze through academic high school." Memories uncovered in psychotherapy many years hence revealed the irresistible basis for my high school choice. My decision was based on a single conversation I had with my father in eighth grade.

We drove into a gas station on a perfect sunny day. The sun beamed through the windshield resting comfortably on our laps as we waited for the gas tank to be filled, and, without apparent provocation, my father turned and began to confess that he had dreams of opening a gas station where we would work together and build a business. "Me and you, father and son, senior and junior," his dream was both hopelessly, excruciatingly alive, and, excruciatingly deceased. "The sign was supposed to say: Ernest Sr. & Ernest Jr." I was seduced. Not by his words but by the depth of the lost hope, false positive of his strivings, his ambitions to be a man of his choice, to be a father as he would choose. Now "open," I could "see" and "feel" my father, a soft gentle man, who desperately wanted to be better than he was, who had a depth of feeling and caring for and about me that had not been previously articulated so successfully.

It was a rare glimpse into the fundamental humanity of a man who was not articulate about his life experiences, disappointments, pain, who could not say to the world again, and again, that he wanted to be, because no one was hearing, only listening, no one saw, they only looked, and looked, and looked.

Why at that moment I will never know, but the magnitude and depth of his passion was awe inspiring and eventually depressing. Perhaps, the refracted rays of the sun broke through the window of his Exile, his jailed aspirations, and for a few memorable moments he spoke like a man pardoned from his life sentence, and together we melded into the unalloyed love of father and son. Most times, I only saw my dad get up and go to work with a work ethic that was as American as any American; driven by what, I do not know, but he retired on two pensions from two jobs—City of New York ambulance driver and parking lot attendant. No matter how much he drank and drank, he always worked and worked, but he never considered himself an alcoholic, publicly, but privately he knew he was in trouble.

Ernest was fortified by alcohol and it was literally a pillar of strength for him, or so he fervently believed. We were having a party at Florita's home when Clarence, a family friend, began taking photographs of folks in pairs or groups. When the camera swung in my father's direction, unlike everyone else, he did not attempt to armor himself with his wife or children or friends. Instead he grabbed a quart bottle of vodka and quart bottle of bourbon and held each one under each arm in repose, and with a Cheshire grin he posed for the camera. Taken aback, Clarence politely said, "Ernie, I want to take a picture of you and Carrie, you with your family and your friends."

Burning in agony, Ernest shifted his weight, jumped into an emotional trench, stuck his neck out. His eyes widened and his grip on the bottles tightened as he stood his ground, "These are my friends, my two best friends, they never let me down."

Swirls and eddies of angst jousted within me, then dropped straight through to the bottom of my feet, and the idea of tears came to my eyes. I witnessed why we always called him Ernest growing up, and why we only called him Pop as adults, and most clearly, I saw why we never called him dad or daddy: he was an empty vessel and vassal to his demanding emptiness. The sustenance he did give me, no matter how genuine, came from a haunted house of brittle and broken memories. He gave like he got, it can be said he gave more than he got, or what I imagine he did not get, but what he did give, he gave with genuine love.

When sixteen years old, I almost came to blows with Ernest—out of raging frustration, he was never physically abusive—and told my mom I was prepared to stab him, as I showed her a knife I held in my trembling hand. But I really did not want to stab him. Breathing heavily, yet smoothly, with tears quietly making their way down the burning knife wound in my heart and my face, my soul felt maligned by his seeming lack of concern for me. It magnified my feeling obscure, not quite solid, not quite liquid.

Growing up I called my father Ernest, not dad, daddy or father, the common expression that denoted parental relationship but not necessarily connote intimacy. Ernest identified himself as my father by his first name but it did not identify me as his son. I never wondered if I was his son but calling him Ernest left me feeling a little cheated, then as I grew up, a lot cheated; cheated out of my natural right as his son. I don't know how it got to be that way, but be that way it was.

Yet, when I think about Ernest growing up, I have no clear memory of calling him Ernest. My memory has erected a "soundproof" wall that keeps out the "noise" from the loud screeching friction that followed every time I called my daddy Ernest. A distance was created that was inherent in our relationship, but not inherent in how we naturally loved each other.

One morning, when we became adults, my sisters and I started calling Ernest, "Pop." I don't recall when and how, but surmise the metamorphosis was due to a mutual maturity, and now delayed recognized need to have more than a formal and nondescript appellation between a father and his children. What is more stupefying than ever, is that his grandchildren knew him as "Erno," not granddad, gramps, or grandpa.

At this very moment, as I am writing these words, I just *now* realized, literally, that I only knew my grandparents by their initials or last name. That is, I just now recognized how odd, how remote, how peculiar a family communication. My maternal grandfather I called H.C. and paternal grandmother, Adams, not the usual generational terms of endearment. This "generation gap," this ponderous gap, rested on my soul, and kept a not so still and swerving distance between us all; distance, full of unfilled longing to be touched, from within the protective barriers erected by them, and me.

I wondered if this was unique to my generation so I made inquiries. I discovered Ernest and his brother John referred to their mother only as "A," a minimal and minimalist recognition of a mother if there ever was one. My mom called her mother "momma" and her father "daddy," but after her mother died when she was thirteen, she and all her siblings stopped calling him daddy, and he became known as H.C. When we were on the farm together, Uncle Charlie and Uncle J always referred to H. C. as, "the old man." Making these meaningful new discoveries and connections for the very first time while reliving the experiences and the accompanying emotional sequelae, feels like a surgeon's knife making an incision, without anesthesia, and uncovering an area of pervasive infection.

What I did not know then, but would later dawn and be welcomed as the rising sun on the dark of night, was that Ernest desperately wanted to be called dad or daddy, but was not able to ask for what was his, and my God given right.

My anger at Ernest obscured the positive impact my father had upon me. I failed, miserably so, to recognize how much Ernest Sr. and Ernest Jr. were alike until after he took his rightful place with the ancestors. Despite all the good enough interactions and good enough memories, his inconsistent and deficient physical presence failed to translate into a complete and fully recognizable internal presence, until after his death. It was the incisive and insightful rendering questions of a most unlikely interlocutor that unlocked a "new" identity during the Jewish days of redemption, so aptly named: The High Holy Days.

My mom was born in 1917, the oldest of five siblings that grew up with her on a one hundred acre farm in Johnston County near Clayton, North Carolina. My mom's mom, Hattie, was a gifted seamstress, dexterous with her hands and made many garments for the family. My grandmother was able, by drafting a pattern onto a paper bag, to transform adroitly, her daughter's wish for a dress seen in a store window. This magical mastery made her eldest daughter feel like a very special girl on the farm. Her grandfather, Henry Charles Delaine Sr., a Baptist preacher owned a substantial amount of property in South Carolina, and his ambition was for his "grandchildren not to have to work," Mom recalled with musing regret. He transferred his liquid assets to what he thought was a more stable bank. His judgment was dead wrong, and he went belly-up during the Great Depression.

Hattie died when mom was thirteen, "giving birth to that last child that was stillborn." The ache in her voice still evident for the ultimate loss a child may suffer and bear, her deep anger at that corpse, that would-be sibling, remained.

H.C. found himself in a new role when Hattie died. It was now his responsibility to clothe his daughter. He purchased her clothes from the Sears & Roebuck and Montgomery Ward catalogues. She was small and he chose "little girl dresses, white pique little jumper dress with a red gingham blouse. It was that or I wore anything and everything that anybody gave me." The incrustation of disappointment and distain still sounded current sixty-five years later. The sudden loss of her mom remained acutely felt, "If momma had been here it would have been different. She gave me everything I wanted." My mom graduated high school but decided not to attend Shaw University in Raleigh, North Carolina because she was certain her father would not purchase the clothes she desired. So instead of college, she got a job as a chambermaid in a rooming house for "Caucasian women" in Raleigh, North Carolina. "The girls, quite naturally," Mom explained, "worked as secretaries and clerks in the stores." When the cook showed up drunk for work once too often, mom got the job. She came to New York in 1938 and lived with her Aunt Alonya Potter who was a superintendent in the Bronx, and also the domestic for a synagogue in the same block.

For mom, a deeply devout woman, God was the centerpiece that provided peace of mind to have the strength and endurance to battle and persevere against the grind of daily life in the Basement. "Give me strength Heavenly Father," Mom would fervently implore. When I inquired about her public prayer she was absolutely convinced, "Jehovah

God gives me the strength to go on everyday. I don't know what I'd do without strength from Jehovah."

From my cynical viewpoint the talk of surviving Armageddon or being resurrected placed too much weight on an invisible and non-responsive Force. I wanted a God sooner than later, in the here and the Right Now. I trusted and believed only in myself. Mom trusted and wholeheartedly believed in the invisible Force. It aroused my distain for a phrase Mom restated often, that I felt and still feel makes no damn sense under any circumstances: "You can't have your cake and eat it too."

My sarcasm would playfully chide, "Who wants cake you can't eat?" When older I asked, "Who needs cake you can't eat?" This phrase smacked of pie in the sky. I made a flippant comment without intending to offend about Jehovah God, "How about Joe bringing some cake I can, need, and want to eat."

Big Mistake.

Her eyes blazed like black diamonds, and locked on me. I was mesmerized. I became afraid a hole would burn through my soul, but I was too intimidated to look away. With a controlled fury I never witnessed before or since, and completely out of character, Mom exploded softly, "Don't be talking about my God like that, you have no right. None! Don't ever talk about Jehovah God that way." Unable to move, I immediately knew I had crossed the line. An Adams will do whatever it takes to defend a principled position or when feeling threatened. I *sincerely* apologized out of the Fear and Awe from which she spoke.

Mom, as she affectionately resonates and prints in my heart and mind, was my reservoir and my saving grace, providing a consistent, reliable physical presence. She was always "Ma," like in, "Ma, what's for dinner…Ma, you got a dime? How you feeling Ma? Ma, can I have this, it's only a quarter? Ma, I can't find my keys. Ma, I don't feel good." She was my sun and my sunshine. If my father's raggedy home attendance record helped to make the world appear a more frightening and less trustworthy place, mom and her faith in God was the antidote.

I was always curious, and mom had the presence and patience to meet my demands for answers and explanations. Also serving as my confidant, I freely spoke about anything and everything, and my observations and inquiries were readily given a platform, from my first notice of Lillian Robinson's breasts blooming under her benign blouse in ninth grade to why if God was everywhere, why not in Harlem helping us out?

She frequently made observations that had psychological parameters. My three-year-old nephew Kevin was asleep, and he awoke in the middle of the night, afraid. Annoyed, I growled he should go back to sleep. Mom heard the commotion, got up, turned on the lights, and explained there was nothing to be afraid of and let him look around. He went right back to sleep. Mom turned to me and explained he was only scared.

"I used to do the same for you, she said."

A "career" woman, mom held different jobs, diligently working eight-hour days whether she was a domestic, factory worker or nurse's aide for the City of New York. She saved her sick days and went to work even when she was not feeling well because, "If something happens, Junior and I get sick, then I will need those sick days."

"Ma, what could happen that would make you need six months off from work."

"Junior, I could have an accident and need an operation and be out of work for a few months."

"But that is not six months Ma, take some days off."

Not a workaholic, she used her vacation days and knew how to have a good time, but she always wanted to be prepared for the worst. She referred to her sick time as "money in the bank." Fortunately she never had a catastrophic illness and when she retired, she was paid for all of her unused sick time. Money in the bank. When I worked for the New York City Police Department I once went to work with a fever in inclement weather and was asked by my supervisor why I showed up so obviously sick. I responded that I saved my sick days for when I was really sick.

Always knowing where mom was provided a sense of security and safety. More importantly, I always knew in the heart of her druthers that she truly desired to be a homemaker, to take care of my sisters and me. She did not work until Audrey and me, eighteen months apart, were able to talk because, "I wanted you to be able to tell me if someone abused you. It was hard financially, but I wanted to make sure you were safe." Mom's genuine desire to be at home made her absence more palatable because I felt her deep care and concern for me. Since I felt like I was a number one priority it provided the proper dosage of narcissism needed to build sufficient self-esteem. No montage needed here: mom was a single complete portrait that was the foundation for being able to order, organize, and adequately negotiate the environment.

In addition to all the obligatory visits to schools, mom was the standard bearer of culture. My sisters studied "toe dancing," better known as ballet. I learned to tap dance, and boy oh boy, did I love my black patent leather shoes with the black shiny glow and oversize taps on the heel and toe. I rehearsed first in my head, then danced in the Basement hallway, where I could hear the taps greet the Basement floor, creating the perky metal clicking sounds that ricocheted syncopated rhythms and fantasies of me dancing with Ginger Rogers, as my tapping feet imitated the grace of Fred Astaire. I then danced a duet with Gene Kelly with the sound of Singing in the Rain in my dancing feet's ear as my body attempted to tap, glide and elevate as athletically as only he did. Then I danced in trio with both Gene and Fred, and I was in the middle, it was magical, like never before and never again, as we swayed through riffs of improvisations and I out danced them that day, and you should have been there. I was cooler than cool, and cooler than Bo Jangles dancing with Shirley Temple, eat your heart out Bo Jangles.

My sisters and I performed in the "show of shows" a community sponsored event that comprised a compendium of song and dance routines. Florita took piano lessons with Miss Archibald and practiced on a neighbor's piano. Because she seemed to have a knack for playing the piano, my parents purchased a piano. I used to watch Florita practice and when she finished I would play what she played. Mom told my dad and he said to her, "Since he can play, send him to Miss Archibald too." Mom had a seemingly natural propensity for middle-class aspirations. We attended theatre, ballet and dance performances and she also took us on excursions outside the neighborhood, to the Bronx Zoo, Ringling Brothers Circus and a variety of amusement parks.

It can be argued I grew up in some reasonable facsimile of a middle-class Basement, maybe. Putting that aside for the moment, I would like to argue my parents did a yeoman's job in raising their three children notwithstanding all the flaws, even the deep and treacherous. They did not have easy personal lives, and the American culture defined and treated them as less than full citizens and human beings. Relatively privileged, I don't know how I would have traveled the narrower path that was available to them.

Individually I salute them, and without reservation love them dearly, but together, they made for a nearly lethal combination. My mom's greatest strength was her weakness and my dad's greatest weakness was his strength.

Dad was personable, affable, warm, sociable with a sense of humor and a big-heart, but he shared too much of his time outside the home. He had the proverbial wondering eye that created a permanent tension in our home. His inconsistency made me feel severely deprived.

Mom was a stable presence, a very efficient captain of the Adams household, but her sense of humor was lacking. She was organized, predictable, and reliable, but she had a propensity for the need to control in order to feel safe. Too often it had to be her way or no way. The energy needed to be the primary organizer and to effectively monitor the environment and have control, or some perceived semblance thereof, no matter how real or not, compromised her capacity to connect her genuine love on deeper levels with me. Mom presented as loving but distant, unable to articulate the depths of her feelings and was only able to see me as she needed me to be seen.

This trifecta, the Basement, the South and my parents, was the dominant influence in the shaping of my personhood. Traveling the Dark highway of life, with no known map, my vision was strained more often than not. The palimpsest of signs and windows on the passing landscape, no matter how blurred or transparent, provided the necessary symbols and information to reach desired destinations, or not. I take credit for my failures and give to others credit for my successes. The only person responsible for the decisions made and the denouement, is the person who experienced, on the journey, all the signs and windows, from Ghetto to Ghetto.

Necessary Education and Education Not Necessary

> Ships at a distance have every man's wish on board. For some they come in with the tide. For others they sail forever on the horizon, never out of sight, never landing until the Watcher turns his eyes away in resignation, his dreams mocked to death by Time. That is the life of men.
>
> ***Zora Neale Hurston***

"Junior, it's time to get up," Mom's voice roused. Our home was a bustle five mornings a week as mom and all the moms of all the Harlems across America prepared their children, however unwittingly, however prepared, however unprepared, for "the life of men," that sadly, devastatingly, had an abundance of boys and girls maturing into men and women who would live such a "prophesied" life, such a truncated life.

I easily fell asleep at night and awoke easily in the morning with the aid of my red white and blue plaid patched soft quilt-like blanket and my two middle fingers in my mouth clutched together in a duet of needy comfort. As I sucked for succor, the self-engendered warmth provided a sense of safety and comfort that the natural world could not. Then came the light of transition from the natural world of dreams to the natural world where dreams were so unnaturally unfulfilled. "Junior, it's time to get up," Mom chimed again.

Some mornings I was reluctant to get up and face the life of men: the world of our fathers. Uncertainty loomed upon leaving the melody of my two fingers and my red, white and blue security blanket, which did not provide security.

"Let's go Junior. It's time to get up," Mom's pleasantness chided me.

I had already learned I could only rely on myself, that there was something wrong both inside me and inside my home, and something was wrong both outside of me and outside of my home.

"Come on Junior, you've got to get up now," Mom said again trying to convince me.

"Junior," Mom's exasperation was beginning to show, "let's go now, let me hear those feet hit the floor." Her voice pulled me up and resistance held me down. I sometimes faked getting up by patting the palms of my hands on the floor, doing my best imitation of me walking.

"Don't sound like no feet to me," Mom said with a tickle in her voice which made me smile as I slid out of bed dragging my trusted blanket. Into the bathroom, I brushed my teeth, washed up, and placed a good amount of Mum deodorant under my arms to ward off the funk monsters. I put on my clothes that were laid out the night before, and I entered the kitchen to eat a hearty breakfast.

Now it was off to school. And school was a must with a very narrow focus, "Necessary education," counseled Mom, "to get a good job, Junior." Before Mom's words had a chance to settle in my brain, she continued without breaking stride, "And just where do you think you are goin' with your hair looking like *that*?"

"Like what?" asked with a boy's genuine ignorance.

"Boy, you better go comb and brush your nappy head. You know you can't be goin' out into the street lookin' like *that*," she said. I did not know what *that* looked like but I often got the same warning from my dad. "Boy, you ain't goin' with me lookin' like *that*, you better go on an' comb that nappy head of yours."

Florita never heard complaints about her hair being nappy nor was she subject, like Audrey, to the hot comb to straighten her hair because she had gotten the gene for "good" hair.

Now successfully off to school, my first stop was the second floor, to pick up Winston McGill, my best friend. The McGills were my ideal family, starting with the three-bedroom apartment they lived in with shiny hardwood floors and nothing but the best furniture. I was unduly envious that both Winston and sister Carolyn had their own bedrooms. Though Winston and I were best friends, our parents were only the most casual and cordial of neighbors; they were separated by temperament, style, their clashing visions of themselves and their children.

Mr. Winston McGill, Sr. was a genteel man by nature and intellect, who studied Spanish at Harlem High School to "keep me sharp," after he was prohibited the opportunity to attend City College of New York (CCNY) in the 1930's because he was Negro. The CCNY campus, with its stellar intellectual reputation, grand gothic architecture stretching a half-mile, sat on Convent Avenue in Harlem, at the top of a steep hill overlooking St. Nicholas Park, and overlooking the young and ambitious Winston, who resided at the bottom.

Steep though the incline, young Winston had the confidence, motivation, intelligence and will to climb, and to succeed. The calculated injustice sank to the nethermost part of his soul; this was a life sentence, and permafrost embalmed his slain aspirations. Every time he walked below on St. Nicholas Avenue, his head and heart would arc and ache upward as his most sought after desire mocked him, grinning, never turning away, in a pernicious perpetuity. Young Winston's soft cerebral humor, impeccably matched with his light rolling laughter, shrouded the turmoil roiling inside him.

In lieu of emotional immolation, young Winston was driven by the very desecration of his dream: stymied, not stopped, he became a visionary who perceived and reasoned beyond his own despair, cynicism, and degradation, and handed down his revivified dream to Winston Jr. and daughter Carolyn, fortifying and guiding them while working as a token clerk for the City of New York.

"Ernie," his voice was heavy with permanent wait, "I had to take care of my family the best way possible at that time," he said apodictically, conveying the strain of a lifetime of continuous disappointment. Young Winston read the "paper of record," the New York Times, every day, even as he matured into Winston Sr., every day, "so I could keep up with the world."

Mrs. Cora McGill, a woman with moxie, challenged Win Jr. to master math and not let math master him. He did not disappoint. Education was more than a value in the McGill household, it was an imperative, a demand to dream and plan and prepare for a life that was not promised, and had little promise: the life of men.

I came home one day and unexpectedly found an eleven inch black and white television sitting in the living room. The eleven-inch screen embedded in the ugly brown-stained box provided an immediate and accessible cultural primer, a conglomeration of events, information, news, sports, entertainment, that enlarged my world as it simultaneously became smaller and more apparent, yet more complex. The visual expanse of communication was mesmerizing and revolutionary. I went on the road with Bob Hope and Bing Crosby; found families unlike any I knew, Father knows Best and Amos and Andy; met Milton Berle but not Moms Mabley; loved George Burns and Gracie Allen; how was I to know I was watching classic TV in I Love Lucy and the Honeymooners? Walter Cronkite and CBS introduced me to politics with the debate between Richard Millhouse Nixon and John Fitzgerald Kennedy. A white racial world beyond Harlem entered my living room.

I was one of two boys and six girls who graduated from elementary school, P.S.129, with honors, and Mr. Stouffer, the music teacher, announced that he hoped there would be more boys next year—my sidekick Winston was the other. The world of school provided relief from the drudgery of the Basement and all was well as I continued to follow the North Star to Junior High School 43.

The lone disappointment the first Junior High School day was that my sidekick and best friend and I were placed in different classes. I was in the "top" seventh grade class but Winston was placed in the Special Progress (SP) class, the prestigious and envious SP, where he would complete both the seventh and eight grades in the same year. I was crushed that I was not in the SP class and could not figure out why.

I sat in Mrs. Sterling's seventh grade class actively wishing that somehow, someway, sometime soon, if not right now, an egregious error was about to be undone. When finally convinced that I was not to be an SP student, it was the straw that cracked my crystal covered veneer of intelligence, and pushed it off the narrow internal wall of confidence, shattering into microscopic shards that ground deeply into my system, and I bled from within, profusely, privately, withering without a whimper. My intrinsic gravitational pull to excel went adios and my spirit and grades followed. I was no longer hungry for honors. Mr. Bernstein opened his grade book and chronicled to mom my steady decline from an A to a C in his English class.

When Mom slowly perused that first ever report card devoid of A's, she lifted her head slowly, made eye contact with me, spoke softly, which was the norm, "Look at this report card, what happened to you?" Despite her best effort a growling sharpness hardened her voice.

"I don't know," which was the sad truth.

"Junior, you always get good grades," she said, looking alternately at the report card and at me. She was genuinely perplexed.

Mom at times had a sensitivity and awareness of her children's problems as psychologically derived and would counter with her psychological approach. As I stood hapless and helpless as the one crowning glory I controlled was crumbling, my mother said: "Junior, your father is going to stomp you." Her expected sensitivity and awareness was nil. I did not recognize this strange mother-like figure who groused grossly before me.

"What happened to you? This is not like you. I know you can do better." My Dad waxed.

Guilty as charged. I remained silent.

"In the garage I like to brag about you, tell the guys about my smart son who does good in school. What am I going to say to them now?"

I was flabbergasted, but being my father's son my face hid my real feelings. This was the very first time I had any knowledge that I existed in the life of my father outside of my presence, outside of our home.

My father said with genial sincerity, "I want you to do better and get back to those nineties and A's you always bring home, so I can have something to be proud of."

Something to be proud of: So, lo and behold, I am bragging-rights, to highlight *his image* as a father to his colleagues.

"Really, son, I want you to do better," said with pleading doe-eyed supplication, with nary a trace of stomp in his demeanor.

Without altering my facial expression, a mental conniption fit was induced. A squall of rage arose and slammed forcefully against my internal foundation, knocking me off balance, "Fuck you and fuck your friends," I thought to myself.

I did not discover I was severely impacted by my failure to be an SP student until I unearthed this hidden source of pain writing this very line.

"Ernie," Mr. McGill said looking down at me, "what happened to you?"

"I expected you and Win Jr. to be together like always," he said with deep affection and disappointment.

And all my friends kept asking, "How come you aren't in the SP class?" To the repeated question I kept repeating, "I don't know."

"It must be a mistake, hound. What do you think happened?" Winston was confused. After graduating from George Washington High School, he went on to graduate number three in his engineering class at City College of New York, and then earned a master's degree in mechanical engineering from Massachusetts Institute of Technology. When working as an engineer was not fulfilling he returned to medical school and became a urologist.

"I don't know," remained my only answer. I felt embarrassingly self-conscious. One day it no longer hurt saying it because self-induced numbness took effect. I have not been academically in sync since.

After I told my parents, they were not upset or curious as to why.

My sister Florita, born in 1940, attended the local elementary school and when she was about ten the teachers, white and black, said to my mother: "Florita is so smart she does not belong here. Your daughter should attend the Hunter College School for the gifted. We can get her in there."

My mother politely refused. Years later when my mother told me the story, I asked why. Mom said, "Because when Florita got older she would not take school seriously, she would play around and not do her work."

Many years after this conversation I resurrected the discussion and mom defensively denied she said that. With utter self-confusion and likely a plethora of guilt, regretting her decision, Mom shook her head and stated, "Junior, I don't know why I did not let her go, just don't know." Mom divinely believed in "the security of government jobs" and steered Florita into being a legal secretary for the City of New York where she worked for twenty years. Mom had no idea what psychological process was working from within.

Predictable, so damn predictable, so damned; by ninth grade I was unmoored, drifting through every day, with no vision of a realistic future that I could impact, beyond mouthing promissory words of ambition, that died as soon as they left my lips and met a reality that demanded a modicum of belief in myself and hard work. Earning honors, I learned to play hooky, drink wine, party with girls, (sometimes in my apartment when my parents were not home) smoke some weed, manipulate and get-over, and hone a psychopathic edge, bluster and talk shit, more shit, bullshit. I learned to "instinctively" say to people what they wanted to hear and became an effective chameleon.

But I was cool, very cool with my Chuck Taylor All-Star converse sneakers. Though I could not play basketball well, well, I still went to the park and played and played and played. *Being* cool took on a more intense and expanded meaning beyond the teenage fashion of the moment. Being coolly dressed and addressed gave me an address where I could be located, seen and heard and presumed happy. My dad took me shopping to Barney's Boy's Town and I purchased a blue suit, my favorite color. Wearing my blue suit made me feel special and loved, and I loved it in return. We clung to each other in ardent rapture, admired each other in the mirror, and when I walked down the street I felt wholesome, and whole.

When I purchased, from the local deli, a spiced ham hero with homemade potato salad spread on the bread instead of mayonnaise, I was wearing my special blue suit. As I was leaving the store my taste buds only thought about devouring my delicious delicious hero but my eyes noticed the stack of wooden round crates and stayed clear of them. The thin twisted metal that kept the top crate closed had become unraveled and stuck out with a sharp pointy edge, with an invisible tip that snagged my pants right above the knee, and left a perpendicular flap with frayed edges.

My Perfect blue suit was no longer Perfect; its love was no longer Perfect; my love was no longer Perfect, and now maimed, I was no longer happy, became sick to my stomach, tasting only my severe loss; losing its taste, I threw my delicious delicious hero away. I felt wounded, as if a casualty to a physical blow, like I lost an arm or leg, or the death of a family member. Shredded with grief, I delicately rushed my injured pants to the emergency room of Mr. Levy's cleaners, who took his dexterous black hands and mended my pants. But the stitched perpendicular flap left a raised edge of uneven blue threads that looked like a keloid and left both my pants and me permanently scarred. I suffered: Post Traumatic Clothes Disorder.

The ruination of my blue suit was a symbol of my plight in life. *Every time* something good happened to me or I felt good about something, something or some thing always impinged upon or obliterated my fun in the sun. It got so bad I assumed nothing good that I wished for could happen or be sustained. So I stopped wishing and thinking about what I really wanted, and began to wish for the opposite, knowing for certain I stood a better chance of success. When my dad told me he was taking me shopping for the cool shoes I wanted, immediately I began to feel excited, but then the likelihood something would prevent me from getting them led me to pray to the capricious gods, "You don't really want them, they aren't that nice, and nobody is going to like them. It's better you don't get them." I became intimidated by my self-imposed irreverent prayer, and was afraid to be proactive on my behalf and would attempt to force myself to act positively by conjuring holy intimidation: "If you don't do homework, you won't get resurrected when Armageddon comes."

James Thomas became my street guru and I spent an inordinate amount of time with Horace, Ron J, Ray, Roe T, Billy B, Craig P, H. J., and Norris; unbeknownst to us all, all, with the exception of James, died sooner than they should have. The common factor: slow deaths, bought and paid for in excruciating installments, that ferociously gripped their lives, in drugs, AIDS, and crime.

One night I was out past my curfew with James and some combination of the above mentioned boys. We had nothing better to do and began walking uptown on Convent Avenue, and as we passed by City College there was a white man walking on the other side of the street, alone. It was a Saturday midnight. I yelled out, "Hey, there's a white boy," and he stopped and beckoned us to come over. I was the only one of the group to respond to his invitation and when I casually approached him, all 5'6", 135 pounds of me, counting my thick brown horn rimmed glasses. I had nothing in mind except as a fourteen year old to impulsively take him up on his seemingly non-threatening invitation in an equally non-threatening response.

This athletically built white man with dark hair, handsome All-American face, about six feet tall, held out a book of matches and greeted me with a bizarre request: "Touch this, please," he began to whisper and whine, "just touch this, please, please just touch this." The insistence in his voice and the menace that lurked in his plea and skulked in his eyes caused me to hesitate and contemplate in a flash and I turned and ran as fast as I could and caught up with my boys.

Asserting my brazenness, in an attempt to elevate myself within the group, I asked why no one else stopped and James answered without breaking stride, "Saturday night, midnight, Harlem, white boy, he was a cop." End of discussion. We turned the corner at 138th Street and began walking down Broadway and as we made like magpies, a car pulled up next to us and the horn blew several times, the window rolled down on the passenger side and we all stopped to see who spent so much energy to get our attention. It was my father. "Get in," Dad commanded. I was more embarrassed than upset as he explained that I was past my curfew, so he came to bring me home.

I will always wonder, if I had touched that white man's book of matches ten minutes earlier, would my dad have arrived ten minutes, too late.

Mom's Jehovah Witness religious affiliation found us in the company of new values, influences and personalities. The Kingdom Hall, the house of worship for Jehovah Witnesses, had "brothers" assigned—from the Bethel headquarters in Brooklyn New York—to local congregations as overseers. One such brother was Brother Bob Hankins, assigned to Lower Harlem, mom's congregation.

But Brother Hankins was not a brother, not a black man. He had pale white skin tinged misty pink, angular nose with thin prominent squiggly red veins, slightly stooped physique and a receding hairline. Brother Hankins was mild mannered and looked like an Appalachian hillbilly. Mom refreshed my recollection and reminded me that Brother Hankins tutored me in grammar, writing and diction when I prepared to give "talks" on biblical scripture at the Kingdom Hall. In addition, Brother Hankins became a quotidian visitor to our home for meals and Bible study.

One afternoon a group of friends led by James Thomas knocked on my door wanting me to come out to play. As James stepped through the front door he spied Brother Hankins and stopped abruptly. Jolted, he stumbled backward, putting distance between himself and the white man eating at my kitchen table. Falling into the group safety net of the friends behind him, James stuttered, "A white man, a white man is in your kitchen," as if there was a white tiger. "He's eating, he's eating," spoken in supernatural disbelief as he looked at my other equally befuddled friends.

Taken-a-back by James' startle response, I huddled with the befuddled in the Basement—not understanding their exaggerated reaction. I said matter-of-factly, "It is *only* Brother Hankins…"

"Who is Brother Hankins?" James interrupted. I explained that he was a member of our congregation. After getting permission to join my friends outside, James, calmer now but still intense, spoke of his disappointment as we walked to the park. "I thought Uncle Charlie would be there, or your cousin Ronnie, Herbie, Charles Fitzpatrick, some brothers," he emphatically added, "real brothers." As we strolled James continued to limn, "our people be over, playin' cards, listenin' to music, talkin', drinkin', eatin', jokin'…"

Actually, we engaged in all those "black" social activities, including Brother Hankins.

Then there was the boy in my eighth grade class who wore brown corduroy pants every day; the same shit brown corduroy pants, and a white shirt. He was expressionless with a tunnel vision stare into the blackboard. I don't remember much about him except that he was dropped into my class in the middle of the semester, talked with a funny accent, and was not athletic. He attended Benjamin Franklin High School, well known for its sports programs, eventually closing because it did such a poor job of educating its predominately black and Latino populations.

After playing a game of basketball during the summer of 1964, my graduation year from high school, I was sitting on the park bench talking with Ray who had also just graduated from Benjamin Franklin. He said, "I signed up and joined the Air Force, I'm going to Lakeland, Texas for basic training in a few weeks. Why don't you come with me?"

"No man, if I go into the service I'll join the marines. You gotta be a real man to do the marines."

Ray chuckled, "So you want to be a real man, huh? How do you become a real man?"

Then for reasons I can't explain, I asked about someone I had not laid eyes on since Junior High School, "By the way, what happened to the guy who always wore the same brown pants in Junior High School, Nikolai?"

Slouching on the park bench, Ray came to life, "Nikolai Berlokoff?"

"Yea'."

"He's going to Harvard," the words popped out of his mouth, proudly. His body became so erect you would have thought that it was Ray going to Harvard, or his brother.

Stunned. So fucking stunned. My ghetto envy's first thought, "Why not me? Why can't that be me? Why wasn't that me?" As the basketball summer sweat cooled my body, I felt the shock of a cold chill, as I angrily wondered why I was not prepared for any college after earning a high school diploma in car repair skills. I pondered how Nikolai did it and I did not; the boy with the same shit brown corduroy pants, no fucking basketball game, and no rap for the girls!

I wept profusely, flooded with dry tears, and did not know it. Unhappy at Automotive High, I had seriously thought about transferring to Benjamin Franklin, but was too afraid because I thought I was not smart enough to pass algebra and biology. But in walks a European immigrant, I believe from Russia, who sat next to me in eighth grade and he was on his way to Harvard, and I was in good standing at Purgatory University, waiting in line to play my next basketball game. The worst part: I wasn't even "All Block." I was a lousy basketball player, no confidence, too nervous on the court.

A few years ago, as I sat in the office of Elliott, my former Junior High School classmate, I lamented that my trajectory might have been different if Mrs. Gordon, our white guidance counselor, had supported my attending an academic high school, and not misdirected me to car repair school. "Mrs. Gordon told me to go to Automotive. She didn't encourage or support the idea of me attending an academic high school," I said.

"Yeah," Elliott nodded. He became animated as he reminded, "Don't you remember, man? We were in the Higher Horizons Program at Junior High School 43."

The Higher Horizons Program was designed to expose public

school minority students to ideas and career possibilities they might not otherwise have considered; we went to the opera, philharmonic, Stock Exchange, etc. In eighth grade we had to research three professions, send away for three college applications, and fill them out as if applying. When Elliott graduated from Andrew Jackson High School with a senior class of twelve hundred students, he did not get a chance to see a guidance counselor, so he filled out his college application by himself, just as he had done in eighth grade.

Then Elliott slipped in matter-of-factly, "Mrs. Gordon supported me going to an academic high school and she readily encouraged me to attend college and become a teacher." He said this as we sat in his office where he was the principal of an elementary school in Baltimore, Maryland.

Elliott, Nikolai, Winston, where did I go wrong? Maybe, just maybe, I should have gone to Benjamin Franklin, George Washington or Andrew Jackson. Maybe, just maybe, the New York City public schools weren't that bad.

* * *

On November 22 1963, I was sitting in the Automotive high school library, when in walked the librarian with her black rim glasses, dark brown page boy haircut that looked like a helmet. Her face was drained pale and whiter than anyone I could have ever imagined, and she announced: "The President has been shot, the President has been shot," her voice quivered in shock as tears formed. She concluded with uncertain certainty, "shot, killed, shot, killed."

Engulfed by catastrophic disbelief, my mind went blank. Then my first thought, "Impossible!"

My denial died instantly; the notion of a mistake was disabused by the librarian's pallid countenance and the words that quavered out of her mouth. As I absorbed her words, my body and mind uncoupled from the shock of the pronouncement, its volcanic message disrupted my porous stability and left me feeling exposed, fragile, flimsy, shaken to my seventeen-year-old core. Negroes being killed, shot and lynched was the norm in my America, even black children were subject to the white man's murderous rage. But the President!

If the President was killed with secret service protection that obviously was not secret enough, and failed in its service to protect, I could be dealt death's blow, sudden, unexpected and right now, even if I was with my father.

In a trembling haze I traveled home numb, feeling Armageddon was about to present itself and that my mom and Jehovah Witnesses were right. No one was home so I walked to the St. Nicholas Terrace Park to find solace with community. It was dusk, and as the light of the sun descended upon our fate and the night rose to stoke our fears, Terry Johnson said with a wide smirk spread by agitation and anxiety, "You hea' the presiden' was kilt?"

I shook my head, "Yea', I know."

Terry continued, "The world's comin' to an end." His words showered me, staining and shaking me, landing in my head and circling like a merry-go-round without merry. But the probability of the world's destruction was now a rational thought, and the immediate credibility created a new layer of twitching reality.

I felt possessed by terror and the abyss, yet in a stunning paradox, I discovered I possessed an audacious, subconscious sense of "safety" and "comfort" beneath my rage at, and fear of, and experience with, American racial brutality—of which I was unaware. Junebug did not feel hopeless despite America's racial resume. Residing ever present in me was a deeper layer of possibility and hope—that cracked open upon Kennedy's death—and an abiding connection to America and American identity, coexisting in the midst of my logical fears of racial violence, rage and frustrations with racism's praxis. But from where did this paradox emerge?

Perhaps, the "safety" and "comfort" I felt was rooted in my feeling that I was right, and had the right to be protected, of being a full-fledged citizen of America, however begrudgingly, though rejected by the living racial reality. In the land of my birth and my forebears, I desperately, and naturally, wanted to be accepted fully as an American, as an American of African descent, wanting to love and wanting to be loved, yet, at this time in my life's journey, I was in transition from being colored and Negro to becoming a black, Black, Afro, African man disdaining the suffix American. Overwhelmed by my youthful pain and unmeasured idealism, my anger, rage, and hate made my visual field opaque; swirling beneath, where the sediment and sludge resides, thick, dark, full of gunk, preternatural splinters of light and life would rise up on a more mature morning—when America's more perfect Light would shine and penetrate my barb wired bunker.

It would be many years and many tears later, that I would come to admit and feel reconciled, if not comfortable and conflict free with my being an American. Despite my angry Black Power rhetoric, large Afro hairstyle and African dashikis I proudly wore, I would come to acknowledge that I was American to the bone: my African American, Afro, Black, black, colored, Negro and indigenous African slave bone. An American tragedy two decades later would be the impetus for my begrudging newfound recognition.

Upon graduation from Automotive Trades High School, I had secret aspirations but no concrete plans. I was drifting on the breeze of a summer carefree day when Mom and Dad powwowed and unanimously concluded, "You need a job, boy. You ain't been raised not to work."

Fair enough. My dad's credibility was impeccable. I could not argue with the man who worked two jobs. When my mom came as emissary, to execute their game plan, she had a job in mind for yours truly. Moreover, she had already secured my being hired and it was only a pro forma interview that had been set up with Eddie, the manager of the Safeway supermarket on Amsterdam Avenue and 131st Street.

We walked over to the supermarket together, making mother and son chatter. I walked up the stairs to Eddie's makeshift office in front of the store while my mom danced outside. Eddie was a cheerful enough chap and I personally liked him, but I did not want to work for him. As he prattled on about "stocking food, the meat section, being a cashier, promotion to…" a curious memory came to the fore. When Mom paid for a rather large purchase of groceries, the cashier asked me to help pack some of the items and I responded, "I don't know how to pack food."

Incredulous, she abruptly halted her packing and challenged me, "You don't know how to pack food? What is there to learn? We didn't go to college to learn how to pack food."

My point exactly.

During the interview I told Eddie, "I'm goin' to college" and elaborated on plans to start in January 1965. With no chance to get into any college given my vocational high school background, I spoke from my underground fantasies. As I walked back down the stairs, my mom gleefully walked up knowing I had a job. When she left his office anger was on her face, in her voice, all over her body because Eddie did not hire me. She was pissed off and in her controlled anger—she never yelled—wanted to know why I did not take the job. As we walked home I told her, "Mommy, I'm going to college." That set her off even further as she moved down to the rage range.

As we proceeded up 131st street, looking straight ahead not wanting to deal with my mother's muted wrath, I walked as close to the buildings as possible trying to disappear from what I knew was coming next. She walked next to me stride for stride, her mouth focused, and she spoke with agitated energy into my ear, peppering me with questions: "College? When are you goin' to college? Who can afford to send you to college? Where are you goin' to college, Junior? You need a job, Junior. You just can't sit around and do nothin'. What are you goin' to do, now?"

I did not look at her, not out of anger; I felt misunderstood. Mom had no inkling of my profound desire to better myself, to follow the exit sign out of the Basement. At that moment I felt like a lone chocolate flower with withering green fern wrapped in a desperate need for laughter—Edgar Clark's Basement mojo.

Unarticulated, but with me every step of the way was my indefatigable Will, accompanied by my boundless *reserve life force*, that comes to my rescue unannounced, without hesitation, with self-love, each and every time I have been in dire need. This was one of those moments.

The "tragic" irony: as we walked up 131st street and turned the corner onto Convent Avenue, and Mom emphatically proclaimed, "Where are you goin' to college, Junior?" there stood the City College of New York, a tuition free institution, renowned for educating the poor, working class and new immigrants, two blocks from my door.

Still I ponder, struggle furiously with at times, if this mental enervation was and is, more of an impediment to escaping the Basement than the discrimination and denial of opportunities based on white preferential treatment.

I certainly could have worked at the supermarket while preparing for college, as the two were not mutually exclusive, or so it appeared.

And Eddie certainly could have hired me as he did not. But Eddie was right for not hiring me, my dad and mom were right for wanting me to get a job, and I was right for not wanting that job and presenting as "unacceptable."

The hidden crucible was implied in my rejection of my parents acceptance of the limited vision of my potential as mandated and legislated by the larger white culture, and not of their prodigious work ethic and their desire to see me "be able to take care of yourself." I knew that if I took my parents job offer it would have irrevocably redefined my surreptitious vision, dampened my Will, and I would still be at the supermarket today, in all likelihood an alcoholic, with immortal pain buried beneath the false positive of my dreams, visions, and strivings.

I did come to hold several jobs, including working in the local restaurant across the street from my home, where the owner had a side business of running numbers, and I would on occasion deliver the "policy."

"Junebug, do you know how many years you can get for carryin' numbers and money?" said Cherry, making me aware of the danger I had placed myself in. I still made the drop. I was oblivious. I was only doing what my boss asked me to do. Noel and I had been hired to work in the restaurant at the same time. The owner was generous and told us whatever money we made on Sundays we could keep. She also said, "I trust you and can count on you."

Simply walking across the street to drop off the money and numbers did not look or feel like a crime, or that I was participating in a criminal act, or that I in fact was an actor in a crime. Everything was familiar: the people who bet, the people who ran the operation; it felt like a "family" affair or business. The long palm of the law mitigated the threat of police action, resulting in my feeling less threatened. My parents did not know the criminal element was courting me.

I got jobs at Bache & Company as a commodity margin clerk, then Paine Webber Jackson and Curtis as a stock margin clerk. I went downtown to Wall Street in a shirt and tie. "You're doin' good Junior." My parents were happy, but I was not.

While working, I made varying failed attempts at starting an educational career. I took classes at night, including remedial courses, at George Washington High School, Bronx Community College and business courses at Baruch College. I was surrounded by men and women, most were black and Latino, who grasped the business ideas readily. After failing a business course exam, I withdrew from the course and my fantasy to be an accountant also ended. I discovered I was no longer in elementary school. Plain, and not so simple, I just was not able to "comprehend," that is, I was not able to synchronize and organize working, taking classes, requirements to read, learn, and study.

I had no realistic idea that serious study required serious study, took a lot of time, and that learning was accumulative. The common thread in my struggle was my inability to sustain discipline and concentration, and having poor organizational skills was a natural outgrowth. I thought just reading the material when I got around to it would be good enough to pass. When something was difficult to grasp, my anxiety would heighten, concentration lessen, and lack of study skills and poor history of studying left me ill prepared to find a tenable solution.

The complexity of the multi-layers and multi-tasking of reading, comprehending, listening, thinking, writing, speaking about and responding to intellectual discourse taxed my lax academic skills, self-concept, self-confidence, and self-esteem, but paradoxically not my self-image and Will; all of the aforementioned component parts joined the latter two to form a union that helped me make it through the long arduous night of learning to be a college student.

Doing the schoolwork seemed harder than the schoolwork itself; intermingled were layers of doubts and fears that came in killer waves of nervousness, difficulty concentrating, and challenges to my resolve. I felt haunted by ghosts—made manifest years later—that I could neither see nor hear but nevertheless spooked and gripped me fiercely, shaking my teeth loose at times as I struggled to pass, and sometimes failed courses. Countless numbers of times my dream of a completed college education threatened to be an ignis fatuus.

In January 1968, without conscious rational thought, something snapped into place inside me—a tangible physical shift was experienced—and I decided to attend college fulltime and saved a few thousand dollars working overtime in six months. Living at home, I said to Mom, "I'm going to quit my job and go to college."

"Junior, why are you leavin' that good job? You started out on Wall

Street makin' $65.00 dollars and now you make $90.00, that's good money, and with your overtime, humph! Don't be leavin' that job."

"But I wanna' go to college, I don't like the job, I'm not happy."

"You'll be happy with some more raises. Don't be quitting that job, boy," said with pleading parental authority. "You wear a suit and tie and you go downtown to Wall Street. It wasn't an easy job to get. You got a good secure job."

"Ma, I'm thinking about the future."

"That job is a good future. It's a good job, good security, Junior."

"Ma, going to college will help me have a better future, better security."

"What are you goin' to study in college? You don't know what you want."

Mom's words were heavy blows beginning to land on my resolve and I had to fend them off to keep myself upright.

"No. *You* don't know what I want. You only know what *you* want, that's all you know."

"You could've been a mechanic making good money, but now you got this real good Wall Street job. You don't know, you don't have any experience. What have you done? Where have you been? A boat ride up Manhattan? Some parties? You ain't been nowhere. I know. Listen to me."

Now I was annoyed and disappointed because I was arguing the strongest logic possible; yet, as she listened, mom refused to hear my ambition and deep felt need. She looked at me but did not see me.

Silence.

More silence.

Dispirited silence.

I was regrouping, trying to sort out why I was in a war with my mother about trying to advance myself in the tried and true American way, make it happen yourself. Having to take a warrior's stand with the person who gave birth to me and who I knew unequivocally loved me, was debilitating, demoralizing and damn sure confusing.

Energy is finite, and to be forced to fight just short of an internecine battle with your mom leaves little energy to fight the real enemy. My dad was not present and involved in these battles between mom and me; he only wanted me to be happy in life, and when I made my decision he did not offer any resistance.

I fought back. "I can't listen to you. I do know what I want."

Definitely.

Damn Right.

Be assured I could not tell mom or dad that I wanted *to be* something, somebody; black, a black something, a black somebody, a black revolutionary of any kind. My consciousness was changing as rapidly as my growing hair, and I went from being a passive Negro with a haircut every two weeks to an angry longhaired black man to *Black Man* wearing an African dashiki. Martin Luther King Jr. was out and Malcolm X was in.

I did not trust one white person. I did not like one white person.

Mom did not let up. "You don't know, you don't know how hard things can be. I pray, Junior, you never know. I know. Listen to me. You don't want to regret leavin' that job."

I was *not* changing *my* mind. Only death could stop me. Having ambitions beyond my mom's vision was debilitating work and a job I did not need, desire or apply for. I felt like an emotional amputee whose severed confidence, self-esteem, and intelligence only existed as a phantom limb, in the form of a neurological "itch" with no real body to support my ambitions.

"Mommy," I regressed as a pervasive need to be taken care of challenged my right to my own destiny, "goin' to college is education, education is good, it's necessary education."

"Necessary for what? Education ain't no guarantee. There are lots of educated Negroes who don't have good jobs. You got a good job, Junior. College don't guarantee nothin', Junior, it's education, but education *not* necessary." She was getting floridly stronger, and as my demons stirred, I had to redouble my resolve so that I did not have to do battle with her and my inferior feelings simultaneously.

I was drained from fighting the cultural inputs of black inferiority; the battle with mom emphasizing a secure job and educational restraint; the constant warring within myself, struggling to find and hold onto just enough courage, and just enough sense of I can do, in order to go forward, to take those first shaky steps toward college, and out of the Basement.

Now twenty-one years old I dipped my hand deep into the bottom of the well of my life force and behold! I found coruscated splinters of "I Can Do." One tiny sliver whispered, "Just try, just try, you can do it, just try."

I turned to my two closest friends for guidance and support. Elliott Burgess was a student at the City College of New York majoring in psychology and sociology. Visiting him at home, I told Elliott how envious I was of his educational pursuit, and that I wanted to go to college. Elliott instructed me not to be envious of him, but to figure out how to make myself eligible for higher education; we discussed some options, then he said, "Go do what you have to do." When I was leaving, I opened my wallet and it was brimming with cash from my recently cashed paycheck. Grace Burgess, Elliott's stepmother, saw my money and said, "Elliott, get over here, look at all that money Ernest got, you need to get a job and get some money in your wallet. I don't know about that school thing."

When Grace left, Elliott looked at me and said with a smile, "That's Grace. Bottom line Grace. Now, just go and do what *you got to do*."

Serving as my own consultant, advisor and cheerleader, I took the necessary but minimum academic courses at New York University's School of Continuing Education to qualify for admittance to New York University's liberal arts college.

Winston McGill tutored me in algebra whenever I needed. On one occasion Winston was tutoring me, and Mrs. McGill came over to see what we were studying, and I leaned over, hiding my book because I felt ashamed studying ninth grade algebra and needing help at twenty-one.

I took the SAT and scored a 369 and having absolutely no idea what the score meant I innocuously asked: "Did I do okay?" My advisor at the NYU School of Continuing Education looked at me in controlled disbelief and said, "You are a plugger." I immediately understood that I did not do well. The letters of recommendation from my teachers at NYU School of Continuing Education and the death of Martin Luther King Jr. in 1968, smoothed over the hole in the road formed by my low SAT scores.

In February 1969, I entered New York University's liberal arts program with maximal determination and minimal preparation for the intellectual rigors I would meet face-to-face and stand toe-to-toe. Moreover, there was no preparation possible for the upcoming simultaneous search for black identity and, by definition, American identity, and how to live with them either separately, together, or merged. My about to be college experience was my dream conferred, but the explosions and implosions along the way, could not be deferred.

Coming of Age: How to be Black Without Really Trying
Was There Real Power in Black Power?

> To refer to their slave holdings…they wrote Negro property…the word most often used was Negro… Lists of Negroes at…Bill of Sale for Negroes. For them, the word Negro equaled slave. It quite literally meant the same thing. They clung to their belief in the natural inferiority of the black race…
>
> ***Henry Wiencek***

> …to be consciously Negro is to be…constantly in turmoil and conflict with your natural state of being, Blackness. Negro is but the outgrowth of a contagious mental anemia that ravishes the brain…a nervous disorder of mental origin, resulting from anxiety, frustration and failure to become transformed from Black people into white.
>
> ***Robert H. decoy***

On a humid July night in 1964, I leaned against the fence in the Saint Nicholas Terrace Park, peering over St. Nicholas Avenue, occasionally looking up, yearning, beseeching the heavens, wondering, taking note of the stars shining, twinkling, energetic, securely in place against the dark night; yet, keenly aware I was not securely in place or secure in any place, still, I wondered if I'm shining, twinkling, energetic, giving off light in the very dark night I peered from to the very darkness I peered into? The immediate surroundings gathered me alone to think about what I was going to do with my life. One month earlier, I graduated from Brooklyn High School of Automotive Trades, and my plans were as hazy and humid as the night air.

It very well could have been the 4th of July, with celebratory popping of sporadic fireworks with wisps of unrest in the faint sounds, the distance muting the rebellious chaos. There was a freedom and freeing of sorts on 125th Street, Harlem's epicenter, Harlem's signature, with the fearless, directionless young black men, much too young to be harnessed and driven by such stinging helplessness and hopelessness. With no particular ideology in mind, they freely sped and fled after gathering and listening to the soapbox raging ramp, vamp harangues about the white man having no regard for the life of the dark citizenry in Harlem, and beyond.

The "Boulevard," as Ray B dubbed 125th street, was by day the place to shop and mill safely, greet and welcome fellow dark-skinned travelers. On this night it was ground zero for every ounce of frustration accumulated in the internal chamber labeled: the deferred American dream: Do Not Wake Up/Do Not Disturb.

A fifteen-year-old boy had been shot by an off-duty white police officer who alleged he was threatened with a knife. I felt betrayed by my mom, annoyed that she believed the cop because, "I heard that boy was a trouble maker." The raw deal in me thought of the midnight the white man on Convent Avenue pleaded and begged me to touch his book of matches. "You are brainwashed, Ma," I angrily dismissed her.

Most of the sporadic popping sounds were gunshots. I knew there was danger. Knew I was now safe, standing alone in Saint Nicholas Terrace Park, facing the American nightmare, overlooking everything I knew of in this world at age seventeen.

To get out of the Basement, I too had to pass through 125th street, to flee from my life for my life. My heart raced and stood still that lonely night, alone, lonely within my racing heart and palpitating musings, I felt something, I pulsated; felt pulled, drawn, to the sound of gunfire, anger, rage and hurt.

I stood at attention, listening to the stirrings of the descendents of Denmark Vesey, Nat Turner, John Brown and modern rebellion; not only talking to myself but also walking outside myself as another soul emerged, its gait became my gate. Shouldn't I be afraid of being bludgeoned, maimed, shot, and killed? Of course I was, and of course I was not; but the soul that emerged unlocked a gate during the gait, and I caught up and joined my fellow dark-skinned brothers. As I gathered to the increasing sound of chaos, the streets were not filled with grandparents, parents, women or children, they were home, safely ensconced. Only fleet-footed young black soldiers armed with sneakers were prepared to do battle run.

125th St. was taut with fear, because the people that peopled The Boulevard were not afraid; fear was contemptuously pushed aside, crushed; not part of their body politic; the young black men were gathering for battle, understood by all, even my mom who subconsciously portending the danger said, "Be careful Junior, stay safe out there," omitting for her peace of mind, the logical last words, "in the war," however willingly, yet unwittingly she sent me off to do battle.

All of us young black soldiers, all infantry men on that riotous night, wanted to reclaim access to our unearthed souls, unearthed spirits, unearthed talents; even willing to pay with a fractured limb or lost life; to let the blood flow freely, with volition, is an act of freedom. We trashed The Boulevard precisely because it only supplied dope dreams and hoop dreams in Harlem, soul city if there ever was one, where no souls were to be found, or maybe us warring black young men did not know where to look.

The energy of the Black Metropolis was galvanizing, as numerous small groups of sneaker clad black young men—stretched across a couple of blocks—attempting to become significant, to enter history, came together on Seventh Avenue and 125th street. The police were war ready. I heard the unfettered voice, unfiltered, pent up, bent up, rent up, gesticulating and articulating, of the soapbox slowing down, the transition, that still moment, from free speech to free-for-all—a cup of water on a hot, hot night was thrown on a police officer, signaled the great chase for black bodies.

I stood frozen near the Loews Theatre as dozens of black blurs sprinted past me. A black cop giving full chase bore down on me; making eye contact, he slowed down just enough to gently push me into the street out of the black traffic. I had no reason to run: no laws were broken by me standing on the Boulevard. I turned to follow this black saint and a black blur stumbled and several bodies piled on top of his. Saintly swinging his black billy club, the black saint lashed and trashed, cracking heads, ribs, backs, arms, and legs; he was beating young black men for running, for running!

No crime was committed.

They ran because somebody they could not see, did not know, threw a cup of water on a cop, and it was off to the races; ghosts from Africa coming through the eyeballs, fingers, mouths, throats, rushing and gushing forth, without thought. What is there to lose if one cannot have a smooth groove, with personal meaning, and not be a reaction to being roped off from society: "If we must die, let it not be like hogs…If we must die, O let us nobly die…" What did Africans feel when chased to be sold to the New World? Nobody, ever really wanted Negroes free I now realized. Except, of course, the Negroes. Unfortunately, the Emancipation Proclamation was not written to free the most enslaved to slavery, the American soul from its white demagogic supremacy. Thus: Freedom Summer 1964

A couple of years later, employed as a commodity margin clerk, at the Wall Street brokerage firm Bache & Company, a white co-worker told me of a white cop he knew who was on patrol in Harlem during the riot. Posted on 125th Street, the white cop, reportedly, described black street protesters who verbally assaulted him, but he did not have any legal provocation to do what readily came to mind. "My friend was thinking, 'I want to shoot you bastard. I would love to shoot you bastard.'" My white colleague laughed as he concluded in sync: "Would be okay if he did."

My white colleague found describing the incident so amusing he could not stop grinning and guffawing for some time. He was oblivious to the fact that I came from Harlem, even though he knew I was from Harlem, and that I lived through the riots. This same white colleague endorsed the idea of "our children playing together."

I told Elliott of my co-worker's sincere expression and enlightened values, that he had some social redeeming value.

Elliott snidely said, "Ask him if he thinks it's okay if 'our children' dated."

The next day I lauded him for advocating that black and white children play together. "Of course, of course," he said with enlightened white pride.

"But once the children are grown, suppose an affection blossomed, what if your son dated my daughter?" I asked ever so inconveniently.

His smile and enlightened white pride slipped from the narrow edge of reason he stood on, and I watched him plummet, free falling, trying to fly with no wings. "No. No! That's different." He quickly shook his head from side to side, looking past me, making eye contact with the empty space behind me, staring into the abyss of his narrow racial contours.

When I told Elliott of my co-worker's answer, he responded with two simple words, "Told you."

And from then until now, every white person who seemingly made and makes supportive statements about black folks, *all* were and are viewed initially with suspicion, then, if I think I can trust them, circumspection.

My white co-worker's antiquated but still modern belief system was the quintessential expression of America's founding foundation. It was this hardcore hand-me-down heritage, as it were, that gave birth to this new time, new change, revived the old and created a new generation of vociferous discontent: SNCC (Student Nonviolent Coordinating Committee), Black Panther Party, Black Muslims (Nation of Islam), and Pan-African thought; accompanied by the arrival of new heroes, Malcolm X, Elijah Muhammad, Farrakhan, Eldrige Cleaver, Huey P. Newton, Rap Brown and Stokely Carmichael's intoxicating cry, "Black Power," roared in a new historical era of youthful black rage, trying to make sense out of turbulent times with no precedent and no road map.

I was inspired by the Negro rising up from the ashes of passivity, which challenged my unrelenting desire for higher education and higher purpose. Since I had a vocational high school diploma, I had to take the necessary courses to qualify for college matriculation. When I received my letter of acceptance into New York University, I was buoyed beyond the belief of my expectation. Finally, I was on my way.

Despite the many sit-ins, lunch counter demonstrations, and riots across urban America in the 1960's, it was the absolute senseless murder of Martin Luther King Jr. in April 1968, that served as "shock treatment" to the prevailing depressed American moral conscience, and rocked the nation from its venomous racial lethargy and status quo.

The white collective guilt at the violent death of the "Prince of Peace," shot humungous holes through the racial fences surrounding Negro exclusion, and down came barriers to open the highway for the Negro to access and success in modern America, the university.

Those of us who were "disadvantaged" and survived the physical and psychological ghettos, seized the historical time, the "equal opportunity," and thus the latent aspirations of the Negro became evident and evidence that our natural propensities had been suppressed and exploited. Negroes passed through the now porous racial barriers to enter major white universities at unprecedented rates. This affirmation of black and Latino talents was dubbed, Affirmative Action.

NYU set up the Martin Luther King Jr. Scholarship fund, and the largess that flowed from King's death actually reached many of the black and Latino youth who were at a "disadvantage," and Asian students were also recipients.

On the subway platform, I waited for the next train and the future. Taking the A train downtown from 125th Street & the Basement "up" to West Fourth Street and NYU is a twelve minute ride, but it felt like twelve light years and a trip to another galaxy; where new worlds, in a New World, awaited to be explored, to challenge and expand my intellectual capacity, curiosity, and imagination. It was a ride not only through "space" but "time." My landing at NYU in the summer of 1968 was by definition, light years away from the world I was born into twenty-one years earlier.

I entered college during the "consciousness" era, as the "new" Negro students were emerging from a passive colored and Negro identity, to "consciousness," an extreme awareness, the changing of the "color guard," of being black and proud, to Black Power to Black manhood, which was paramount, became the to be all and end all, the Negro as artifact was history, so to speak.

Malcolm X's mocking humor and blistering logic about Negroes and Negro life under the white man's domination, tapped into a vein that was longing to receive an infusion of new blood to the pallid Negro identity. "I am black," I proudly waxed, and thus forever, therefore I am; no longer a Negro, no longer colored. The stigma of being called black was washed away with the cleansing and caustic cry of Black Power; with the new focus on black self-determination, pride in being of African descent. "Say it loud, I'm Black and I'm proud," James Brown, the king of soul sang triumphantly. My parents and my grandmother thought I was going through "a change of life." Florita, six years my elder was living on her own, while Audrey, eighteen months younger—was a teenage mother struggling with meshing her youth and unexpected parental responsibilities—were not caught up as intensely in the black historical tide.

Being Black included being a man, who defined himself, loved himself, protected his family, and who demanded respect, no longer a boy. The need to be a real man, real Black man that is, and treated like one, respected like one, and most importantly, feeling like one, regardless of how treated, roused my somnolent consciousness to which I gave voice to in a poem I wrote and one line read, "Be a man Black man be a man."

Amid the attainment of this new prestigious stature of being Black, psychogenic lava from the volcanic eruption of Black Power, "blackness," flowed with raging certainty: defining, defending, and encouraging black pride, aspiration, and achievement; as it roiled forth, this exploding blackness gushed hot, scalding, scarring, saturating every pore in the newly minted black body and soul. Blackness morphed into a perceived, deep-set, intrinsic commonality, rooted in our African heritage; the pigmentation adorning our flesh was the common bond. Functionally, blackness came to be defined as: Complete distrust of white culture, white institutions and white people; belief that racism and being racialized due to African ancestry are recalcitrant cultural parameters that permanently define, limit, and lead to mistreatment of black citizenry; that exclusively perceived group solidarity and groupthink, as the only legitimate way to conduct one's affairs. And when the black lava cooled, it hardened into a rigid posture that proclaimed blackness as the soul and sole legitimate expression of black people, expressed quite simply, in a t-shirt popular a few years back: "It's a black thing, you wouldn't understand."

On one occasion, my mom referred to me in conversational context as "boy," which was not uncommon. One evening mom was cooking and I tasted one dish, then another. Mom said, "Boy, what are you doin' in those pots? Stop all that tastin', one spoonful is enough," said with the usual delight of a mother whose son enjoys her cooking; Of course, I kept tasting. "Boy, don't be eatin' all that food, it's for dinner."

"Ma! I am a Black man not a *boy*, a Black man, who commands respect," I said emphatically. At that moment the need for external respect was salivating all over me. "You can *never* call me boy *never ever* again," I said with righteous indignation for every historical slight and offense received.

Standing in the kitchen, Mom looked at me and looked at me and looked at me. I assumed she was trying to find a graceful way out. Then her neck leaned slightly to the right, as if she were trying to glean a different perspective on my statement. Her neck straightened out and so must have her thoughts, she countered with: "I gave birth to you; I brought you into this world; you are *my* son, no one else's son; you were my boy when you were born; you were my boy when I changed your diapers, when I fed you, took you to school; when you were sick, I took you to the doctor, you were my boy; you were my boy when I raised you; you were my boy when you left home today; you were my boy when you came back; you are my boy now; you will be my boy when I die; you will be my boy when you die."

As she spoke, I knew I was wrong.

"Boy?" mom sarcastically belched a laugh, "Boy. You always gon' be *my* boy."

My Black manhood and I never pursued that line of thought, never, ever, again with my mom.

My grandmother was a nurse in the army, a conservative Republican, and headstrong. She voted for Senator Barry Goldwater for President, and presciently said that Ronald Reagan would become president when he was governor of California. We argued infrequently but furiously, about politics. Knowing for sure I could not be refuted I said, "Black people are angry at having been enslaved, treated brutally, and not set completely free."

"We are free, absolutely free. I don't see any chains on you. You see any on me?" Her sarcasm pricked and annoyed me. "All the slaves cried when they were freed because they didn't want to be set free," she said robustly.

My grandmother Adams alleged she was told such stories as a little girl. Maybe? But I don't think she really believed them as an adult.

How could any person, especially a black person believe such utter nonsense? At minimum the idea is counterintuitive and maximally, it is untainted absurdity.

Now I am pissed off that I have to entertain such a ridiculous assertion. "That ain't true, slaves didn't like being slaves and didn't want to be slaves. They were stolen from the African homeland by the white man and put in chains to pick cotton," I asserted.

"Some Africans were stolen from Africa, but a lot were sold into slavery by other Africans," she countered. I was distraught the first time I heard a black professor say that Africans had to teach Europeans how to navigate the African interior, so they could get into and out of villages; that slavery existed in Africa before the European's appearance. In college, I met a Nigerian who worked at the United Nations. We were having an intense and serious conversation about Africans and Afro-Americans when a big amused smile took shape on his face, and he chuckled: "My great great great great grandfather sold your great great great great grandfather."

I was not amused by his cavalier attitude and effervescent insensitivity.

I said to my grandmother, "Slaves were made to do whatever the white man wanted. The white man controlled the black family, selling mothers, fathers, and children. He lashed men with the whip, had sex, I mean raped the women." I paused for effect, "Raped the women."

"We are absolutely free now, and nobody is getting raped," she replied.

Recently a white Jewish friend told me that a prominent rabbi said in his class that black American slaves did not want to be freed, that they cried. My friend confidently believed it as he said it to me.

"There were violent slave rebellions," I asserted, "the Underground Railroad, sabotage on work sites and slaves en masse deserted plantations and fought in the Civil War. Because some Israelite slaves longed for the 'flesh pots' in Egypt, did that mean they really wanted to be slaves under Pharaoh?"

I was livid with my friend's facile acceptance and how he tried to pass it off as accurate information about the African American experience. The rabbi needed some education about the African American experience. I wondered about the source of the rabbi's misinformation and how many other students had he misinformed?

I was ripened for the activation of my latent black consciousness and rage, with the heinous murders of Emmett Till, a black fourteen year old boy, brutally mutilated, and four black girls murdered on Sunday morning inside the basement of their church by a white terrorist bombing in Birmingham, Alabama. The Sharpsville Massacre, the slaughter of unarmed black South Africans by white South Africans made me frenetic with fear and dread. Reading the headline and viewing the carnage on the front page of the Daily News, my heart collapsed with dejection as my mind nervously raced to phantom why the Negro was so hated whether it was at home in the United States or the African "Negro" in his own homeland. With no nightmare to awake from, I felt maimed and depressed.

The norm of American violence and discrimination, the powerlessness that resulted, was felt daily and felt "normal," but with each screaming headline I felt more wounded and more helpless, and the new wound, forming a new layer while aggravating the old, cut deeper and deeper into the energy of my life force. The Post-Reconstruction "lynch law," reinforced the American standard of justice for the value of the life of the newly freed Negro. This insidious "covenant" was and is "renewed" each generation, with heinous acts that tap the acceptable brutal evil core of American racism. One result is that undischarged pain and suffering, fearfulness, anxiety and depression find discharge, sometimes violently, sometimes without notice.

With shame and dread, I look in the rear view mirror of time, and see myself at about age nineteen, exiting a parking lot in a suburban mall. I saw a white man walking with his six year old daughter on his left, holding her hand, and wife to his right. Sans premeditation, a hungry and malicious carpe diem impulse raged forth, and I intentionally drove my car within a foot of the girl.

"Take it easy," the father said with alarm.

I was delighted with his alarm because he should now know the daily alarm black parents live with, that I live with, I thought without thinking. I shudder and shake to this very moment when I think how I could have injured an innocent child due to an impulsive hate-filled moment in time.

Now, listen and understand this clearly. I was essentially a law abiding, ambitious, respectable, friendly, popular, upwardly mobile black youth and, unlikely candidate for violent anti-social behavior. What triggered such an outburst?

The sun was shining, it was Saturday, it was America, and I was treated as a black man, not a man. That is, nothing in particular, nothing out of the ordinary. Hate: meant I had a moral case that justified my mood swing, my near murderous impulse. Hate: meant I did not have to experience my true lot in life as it anesthetized my ranking in the American hierarchy. Hate: is hopelessness and hopelessness hates. Hate: masks pain, hurt, and fear. Yet, Hate: is a manifestation of pain, hurt, and fear. Hate: organizes and disorganizes. Hate: is thinking without thinking, being without being, avoiding the complicated, voiding the complexities of life, blaming the white man, then blaming yourself for not understanding why you cannot do better and afraid to look closely at the reasons why, because in reality, no simple solutions can be found today.

When I was in college, an off campus event impacted me profoundly.

I was in the North Bronx, observed a moving tractor-trailer when a black girl about age seven playing with friends darted out into the street. The driver slammed on the brakes and the screeching sound of the tires froze the girl wide-eyed in fear; as the skidding and shimmying truck was about to crush her, it came to a heart-stopping halt, inches from her; unceremoniously, she ran back to play with her friends.

I too was frozen and exhaled the so-near tragic horror. The driver, who looked like your everyday dark haired white truck driver, turned off the engine, got out shaking, sweating, and sat on the side of the truck and gripped his flushed red face in his large hands. I did not merely observe this white man, I kept watch over him, studied him for thirty minutes, measured every reaction, the depth of his sincerity, as he tried to purge the trauma of his so nearly crushing the life out of a colored Negro black Black Afro-American child.

I was equally dazed and skeptical to see a white man have any concern, much less genuine trauma, at the actual possibility he might have killed a black child, no matter how accidentally. The exploded and torn bodies of Addie May Collins, Denise McNair, Carole Robinson, and

Cynthia Wesley, in the Sixteenth Street Baptist Church in September 1963, seized my memory.

Being an eyewitness to this, thank God! Near miss! For the very first time in my life, I now had direct evidence that below the white epidermis there lie a soul capable of genuine compassion and human regard for fellow Americans with black epidermis. I now inhaled the fresh misty air of compassion emanating from God's white creation. This pristine "white oxygen" revived my faded hope and belief in the potential goodness of humanity.

There were countervailing forces that offered outlandish theories about the United States Government planning to exterminate black people; there were many who did not readily disbelieve the proffered provocation. I was having lunch at a black friend's home when another black guest smugly said, "Is there anyone here who really thinks the American government wants to exterminate black people?" I kept silent as my heart raced to the tune of, "I don't think you should be so cock sure."

In tandem with the shifting of the color guard, was the skewering of traditional labels—the name game became prominent. The new black students placed their hands on their knees and mocked, "This is how tall 'knee-grows' get." Colored was out. "Yo bro, if we are colored what color are we?" asked with searing sarcasm. "Purple? Green? Pink? They ain't got no color, we do."

Nigger—the American name game at its worst—is an epithet so vile and reviled it has a socially sanctioned euphemism, N-word. The "black street" appropriated nigger long before Richard Pryor brought it into the mainstream of public American life—though out of the mouth of black folks it was never used to dehumanize the race: but served to reduce its intended toxicity and invert the white man's lethal aim to maim, degrade, and dehumanize the black psyche; the "in-house" use of nigger continues in the twenty-first century as both term of endearment and caustic critic.

After having been colored and Negro all my life, the search for personal identity could not be found where most people begin, with their name. Some black folks changed their "slave" names, American names given at birth, and adopted African or Islamic names; most did not. Since there was no recent direct connection to Africa in most families, some chose names after researching their meaning, some chose names because they sounded cool, while others were given names by people they respected. Many parents and grandparents were astounded by, "all that foolishness," and some were offended.

The name game was in full tilt. William Mixon *became* Kujaatale Kweli, Nesbit Pringle *became* Mtendaji Kuweza, Eugene Robinson *became* Saba Mchumguzi when all three legally changed their names over thirty years ago. Linda Youngblood became Mtamanika Yetumbe and is currently known as Mtamanika Youngblood; Marcia Adams became Zoleka Mtendeka and is now the Reverend M. Zoleka Adams. Some only changed their first names and some mocked the process. Abdul only wanted to be called by his new name, "I will always be Abdul." When I saw him years later on the Westside, I greeted him, never having known his slave name: "Abdul, how are you?"

Employed on Wall Street, he said with pursed lips, "My name is Herman."

Lenny Burg told friends to call him, Lehebg, his new African name. But Leonard Herbert Burg took the first two letters from his first two names and the first and last letter of his surname and created the African moniker, Lehebg.

Among those who did not change their names, quite a few gave their children African and Islamic names. One couple named their daughter Kenya, because she was conceived there. As a psychologist I treated several children who felt burdened with these African and Islamic names, and many voiced their displeasure at being the recipients of their parent's college or ideological hangovers. "Why can't my name be Michael?" "I hate my name, why can't I be Charlie?" "I'm not African; I'm going to change my name to Karen," "I'm not African, they don't even look like me," and so forth and so on.

I never considered changing my name, likely because I was too busy in search of the real Ernest Adams, and the underlying potential I possessed and it did not seem likely to be influenced by adopting an African or Islamic name. (I would discover many years later that I had Algerian and Islamic ancestors.) Mtendaji pointed out that of all the black folks he knew that changed their names and identified with Africa, "I am the only *been to,*" that is, he is the only one amongst his close friends in the more than thirty years since college who has, *been to* Africa.

The name game, its transformations from colored and Negro to black, Black, Afro-American to African American, all these names and changes of names and changing names, all determined attempts, at finding self-expression and self-recognition, was and is an uncompromising search for identity, humanity and divinity.

When Negro and colored were jettisoned and "black" and then "Black" became normative, the question of who was *really* black came up. Simply having a Negro parent was not enough. People were measured with subjective standards, and a "blacker than thou" attitude quickly emerged from the former Negroes and colored people.

It was a big help if one came from Harlem, Watts, Southside of Chicago, and Newark, New Jersey. Anyone who came from any ghetto was looked upon as having veritable "street" credentials; such a person was automatically assumed to be authentically black, with nothing to prove. Even if this criterion were not met, if one associated with the authentic black students and forged the rhetoric and slogans, then one could "pass" for black.

Deference was shown to Black Muslim students or their advocates and we engaged in the Muslim greeting, "ah salaam a lakim, a lakim salaam." But when they were out of sight some folks mocked, "ah salaam a pork chop, pork chop salaam."

A new standard of beauty emerged, "Black is Beautiful," trumpeted with a newfound source of genuine pride. Africa became cachet. All shapes, shades and features of Negroes were transformed, whether one had 100% African/black blood or 1% African/black blood. With the white culture's defensive bulwark, the one-drop rule, *all* became black, proud, and beautiful.

My girlfriend Juanita did not want to get an Afro, and I badgered her and threatened our relationship until she got one. She was prone to be chubby, and when a poster size layout of Rachel Welch in a bikini appeared in the Daily News, I pasted it to the back of her bedroom door and told her that is how she should look. I forgot about the poster until Juanita reminded me during one truth telling moment.

"Excuse me Mr. Black Man," Juanita said with ridicule glued to her words, "Excuse me Black man, *excuse me*, Mr. Black Man, but, which one do you want me to be?" She closed her bedroom door, pointed her index finger sarcastically at Rachel Welch while steadfastly looking at me. "Do you want me to be a black woman with black hair, or do you want me to be like the white girl?"

Caught in a vise of my own making, though I was emphasizing her body and not her hair, I stood at attention for an instant, then in a flash ripped down the poster of Rachel Welch. "You be a sister, a Black woman. Fuck the white standard." Years later Juanita expressed vehement anger at having been bullied and coerced into getting an Afro. I had no awareness that she was even mildly upset.

When I went from getting a haircut every two weeks to a big bushy Afro—thick wooly Afro that matched my new thick wooly pride—it caused quite a commotion. "Look at all that nappy hair. You need to cut it Junior. You can't be going around looking like *that*," Mom and Dad said.

I finally understood, painfully, that my wooly hair was not acceptable to my parents, but only tolerable when cut every two weeks. Mom, who looks like she is straight out of the bush of Africa, and my grandmother Adams, who had straight hair and passed for white, were united in their reprimand. Infused with the new generation of black pride, one day, with no fanfare, mom wore her hair natural. My father was philosophical. He said it was only a hairstyle and it would change like every other style he had seen.

African garb became fashionable. I wore my new large flowing dashiki like it was a tuxedo. One day I walked up Convent Avenue with my new dashiki, big Afro, feeling very black, and very connected to Africa. Jean was sitting with some of our neighborhood friends and had a new ponytail extension and newly arched eyebrows, heavy makeup, glossy lipstick—so *not* black. "I didn't recognize you," I said with disappointment.

She retorted sarcastically, "I didn't recognize you."

"Got a new ponytail, you look different."

"No, you look different. *Nobody* here recognized you."

The age of black puritans was upon us. At a college poetry reading I will forever recall the last line of a poem/diatribe: "You in your Afro wig…Pig."

During this ferocious period of upheaval and transition, we scoured ourselves and the American culture, seeking an identity where our humanity was assumed and not assailed. We looked to Africa even though it was not on the map of our origins as Americans nor relevant to our recent experience; Africa, a mother we resembled, but we had virtually nothing in common that we could consume. Yet we embraced Africa as the "motherland," even though we were not able to look back and embrace it as our country of origin, as other immigrants were able to do as a source of solace during hard times.

A few years later, I sat with Winston McGill Jr. listening to Alex Haley tracing his ancestry back to a specific tribe in Gambia. Haley's mother told him a story handed down through the generations: the circumstances of how his African ancestor was kidnapped from his village in Africa. When Haley went to Gambia, the griot, the tribal historian, narrated the same story that Haley's mother had told him; it was a galvanizing confirmation of his African ancestral heritage, and mine. Every person in the auditorium stirred viscerally. I felt my psyche elevating as my spirit gushed forth, reopening a portal that had been closed since my African ancestors passed through the Door of No Return. I recognized my humanity as it existed outside of and prior to the imagination of America. An ocean of sensations erupted that left me trembling with an overwhelming and overdue pride, and undue joy.

Reading the New York Times in July 2003, I was amazed to read that the Nigerian singer Fela, stated that it was the photographs of African Americans in traditional African dress that made him feel comfortable in African style clothes and with the idea of Black Power.

NYU was as segregated as the South of my youth—there was virtually no sense of commonality or common purpose between black and white students, despite the un-civil Civil Rights struggle. The signs advocating and supporting the separation of the races were displayed, not so conspicuously, in the windows of black and white hearts and thoughts. The mask I learned to wear and continue to carry, to use when needed, was contingent upon whom I was around. All African American people wear or carry masks when traversing in white America, even those black folk gracing the top of the American echelon. The questions that lurk, right below the surface, in the most balanced black minds: "Am I being challenged? Doubted? Mistreated? Rejected?

Harassed? Accepted? …because of my black blood?" This peristaltic process took centuries to evolve, and may take even longer to cease.

As I began my sojourn on campus, I was leery of every white face; every black face I saw offered a portal of asylum. It did not take long to evaluate the individual black student on their individual merit, but it would be years in the making before I would be able to distinguish the blur of white faces. In the Loeb student cafeteria black and Latino students sat together as did white students, separately.

I signed up for English, biology, psychology, French, courses of my choosing. For the first time in a very long time, I did not wish for the negative hoping the opposite would come true. No longer in its pure childhood form, this bastardized prayer morphed into severe self-doubt. Despite the hope and joy of being in college, I could not calm the endless "noise" in my head.

The reality: I was in a state of continuous anxiety independent of and exacerbated by my lack of a study discipline, limited experience of learning as cumulative and hard work, and afraid of subject matter not easy to learn. I had difficulty with French, trying to cram to learn it, because I was both intimidated and not able to sit down, concentrate as needed, and learn it accumulatively. Knowing that I was not likely to pass, I weaseled my way out with a self-serving lie to the head of the department and took it again the next semester.

The natural spark invigorated by Black Power and the ever-true beauty of Black is Beautiful, in its most positive sense, failed to fully erase the embedded deep structure of inferiority, and the negative thoughts and images permeating the American culture and mind. I sat trying to rebuild, versus renovate, my confidence one new black brick at a time. Doing homework was part of the rebuilding process.

Zoleka came to study with me in my dorm room, and after sitting at my desk for an hour shuffling papers and turning pages meaninglessly, she accurately observed, "Ernest, you have been sitting there an hour and have not done a thing."

I wanted to study, God knows I wanted to study—that's why I invited Zoleka hoping she would serve as a calming agent. Try as I might, I could not organize myself into a coherent regime or pattern of sufficient work habits, despite my belief I could do well if I buckled down, and goodness knows I wanted to do well.

Among the books I passionately purchased about black American life and African life, even the ones that were required reading, I was unable to completely follow-up and read. When A. Phillip Randolph spoke to black students on campus he said angrily, "You students go around calling people Uncle Tom, to criticize those you don't like when you have not even read the book, because if you did then you would know Uncle Tom was someone to be respected and admired."

I was one of those students quick to use the term derogatorily about some black person who failed to register enough racial bile and mistrust of whites, or who too heavily criticized black folk for not doing enough for themselves. The truth of his words embarrassed and stung where it hurt the most: I had not read Uncle Tom's Cabin, even though it sat on my shelf with pleading pages every time I passed it by.

Despite my inability to organize my academic discipline, I did organize time to improve my basketball game. I was always a lousy basketball player in the playground and always wanted to be better. I practiced so much that I heard the voice of heaven on earth when warming up for an intramural game, someone shouted, "Leaping Ernie," after I dunked the basketball. It was the first time I had dunked in my life and I was orgasmic with pride flowing from every pore in my body. And when a sister flirtatiously said, "Ernie, dunk one for me," and I did. I felt as if I had followed one of the Ten Commandments. While playing an intramural game I was leading a fast break, rose high and laid it in for two points. Afterwards one of the spectators said, "Why didn't you dunk it, you were high enough?" I did not know I was high enough; I was not able to fathom I could actually dunk in a game.

I wanted to take an algebra class and met with the professor and told him of my reservation. He put a rudimentary algebra formula on the board and I explained it. The professor cheerfully said, "You have the basic knowledge,"

I nodded and grunted, "umm huh."

"You know enough to be in the class," said with confidence in me.

"I don't know…if," my hesitation thick with doubt.

Becoming my advocate and cheering me on, "Take the class and I will tutor you personally. I will take the time, and *we* will get you through this together." He said with sincerity that I could not grasp and I did not take the course. I am uncertain if my lack of confidence weighed more than my discomfort because he was a white man and Jewish. True, he could easily have become another Brother Hankins, however, the professor was not in the safety of my home and the ghosts of historical times past were hiding, yet presiding, between the synapses of my psychological makeup.

Black Power, now a revolutionary motivator in full cry, ideological and emotional prosthesis, profound to black folk, became a curse word for white America, experiencing it as frightening rage with pumping fists in the air, rifles lofted heartily in the national media, and shouts of "death to pigs," the very police officers who were seen as keeping Black Power at bay, keeping white people safe.

Many black students believed that everything was "political," and required to be "relevant." It became a mantra and the currency needed to afford our racial circumstances. There was one problem: I did not fully understand what being political meant, and uncertain what was relevant.

A meeting was about to begin with black students to discuss our grievances when Professor Roscoe Brown, World War II black decorated army pilot, whom black students referred to as "Uncle Tom," suggested we use the parliamentary model as a democratic tool to facilitate an orderly discussion.

A student mumbled, "The parliamentary model is not relevant. There must be a better way."

The students sitting within proximity grumbled to each other in short huffy bursts, "Yeah…right on…got to be a better way."

A student stood up and spoke, "European based democracy, there must be a better way, black way. How did the kings and elders of the great ancient African kingdoms make decisions? Let's use something from our heritage." In response the entire roomful of students lustily assented, "Right on brother…ump hmp…that's it…yeah."

As the unifying good feelings brought forth a bite of black satisfaction, Professor Brown, respectfully, in his best "Uncle Tom" voice, said, "What is this ancient African democratic way?"

There was silence, cold, dreaded, and full of shame; the silence was silent, with the terror of falling through the trapdoor of history, vanishing without a trace, settled like a thick mist on our good feelings, then drenched sour our bite of black satisfaction.

NYU created an Institute of Afro-American Affairs (IAAA). Students were encouraged to submit their ideas for classes to be held within the university. Eager to have relevant courses, I sat down with Professor Miller and said, "I want a course on the works of Richard Wright, just like there is a course on Shakespeare." I had read Native Son and thought Richard Wright deserved his own course.

Professor Miller was patient and respectful, "There has to be a large body of work an author has produced, like Shakespeare, to have an entire course. Richard Wright has not produced a large body of work."

I was offended, but with equal sincerity I said, "Well, what about a course with Richard Wright and Ralph Ellison's writings?"

Professor Miller reiterated the same point. Enough students had made similar appeals and a black literature seminar—open to all students in the university—was born and taught by Edward Braithwaite, author of *Too Sir with Love*. Only about ten students signed up for the course, and one was a white girl. Shakespeare now seemed whiter and, definitely not relevant: "Fuck Shakespeare." I never took the course on Shakespeare.

Seeking to add diversity and creditability, NYU hired black faculty members, including Ralph Ellison, author of *The Invisible Man*, as adjunct professors. Mr. Braithwaite, a native of Guyana, was accessible and down to earth. He greeted students with an open smile, shared his experiences and tolerated our youthful impropriety and sloppy enthusiasm. Ellison offered a different paradigm.

He designed a literary course that only upper classman were qualified to take, which meant leaving out most black students. A black upper classman went to see him privately. He beseeched Ellison to admit lower classmen or teach an introductory course and he refused. The upper classman reported that the conversation became heated when Ellison resisted his continuing entreaties. Feeling as if he had been a phantom and not seen by the inner eyes of Ellison, then bumped out of meanness, the upperclassman and Ellison ended up in fisticuffs rolling on his office floor. Remaining unconvinced, Ellison was the winner and black students were the losers.

In Ellison's class there were about twenty white students. As the only black student, I felt like I integrated a segregated course. Ellison did not focus on any material "relevant" to the black experience. Disappointed, I did not attend class for a few weeks. When I returned Ellison had his back to the blackboard. He turned around and saw me, and with a wide smile said, "Mr. Adams has returned." The genuine smile and affection attendant in his voice did not blossom into the relationship of mentor to student that I craved.

After class, I was in conversation with a white student who wanted to know why I was not attending the class. Dissatisfied with the pabulum I fed him he said, "Tell me the real reason."

I said, "I expected a black man of Ellison's experience, prominence, intellect and accomplishment to serve as teacher, model and guide to black students, to relate what he learned in life as a black man."

Given his stature he was expected to help craft a concrete roadmap in non-fiction life. Why didn't he see the potential for a second Harlem Renaissance in the eager black students? Didn't Ralph Ellison long to help develop an inchoate Ralph Ellison? Why didn't he long to find the next Richard Wright? Frances Harper? Claude McKay? Zora Neale Hurston? Langston Hughes? Moreover, I would have loved to hear history and the struggles of the "privileged" young black intellectuals and black folk of his generation. He could have set high standards and challenged black students to reach them as only one black person can to another without pre-supposing white arrogance and superiority. Ironically, I felt invisible in his class.

Maya Angelou gave a talk and read poetry at Teacher's College, Columbia University. In the question and answer period that followed, a black male student made some observations, and in mid-sentence Maya Angelou corrected him grammatically, then proceeded to correct him a second time.

I felt it was totally appropriate, educational, and did not feel a wave of black embarrassment or black shame. I looked over at the white professor who was her host, and as his eyes circled the room with a smile of incredulity plastered to his face, he was amazed that not one black or Latino student was perturbed. The thought that ticker-taped across his forehead was, I imagined: "I know damn well I could not do that and have black and Latino students feel I was trying to make them better students and better prepared for the workplace."

Ellison should have been a ripened fruit of virtue, on and off the Civil Rights vine, that nourished young black minds, not a common everyday street fighter between two frustrated and angry black men trying to beat and best the shit out of each other because they cannot best and beat the shit out of the white man for the centuries of ongoing oppression.

Or, perhaps, he could not be the all-knowing and intellectually powerful black father or a big enough black breast to feed and soothe the roiling black unrest, not because he did not care but because *being* The Invisible Man, took a toll that was not readily available to the naked eye, or naked aching heart.

Looking over my shoulder into my past, the irony is that a white professor saw my black need, lack of confidence, and sought to encourage, guide, and support me. I politely demurred because his humanity was hidden by the glare of his whiteness. Yet Ellison, whose humanity I assumed because of his black skin, could not see me as I needed to be seen, a need for encouragement, guidance, and support.

Now I realize that if I had allowed myself to be taken under the mathematical wing of the white professor, my confidence and sense of self would have soared higher, that my need to be and feel like a real man, a real Black man, would have been bolstered.

* * *

The talk of black unity was ubiquitous when I was growing up and continued on campus. The common greeting that originated in the Negro community was transposed and every black man was greeted with, "Hey brother," and every black woman, "Hey sister." The lack of unity was portrayed as a major reason why the Negro and now black folk had made so little progress despite racism's woes. A significant change was that emulating Jews was now eschewed. The rupture that occurred during the Civil Rights struggle led to a distrust of Jews as white people.

There were some black revolutionary brothers by day and sleeping, unbeknownst to others, with white women at night. A black young man, now a wealthy entrepreneur, openly had white girlfriends while still maintaining friendly relationships with black students. One day I asked him how he could openly date white women, especially with the sisters scrutinizing him. He said, "Ernie, don't confuse the ass struggle with the class struggle."

"Would you ever sleep with a white woman?" A black professor asked me as if we were peers.

"No, I'm no political dog," I said self-righteously.

He offered the following supposition, "Suppose no one knew?"

"No," I responded angrily, "What difference would that make."

"But suppose she was beautiful?"

"No."

"But, if no one knew and never found out, would you?"

"No."

He chuckled, enjoying my unspoiled attitude. Of course, of course, I later discovered he had fucked white women galore, and sadly, he exploited some of the black undergraduate women who looked up to him.

We were black youth living in the first-world but identified and aligned ourselves with the third world peoples around the globe. The commonality was the oppression of people of color by European imperialism, colonialism, and its American racial offspring and other descendents. America's friends, whether in South Africa, Portugal, France or Israel, were considered the enemies of justice, precisely because they dominated and exploited indigenous populations.

Some friends and I started an intramural basketball team, and we sat around trying to come up with a name. After a few titles were bandied about someone said, "What about Al Fatah? That sounds like a cool name." We unanimously agreed.

One friend of reason cautioned, "Those Jews aren't going to like that."

"So what the fuck do we care what they think? Do they care what we think?" Someone asked sarcastically.

"Hey look, this isn't simply NYU this is NY-JEW." An angry voice chimed in.

"Who supports apartheid in South Africa? Huh? Tell me? Who? Who?" Righteous passions and several voices were rising together, fearlessly.

"Israel." Said with and by a cold chill. "In case you didn't know, *Israel* is one of the biggest arms supplier to South Africa, in case you didn't know."

"Look, there are a lot of Jews here and they won't be pleased with a black Al Fatah," the lone voice said trying to be reasonable. Reacting all at once, a cacophony of angry jumbled words spewed forth.

Drawing a deep breath, and turning to look into the eye of the lone voice of reason, the cold chill had the final word, "Them Jews can't do shit to us, *to hell* with them." Thus, we entered the basketball tournament with the name of a Palestinian guerilla group.

Al Fatah made the semi-finals of the intramural tournament, and we played a team comprised predominantly of white Jews, some from the medical school. We were a shoo-in as the favorites to meet another black team in the final. But a funny thing happened on the way to the championship game, we got outplayed as the Jewish team was quicker, out rebounded us, creating fast break two on one plays and we lost by ten points. Jews won the game and defeated two stereotypes—without one slam dunk.

With a few seconds left in the game and now obvious we were about to lose, the "crazy" member of the team deliberately punched one of the opposing players—I believe a medical student—in the mouth knocking out his tooth. "That's what you get, white boy, for elbowing me," was the false pretext. The injured white student went to retaliate and his friends grabbed him and yelled, "No, no," and pulled him off the court. Our team left the court embarrassed and bickering about how we lost and pointing fingers. Over thirty years later, the "crazy" one became a judge.

Sitting in the Martin Luther King Jr. student center, I read a New York Times article about the Palestinian representative to the United Nations who said that Israel was in his "living room," that Israel was geographically located where he grew up as a child. After reading that article I solidly believed the Palestinians had the moral high ground and Israel was no different than their European colonial counterparts. On NYU's campus and in the minds of many black people, Palestinian support of black South Africa enhanced the perception of third-world solidarity, and many black students cast Israel and Jews as enemies of black people everywhere. I was one such student.

A group of black students were sitting in the Martin Luther King Jr. student center, relaxing and communing together. We began a dialogue about how we arrived at NYU, and with a light chuckle Fred Beauford said, "It's a good thing," and he looked around the room making note of all the students present, "Martin Luther King was killed, otherwise none of us would be here." All of us chimed in with concurring laughter and nodding heads.

When Martin Luther King Jr. was murdered, as heirs to his American will, we first generation black students were hastily flung from our individual and community ghettos onto the tumultuous "world" stage. We were not mere students sojourning through college to simply make a place for ourselves in American life, but legatees to suffering that motivated us to find a cure for the racial ills that had denied our parents and grandparents.

I felt impelled to do something, to put the "money" of my revolutionary fervor with the idealistic words flowing from my revolutionary mouth. I was impressed with the energy, boldness and ideals of Rap Brown and Stokely Carmichael. When Rap publicly said, "Racism is as American as apple pie," it was easy to digest because it tasted like the truth that it was, and despite its bitterness, truth tasted real, and real good.

Duly inspired, I walked up Fifth Avenue from the NYU campus after class one August afternoon and entered the SNCC office, at Fifth Avenue and 14th Street. (It literally just struck me: it now seems kind of peculiar for SNCC to have an office in a high rent white district) A black woman with freckles and a big red Afro greeted me, and she was absolutely gorgeous. She shook my hand and my heart muscle softened. After telling her I was a student at NYU and wanted to become a SNCC member, she had me fill out an application. It was a typical employment application, and had a laundry list of job descriptions including security, typing, bodyguard, and driver. Merely checking off "No" to security and bodyguard made me nervous. I could not type fast, and checked off "No" to all the job descriptions. I wrote I could file and was good at figuring things out.

After completing the application I sat in the waiting area drooling over the beautiful sister and hoped I could work in the office with her. Out comes a slender black man with the manners of a saber tooth tiger. He stood over me and screamed, "What kind of application is this? You're in college and you can't do anything? What can you do?"

Shaken by this outbreak of venom, I was confused. I had expected to be welcomed as a comrade in the struggle. Instead, I got a taste of an angry, bitter bureaucrat, and a black revolutionary one at that!

He turned on his heels and went back to his office as if he had just fired me. I sat there with some of my idealism leaking from the hole his arrogant anger had punctured. The beautiful sister approached: "Look, someone will call you. When is a good time to reach you?" I answered drooling and left feeling that some good may have come of this misadventure. A few days later I received a phone call, and was told I would be contacted again about something specific for me to participate in. I am still waiting for that phone call.

Daunted, but not defeated, a few months later I next went to the Black Panther office in Harlem. I came after class carrying my books, opened the door, walked in and greeted the one person there, "Hey brother, how ya doing? I'm Ernest. I want to join the Black Panthers," said with casual enthusiasm as I reached out and we shook hands. He did not reveal his name.

I was struck by how dark, plain, and empty the storefront room appeared. There were no posters on the walls of Black Panther leaders, no signs proclaiming the rights of black people, no signs or posters about the lunch programs provided, and no Black Panther newspapers. Devoid of inspiring energy, the Black Panther office was virtually lifeless.

My nameless greeter's eyes and nostrils widened and seemed to inhale my essence, like an animal sizing up prey. He held his gaze impassively. Nothing registered on his face as he said, "We are not taking any new members now."

"Really!" My curiosity asked, "How come?" Was the revolution put on hold? Did they have too many applications? I read the Black Panther newspaper and there was no indication of an over subscribed army. "When will membership open up again?" I persisted.

"I don't know," came the disinterested response. There was no fervor, no fire and for damn sure, no ire.

"How come you're not taking new members? You don't need new members?"

"Look man, I only work here. I'm not in charge of new members." He was polite as he scrutinized me without exhibiting his scrutiny. "Leave your number and someone will call you." I felt like I was being rebuffed by an exclusive white country club.

I am still waiting for the call.

Looking back with no concrete evidence but my gut, I hypothesize that the brother at the Black Panther office was an undercover officer, and possibly the SNCC employees also. I remain uncertain because I don't know what a revolutionary black man or woman looks or sounds like, just as I don't know what an Uncle Tom looks or sounds like.

* * *

The hearts and heart-felt souls of black youth wanted to have a significant impact in the everyday lives of ourselves and all black people. We wanted to effect material change in the failures of American ideals. In a chance meeting in Atlanta, Georgia with students working in the 1970 summer program for the National Urban League, Dr. John Cashin, running for governor, broached the idea of black students coming to Alabama to help get first time black candidates elected. Historically, black counties in Alabama that had predominant majorities, failed to get black officials elected due to methods designed to limit black participation. Included were literacy tests, intimidation, and voter fraud. Dr. Cashin did not expect to be elected governor, but his candidacy was expected to inspire a larger than usual black turnout in the Black Belt of Alabama, to elect candidates at the county level, including Probate Judge, Sheriff, seats on the Board of Education and County Commissioner Court.

The inspired descendants of American slavery, eager to be political and relevant, leapt at this pragmatic and paradigmatic historical opportunity. Southern experiences of trying to get a mere drink of water, ice cream cone, and hamburger, and Northern experiences of ghetto life and recipients of discriminatory practices informed our motif: "Black Students Up South Go Down South."

On NYU's campus our specific determination, idealism, and commitment were eloquently articulated in going to Alabama to work in the historic election campaigns in 1970, to support the National Democratic Party of Alabama (NDPA), a black insurgent political party. The Democratic Party in Alabama white ruled since Reconstruction had been a major suppressor of the political rights and aspirations of its black citizens.

In October 1970, two busloads of enthusiastic Black students headed south to the Black Belt. From the sheer spirit, bubbling, bundled energy we possessed, we frequently broke into familiar songs and a chorus of soul and gospel that the bus driver later said kept him awake during the eighteen hour trip to Montgomery, Alabama.

We disembarked and went to a cavernous Baptist Church. The town storefronts lined uneven wooden streets that creaked, and reminded me of a western movie set. The air was heavy and stale with the stench of slain and compromised black lives. After being welcomed we were greeted with a dire reminder, "*This is not New York.*" The speaker's voice was coarse, and the alarm in his voice registered new and resurrected old fear within me. We were warned, "*not to ever walk alone*," and to remain in the presence of local black folks at all times. We were then dispersed to local counties.

I was stationed in Lowndes County and lived with a family in a rural area where the moonlight and black night kissed your face and closed your eyes. I don't recall their names, but recall their hospitality, as they and their children easily shared their meager goods. I pointedly remember eating some of their government allotment of spam and its salty hybrid after-taste.

Lowndes County was notorious for its racist, venomous, practices against Black folk. In 1965 Lowndes County had an eighty percent Black population but not one Black American citizen was registered to vote. On March 21, 1965 two weeks after "Bloody Sunday," led by Martin Luther King Jr., 3200 marchers on the third attempt marched from Selma, across the Edmund Pettus Bridge, to Montgomery Alabama, passing through a part of Lowndes County, protesting for the right to vote for the Black citizenry. Among the participants was Rabbi Abraham Joshua Heschel who described the marching as "praying with our feet." Five years after the 1965 Voting Rights Act, on November 3, 1970 Black American citizens were running for office in Lowndes County and throughout Alabama. After a day at the polls escorting people to and from the polling places, a historic time was in the making. As we headed back home in a pickup truck with folks piled everywhere, everywhere there were guns. The driver said, "Take this," and he held out a gun like it was a ballpoint pen. When I did not reach for it the driver placed it in my lap.

I recall the time I was visiting my grandfather as a child and going through his jacket pocket, hung up in the closet, and found what I instantly knew was not the usual toy gun. At seven years of age the weight of the gun prohibited me from lifting it with one hand. Even with two hands I still could not get an easy grip, and let it slide back in his pocket. Finally, I maneuvered the gun out and delightedly showed my mom the new toy. As I lifted it up with all my might, in horror and with lightening speed, Mom swooped down and took the gun from me.

The gun placed in my lap was heavy. I then heard the stern childhood recording of my mother's voice: "Leave that gun alone, Junior, don't you ever touch it again, you can get hurt or hurt somebody." She continued, "Junior, somebody could get shot. Killed." My childhood enthusiasm was wounded.

I was frightened as I looked at this curio now resting in my lap, like a baby, waiting to be touched and attended to. The truck rumbled along on the narrow uneven dirt road lined with overgrown vegetation, making it the perfect hiding place for evil; it was pitch-black and the car's headlights were the only illumination. The only thing visible was the dust from the road swirling in the concave shaped light. My heart rumbled, and each beat pounded with more fear.

As I picked the gun up I made a relevant inquiry, "What is this for?"

"For the white folks, in case dem' white folks hide and ambush us," said like a soldier on routine patrol. "They ain't happy wif us runnin' for office and defyin' them. Fo'sure they'd kill us if they gets a chance." This was the real-life definition of relevant; now I had actual experience of what it meant to be political and that everything was political.

The circumstances dictated, and I accepted my duty. I picked up the gun and began to scan the side of the road for white people who would kill us for merely voting, for exercising our constitutional right. I was ready to hurt somebody, ready to get hurt; though not ready, not willing, not ready to die, but made ready by necessity.

The natural hazy black shadows that bounced on the vegetation from the moon, I monitored for hidden danger. "Son," the driver said affectionately, "you just point and shoot and you be okay." He smiled a glinting veteran's smile, trying to relax the new soldier in the war. The fear riding in the car engulfed me, consumed me with uncontrolled dread. We bore down the dirt road and cold pure fear rode ahead and followed us simultaneously, as my eyes darted and searched frenetically.

We arrived at my host home unmolested. I remained outside, alone, and inhaled deep breaths in an effort to de-cathect from my "freedom ride" and reflect upon the new "State" of Alabama. The moon was round and high, and the pale light painted a shadowy skyline of trees and black grass. Compelled to release the massive energy of fear and anger, angst and morbid uncertainty accumulated in a half-hour ride; I went inside and asked permission to fire the gun. On this historic night, I had helped in some miniscule measure to make American ideals come to life for black folks nonviolently, and white folks too. I needed to violently discharge my joy.

"Sure," he said without hesitation.

With acres of empty land before me, I looked at the gun, pointed it, pulled the trigger, and felt the jerk of death explode forward as I rocked backward; the open expanse and anonymous night swallowed the explosive sound and whizzing bullet. I wondered if I could have done the same, with such ease and poise, if we had been attacked?

One man, one vote.

"Leave that gun alone, Junior, you can get hurt or hurt somebody."

One black man...one black vote...one gun.

"Junior, somebody could get shot. Killed."

Upon returning to New York my experience in Alabama left an afterglow that has not completely worn off. One continuing image that replays itself with uncanny clarity is of a one hundred year old man speaking to students in a rural church in the woods of Alabama. Standing erect and physically and spiritually defiant, he emotionally implored, "You young people, *don't give down.* I rememba when the Klan was born, when the Negro was lynched for nothin'. I rememba when Hardy and Coolidge was presiden' and the Negro was treated like dirt. You young people, *don't give down.*" His voice boomed passionately, youthfully, as the one hundred years of pain he witnessed and lived every single day, appeared to be lifting and soaring as was his voice. He stood and spoke as the Witness, connecting disparate and distant times as he chronicled the nineteenth and twentieth centuries as historian qua historian. It was now his time: time for redemption, to pass the torch of light he had harbored for a century, notwithstanding the oppression and pain; he was representative of what came before and a harbinger as to what was to come. "*Don't give down, You young people, don't give down.*"

I replay his words and his spirit every day, wherever I go. Every day.

He was a Black angel and his spirit and message was heavenly. I remain proud to have been part of the historic moment witnessing John Hewlett elected the first black sheriff of Lowndes County, Alabama.

What I did not know then and proud to now know was that my mom's uncle, Joseph Armstrong DeLaine, known as J.A., was an African Methodist Episcopal minister and Civil Rights pioneer from South Carolina. J. A. led the fight for school desegregation in Clarendon County. The case became known as Briggs v. Elliott, and it was the first case in the twentieth century to be filed in the Federal Court fighting for integration and overturning the Separate but Equal doctrine espoused in Plessy v. Ferguson in 1896. Briggs v. Elliott reached the Supreme Court in 1951, and it was combined with four other cases, with each case heard separately. The Supreme Court rendered its decision under the name Brown v. Board of Education.

J.A.'s home in Summerton was burned down in 1951 and his family fled South Carolina in 1955 after his church was burned down. When I discovered this information at the first DeLaine family reunion in 1982, I was shocked that I had not heard about him from my mom or my Uncles J and Charlie. Mom shrugged when I asked why such courageous acts were not told to my sisters and me as a source of family pride. Sponsored by Senator Ernest Hollings and United States Congressman James E. Clyburn, my great-uncle received the Congressional Medal of Honor, posthumously, in 2003.

I passed through history not recognizing there would be a complex future that would not fully respond to the very moral, just, fair ambitions, and protestations of black folk. My father as pessimist or realist told me that despite the new hairstyles, African garb and sententious rhetoric, not much would substantively change and that my generation would grow weary. I vigorously defended my generation as unique, enduring like no other, and achieving beyond the scope of his vision. Dad recalled the passion he felt at the racial injustice when he was young. "I used to get angry and get all worked up," he shrugged, "It's not going to be like you think."

I graduated from NYU in two and one-half years attending summer sessions and taking extra credit during the semester. In retrospect, it was not in my best academic or intellectual interest to rush through college for college sake, for the sake of having finished college. I could have used the entire four year period (no doubt, even a lot longer) to learn in depth and develop a true confidence, discipline and broad breathe of knowledge, without major concern for time and grades. Overall I had a GPA of 3.3 and my last four semesters of credits I earned a 3.8 GPA. Then I was impressed with my grades but not now. I crammed and got good grades but did not indulge in the process of learning. I did not appreciate the philosophy of learning, did not examine reason and methods across disciplines, history, science and literature. In short, I used my intelligence to figure out the minimum I had to do in order to pass courses, with high grades, if possible.

I was advised, when I first arrived on the NYU campus, by Martha Pitts, "to hang out with white boys like Josh and Mike because they know a lot about everything and you will learn a lot." Listening to them discuss Hebert Marcuse, Hegel and Aristotle like I discussed Malcolm X, Rap Brown and the Boston Celtics was impressive, intellectually stimulating, enlightening, and intimidating. Though I was welcomed, my feeling that I had nothing intellectual, learned, or academic to contribute, ruled out a relationship of any kind.

Yet, my self-image projected me in grandiose fashion. During a conversation with my political science professor I informed him of my ambition "to study at the London School of Economics after graduation," I said it as if it were on 125th Street and Seventh Avenue. Jolted by the enormity of my ambition, he ceased moving and became mute.

I certainly did fathom that the London School for Economics was a prestigious institution to gain entry for scholars and intellectuals. But I thought an intellectual was someone who studied hard and got good grades. Thus, I thought I could become an intellectual by studying hard and getting good grades, just like in sixth grade.

Graduating college in 1971 made me feel as if I could accomplish anything in the world. I felt wholesome, in some ways I felt whole; no longer a nobody; now, I was somebody; I mattered, at least to myself; I now had a future to think about and plan for. My mom, who fought against me attending college, proudly attended my graduation with the rest of my family. I could not stop looking at my college ring, mesmerized by its brilliant sparkle. I no longer merely walked down the streets of New York; I graced lightly, as if walking on water, proud that I had achieved what I set out to do, and do it as well as I did. Now, I had a sense of a future, with options of my choosing. Thus, I sparkled like my college ring, shining, twinkling, energetic, giving off light, like the stars at night; still, I did not feel securely in place; yet, I now felt I had a place at the American table, unlike seven years earlier on a riotous humid July night: Freedom Summer 1964. My All-Star Converse sneakers fell from my throne of fashion.

Graduating college also led, at times, to clashing of the classes. I saw Junior High School classmate Ron J from the Grant projects at a local nightclub. We greeted each other warmly, talked, and rekindled good feelings, then reminisced about the crazy fun times growing up. I observed Ron J as he observed me, as if I were a subject in a social-psych experiment; he kept a steady eye on my finger, which wore my college ring.

Ron J was now an elevator repairman. He angrily observed, "The Irish, straight off the boat walk in and get a union job because they have connections. They won't hire no brothers straight off the block. I see that shit all the time." I felt the pang of reality in his story. But I was not about to tell Ron J that I turned down Columbia University's acceptance of me in the political science department with Charles Hamilton as my advisor, as stated in my acceptance letter. And for damn sure I was not going to say I decided to attend Yale University as political science graduate student—to get out of the neighborhood.

Later in the evening Ron J said, "I watched you, listened to you, wanted to see if you thought you were better than *us*."

Us? I thought I was us! I am us! I grew my long Afro and anger and wore my African dashiki to be us! I went to Alabama in the name of us! I was going to Yale to be one of the chief theoreticians of the black revolution. I did not trust white people nor like them any better than he did. Us versus them? Us black folks verse us black folks? I did not identify with the black bourgeois. I was still a brother from the street even though I was now on a first name basis with the black bourgeoisie. I had not changed substantially, though my sense of self changed, ambitions altered, projected in new directions, new and larger vocabulary, my diction and grammar improved. I was rejected from Harvard, but I applied. I was still the same man with the same core, yet different man from Harlem's ghetto. My humanity had not altered, but Ron J was not concerned about my humanity, he simply wanted to know if I now looked down on him. Perhaps, without conscious realization, he was looking up at me.

"I could never think I was better than you or anybody from the block," I said with steady cool. "Nah man, not me. You know me better than that."

"I checked you out, you're okay." Before he died of HIV drug related complications, Ron J confessed a confession of wished and wanted, in his internal secret chamber. "I want, I hope my son," who was attending a community college at night while working fulltime, "to be the first member in my family to graduate from college."

I was stunned, not at his wish, but his seeming insistence to look right through me, ignore our proximity, and not recognize that we were in the same ninth grade class, we attended vocational high schools, ran track and got jobs after graduation. The core of my discomfit was the empty chamber in his voice, devoid of any prior hope or possibility of achievement. Eerily, his implied self-evaluation, felt hauntingly familiar. The ghosts of the Basement past and present would present, sometime later, serendipitously.

I had just come from a dinner with Juanita, and I was wearing a sport jacket and tie. We stopped by Sharon's apartment to join a group from the block hanging out. During the conversation someone said, as neutral observer, "Ernie, not only do you look kind of spiffy, you sound kind of spiffy, you sound like a professional now."

I said nothing because I did not know what to say. The comment was so unexpected, but it was just as welcomed, making me feel proud that my metamorphosis was now making my childhood friends take notice.

To leave the ghetto, this comfort zone, was the quintessential terror; it was my ghetto, my home, the ground zero of identity, safety and opportunity, no matter how limited.

Each new step for me was fraught with fear of the known and the unknown. At NYU, we idealistically championed going back to the black community and being relevant but the sober voice of Martha Pitts sliced through with knife-edged clarity, "You are not preparing to return to the ghetto, you are preparing to leave."

Martha Pitts, prophet extraordinaire, was painstakingly correct. We as revolutionary black students were not being educated to return to the ghetto.

"Bullshit," said the Present, "I'm going back to help my people, not leave them. I'm taking the skills I learn and tools I develop and knowledge I gain to uplift our brothers and sisters."

The Future, meek and humble, spoke tentatively: "I don't know. I did plan for today but did not plan for what actually took place. I can't predict…can't forecast tomorrow…really don't know, just hope I'm ready, better ready for tomorrow than I was for yesterday and today. I just don't know."

"Right on!" bellowed the Past, "Return to where it is safe, with fewer risks, less threat and less challenge to your ego, come back and survive to live another day, though the sun rises slowly, ever so slowly and the nights are never-ending. This is our creed and morning star."

Einee minee miney mo catch the future by the toe, if it hollers, whatever you do: don't, let, go!

I wanted out of the Basement, desperately, yet I loved so many people and so much of the experience because there was a lot of good stuff there that had shaped me and still informs me. When my childhood friends died prematurely, a part of me died also, sometimes terrifying me because: "But, for the grace of God, go I."

When you leave your home, and for sure the Basement was my home, the loss is a zero-sum phenomenon because my new address placed me in a new zip code, with new friends, new values, new ideas, new perceptions, new opportunities, and realized ambitions. As time does what time does, graduation presented itself and new challenges and new fears arose, but mostly old fears refused to die. I humbly, but happily chose the future, knowing I was not going back, ever.

High Ambition Meets High Anxiety
Why Do We Have to Take Exams When Life is One Big Test?

> White supremacy lives in the conscious and unconscious mind of every American, white and black. Up rooting it might take centuries of sustained effort.
>
> ***Mark D. Naison***

> If people bring so much courage to this world the world has to kill them to break them, so of course it kills them. The world breaks every one and afterward many are strong at the broken places.
>
> ***Ernest Hemingway***

After traveling the now open American educational highway to NYU, I continued my journey and next exited onto the campus of Yale University in 1971 as a political science graduate student. What was written in the letters of recommendation by my professors, still, I can't imagine. In class with my fellow students (all white) who flowed with articulate confidence, I shuddered when having to speak, and then only when forced. They had a lifetime to prepare while I was struggling for a life with a recently found lifeline. I was so reticent one professor asked me after class if I was an undergraduate. "No," I murmured, "I am a graduate student."

All the students in class were friendly and the faculty supportive but my nerves were frayed from having traveled so far, so fast, by my lonesome. I got to know some of the black graduate students and law students and they were cool, for the most part, providing a respite from my fears. But I even felt pressure and judged by them when asked, "What are you studying in political science?"

I met African and West Indian graduate students. At dinner one evening, they inadvertently stumbled upon contrasting statements of one tenured white professor. At different times, he told the West Indian he was "superior" to black Americans; he told the African he was "superior" to the West Indians; he told the black American he was "superior" to the Africans. I shook my head in disbelief. The sheer malevolence of racism left me aghast when a student added, "In Africa the West Africans are told they are superior to the East Africans, and the East Africans are told they are superior to the West Africans." I quaked inside as the term "divide and conquer" was treacherously manifested.

My motivation to attend Yale, to become one of the "chief theoreticians of the black revolution," despite all the signs to the contrary—especially my being on campus—was fantasy squared. Juxtaposed, was George Bryant, father-in-law to be, who used Ralph Bunche as black role model for me to emulate. Moreover, Yale was the right place and right time for the Ralph Bunche comparison. But my confidence was in the wrong place at the right time. Even as the fantasy crumbled in the light of reality—reading assignments and term papers—I maintained the need for the black revolution, because I did not believe I could live up to Ralph Bunche as a realistic role model and the academic demands required. The fantasy for a black revolution masked a deeper set of aspirations. That is, I could not otherwise have gone to Yale, because in the closet of my ambitions, I really wanted to be a successful human being first and black man second.

Yale, by dint of its mission, did serve a useful purpose. I finally had to admit that the black revolution was not going to be, and that I had to find a way to be. Still, I was unsure how to fit in conventional society. I left Yale at the end of the first semester and got married in August 1972. In September I entered NYU law school. In college I learned that America is a credential-oriented society, and I imagined that having a law degree would open doors of opportunity even though I entered law school stating, "I don't want to be a lawyer." (A conundrum: I do not understand why my sisters and I pursued legal training commensurate with our education. Florita became a legal secretary and Audrey trained as a paralegal. I believe there was something in the "culture" of our family that motivated us.) Meanwhile, I experienced law school as a personal Hell; it was as if I had a wet finger in a live socket for three years.

During my first final exam my brain froze like an engine in the Antarctic Circle. The churning of my mind would not cease until the grinding smoke and flame of friction consumed itself. My brain quailed, my hand trembled as I wrote mindlessly and the letters I scribbled in my booklet I could not read and neither could the professor. When he handed me my exam to read, I opened it, attempted to read it, and said, "Was I that nervous?"

During my last final exam I began to read the fact pattern, the words rapidly went limp, melting like black snow in a torrid zone, forming into small black puddles of ink, and in the next instant they coagulated and flowed like hot lava rushing down a mountain until the entire white page swirled violently in black waves.

In panic, I pushed away from my desk. Earthquakes on distant continents are measured instantly and accurately, yet not one person in the room was aware of the seismic fissures that blinded me. I looked around the room and nothing was blurred. I looked at the exam again, and it remained a raging sea of black ink. In an attempt to regain my vision, I stood up, took a deep breath and tried to bring calm to my stampeding distress.

I walked into the quiet of the hallway—oblivious of my classmates writing furiously. I placed one finger in the cement line under the evenly spaced stones that made up the hallway walls and dragged my panic-stricken soul around the full length of the T-shaped hallway until the volcanic intensity subsided. I returned to complete the exam in the truncated time left. This was the pattern I suffered and endured throughout all law school learning and exams. My grades suffered as well, which only served to reinforce my sense of inadequacy. Notwithstanding, I believed I should have done better.

Being a law school student was an object of awe for family and friends. With some degree of pride or reverence folks vicariously needed to know, "How's law school doin'?"

"It's okay, a lot of studying, but things are going okay," keeping my struggles with anxiety hidden. How do you tell your family and friends that you are scared and have little confidence in yourself when they look up to you as "the smart one?" The Hope. "You makin' it boy, I'm so proud of you," a common sentiment from folks of my parents generation. "You ain't no regula' nigger off the block Ernie. You doin' good, man. Keep doin' that school thing, man," words of encouragement from neighborhood peers.

My father and I were watching a black male political personality being interviewed on television and he said, "When are you going to be up there, big-time, so I can see you on there," pointing to the television, "so I can be more proud of you."

Insult, anger and inadequacy rushed into the same emotional room simultaneously. My chest tightened, feeling certain that dad viewed me as a failure, but dubiously happy that he had such high expectations. Years later I came to understand that my father was living vicariously through me.

Upon graduation in June 1975, I told family and friends for the first time, that I did not want to be a lawyer. Uncle Bud looked on as his wife, Ruth said, "You would be the *first* one in the family to be a lawyer. You would be a professional," said as if I was about to land on the moon.

With heads shaking in disappointment my parents stated, "Boy, you don't know what you want."

Mr. Winston McGill Sr. looked at me through the prism of the life he desired, trying to conjure a way back to the past to bring the future I was rejecting to the young Winston who stood at the bottom of the hill in the 1930's gazing up at the City College of New York, then a white fortress that he could not penetrate, though he had the will and the intellectual way. "Ernie," said Mr. McGill, his voice shaking as he took flight back to the present, "why don't you want to be a lawyer?"

I humbly said, "Because I want to become a psychologist."

My friends hunkered down for the summer, preparing for the New York State Bar Exam. I declined to take the bar exam with the promise I would take it in the future. All my friends offered the obvious appeal, "Now is the best time to take it when everything is still fresh in your mind."

Immune to the pressure, I began to parry, "I want to be a psychologist so I can help people." I entered individual and group psychotherapy in July 1975.

In 1976 I was one of eight students accepted into the clinical psychology program at Teachers College, Columbia University. During third year I began to work with Professor Joel Davitz to develop a dissertation topic and formed a preliminary interest in moral development. He instructed me to research the topic and come back and discuss it. After doing the research I worried if I understood what I read. I cancelled several appointments with Professor Davitz for fear I would not have anything intelligent to say. When I finally found my way to his office, I spoke a half-hour nonstop. When I finished he asked, "Have you ever thought about teaching?"

Gripped with surprise, I said, "Me? No."

"You should. You would make a good professor."

"But I told you there was one thing I didn't fully understand," I said.

Shrugging and waving his hand, he continued, "You explained everything clearly, there was only one thing you were not clear about; you did fine."

When I left his office I was experiencing "Post No Traumatic Stress Disorder." I was giddy, pleased with myself, and recognized that my true potential was apparent to Professor Davitz. When and why my anxiety accelerates and disrupts my functioning around any given event remains baffling.

I chose to do my dissertation on the relationship between prejudice and moral judgment reasoning, using the theory of Harvard professor Lawrence Kohlberg. Professor John Broughton recommended I go to Harvard to learn Kohlberg's scoring method and study at his Moral Development Institute during the summer of 1983.

I prepared thoroughly, actually over prepared as is my wont at times when feeling anxious. In class I solved a problem in a way that had not been previously thought of as thirty-five students from around the world listened as I spoke.

"Hmmn," the professor murmured as he mulled over my presentation. He looked in the scoring manual—prepared by Kohlberg and his staff—to ascertain if my reasoning was accurate, but my proffered answer was not there. "You are right, it is not an answer that we came to, but you are right for certain," he said with surprise and respect.

Near the end of the course Professor Kohlberg asked, "Ernie, do you want to come to Harvard?"

Kohlberg invited me to come to Harvard to complete my dissertation, become a member of his research team, and teach in his graduate school program. Harvard invited Harlem to become a member of "The Club!" Junebug, from 129th Street, was keenly aware that he was being recognized as intellectually capable; yet, his invitation sent me into a stupor. When I did not respond Kohlberg said, "Think about it Ernie, we will talk later."

In lieu of responding with enhanced confidence, the deadly sotto voce Whispers War began to rage throughout my entire being. The Whispers War: competing voices, one saying I am inferior and not intelligent, the other voice challenging that I am intelligent, not inferior. An internecine battle with my true intelligence and humanity ensued. Intermittent surges of electrical charges shot through me. I felt weak with dread as I walked through Harvard Square; that Professor Kohlberg and his staff would expect me to always find the answer no else could find, or come up with a novel perspective or solution and if I did not, and I knew I could not, they would me see as a dumb and stupid nigger: "Because that is all you really are, a dumb and stupid nigger," so said the warring Whisper dominant at that moment: "Whiteness"—the belief propounded by the Founding Fathers, that Europeans were superior because they were white and Africans were inferior because they were not white, but black.

"No, no thank you," I replied to Professor Kohlberg. My tone was neutral, conversational, but I was still in shock. Yet there was no accelerated heart rate, no conscious thoughts of fear, no conscious thoughts of failure, or abject sense of inadequacy, only a mundane zestless rationale: "I have a nice apartment in New York and a good therapist so I can't leave now." Just like my Mom's rationale when she rejected the invitation from Florita's school teachers to place her in the Hunter College School for gifted children.

When I told friends that I turned down Professor Kohlberg's offer, each one reacted in astonishment. Robert Jekyll and I were running in the calm air of Riverside Drive, a street lined with trees thick with spring foliage that formed a beautiful and shady vista. Sweating profusely in the tenth mile of our fifteen mile run Robert stopped abruptly,

"What is wrong with you?" He said exasperated. "Harvard. You have a chance to go to Harvard. You better go, man. If it were me, I would go; no question about it. It's a once in a lifetime opportunity. Fuck! Go!"

Once the initial shock wore off, he began to lobby me in a more measured way, "Look Ernest, you will not always have this door open to you," as if his change of inflection would soften my rock solid decision. In his sincere plea, I could hear his longing for success in whatever form his Harvard would take. Even louder, I could also hear the cries of generations past.

When I discussed my decision with my psychologist, she observed, "Ernie, you still don't know you are a lawyer."

"What are you talking about?" I asked.

"You know you finished law school, but you don't know you are a lawyer," she said.

Bristling with annoyance I sneered, "I graduated from NYU in 1975 and my parents came to the graduation. With all the pain I suffered and endured, I hung in there when Quit slapped me upside my face many a day; that tells me I know I am a lawyer."

Then one cloudy day while walking to class on the Columbia University campus, I felt my gait involuntarily slowing down. As I tried to make sense of it, I became acutely aware of taking steps in a place I had never been, though I walked these same steps many yesterdays. In a dream like state I found myself walking ever so slowly, then stopped. I felt the history, majesty, and Ivy League aura of Columbia University from a hazy remembrance that became sparkling clear and cleansing in an instant. Poised like a statue and staring up into the graying skies, I looked straight at the heavens and a "Light" emanated from within me, shined up—like an El Greco painting that moves from the concrete and material and rises to the spiritual and celestial—connecting with a sparkling voice that shouted in quiet and amazed joy, "You graduated from college, NYU. You graduated from NYU Law School! You are a Lawyer! You are on The Columbia University campus! You are in a PhD program! When did I get here? How did I get here? I did this. I Did this. I Did This!" Suddenly, the cloudy day broke forth with a luminous glow. Heavenly glow. I basked. Just as suddenly, the Light contracted, the excited sparkling voice became still. This emerged truth? This submerged truth? This escaped truth? Unsure how to characterize it, this pristine moment of moments, took refuge, returning from whence it came, in the bedrock of my humanity. I presume.

I resumed walking on the still cloudy day toward my destination, conscious of my fantastic interlude with myself, and continued the day as usual. The illusion of control I thought I exercised with my conscious choices was deluged with humility, perplexed as to why I could not, and still cannot, summon my human worth and value at will.

In the summer of 1984 I planned a trip to London, when a tangible physical shift was experienced—something snapped into place inside me. I cancelled my trip to focus on my dissertation. When I got to the writing stage I was able to work all day, take a break, and then continue into the late night playing classical music to keep me company. Mozart, Beethoven, and Mendelssohn were among those who soothed my mental and physical exhaustion. Sometimes late at night I would decide to complete a section or idea, and would will myself to stay up, even as I began to fall asleep, with the words, "I want to finish this tonight." Instantly, I felt refreshed and alert. It was a discipline and control I was not aware I possessed and have not had since completing my dissertation.

I defended my dissertation, and the committee of five professors sent me out of the room and when I returned, everyone was all-smiles as they greeted me: "Congratulations, Dr. Adams."

Having defeated the all-star cast of demons that had impeded me for a lifetime, finally, law school Junebug was now Dr. Adams. After the euphoria subsided, I thought out loud, "Is that all there is?" I recalled all the angst I experienced and it did not seem commensurate with the outcome. The mountain was actually a molehill. The degree of difficulty did not require the nine years it took to complete my doctorate. The reality I created in my head was unrelated to the actuality of the task.

I became friendly with a woman who lived on my floor. She was a graduate student in psychology and had some trepidation about whether she could complete a dissertation. I encouraged her and gave her my dissertation to peruse. Talia Matalon, a charming woman, always with an effervescent smile when she greeted me, went on to earn her doctorate in psychology. Her husband Roly Matalon was a rabbinic student at Jewish Theological Seminary. One Saturday evening I passed

Roly as he was entering our apartment building and I was leaving. We greeted each other, made light chit chat, and continued on our respective ways. I was invited to a party sponsored by Latin American Jews. At the party, I was surprised to see Roly and he bluntly said, "What are you doing here?"

Now, I felt conspicuous, and out of place. I countered, "What are you doing here?"

"I am a Jew and Latin American."

"I am here because a friend invited me."

With my doctorate in hand and Professors Kohlberg and Davitz support and encouragement, I did not seek a university teaching position, because I believed I could not be a successful professor. Instead, I got a job as a psychologist with the New York City Police Department (NYPD). I evaluated candidates for the police academy, worked with police officers having difficulty in their private lives or on the job, did trauma debriefings with police officers involved in firing their guns in the line of duty, and removed the guns of police officers suffering psychological disturbance.

Sitting at my desk in the early afternoon on January 28, 1986, a colleague said, "Have you the heard? The space shuttle Challenger exploded and all the astronauts were killed."

Disbelief and numbness vied for supremacy, and as I reacted through the sequelae of both responses, an incredible sadness enveloped me. Being the veteran of many horrific events in my life, I shook-it-off and continued my day; but debilitating feelings began to regroup, and when I left work, they had returned in full force. After watching the graphic retelling on television, I went to bed that night feeling sadness for the loss of life. The next few days I was perplexed, because the losses felt personal, like people I cared deeply about. The hurt began to throb mildly but consistently; as it grew I asked myself: "Why are you still feeling this way? What is going on with you, brother?"

The intense ache spoke, "You feel the losses of the astronauts as a horrified American citizen." Surprised at what I had said about by myself, I gave plenty of thought to understand my feelings. I, Ernest Henry Adams Junior, experienced the losses as a full-fledged American; feeling like I was a part of one nation, with one identity. Why and when did I come to feel apart of being a part of America as a complete human being who was of African descent?

The answer: I really do not know. I guess that it lies in both my failures and successes, that I came to feel I was a significant American, a real American, because I was in the "hunt" for the proverbial American dream; that what I wanted most, I achieved: the opportunity to exercise my free will to become the person I would choose to be.

The next mountain to scale was passing the New York State psychology-licensing exam; the mere thought of taking the licensing-exam stalled my thinking. I took the necessary preparatory course, studied sporadically, and on the day of the licensing-exam my supervisor at the NYPD stared at me in surprise when I showed up at work. When he came to my office I found some tasty pabulum to feed him. The terror inside me had formed a blockade that prevented me from taking the exam. It was a palpable terror, felt as rampant and restless agitation, which I was now aware of, but unable to contain. The passage of time lessened my terror to tangible fear, and permitted me to enter the psychology-licensing exam room.

When I took the licensing-exam the first time, I came to an essay question that I immediately understood. I had the knowledge and my heart nervously leapt for joy, but when it was time to write the answer, the knowledge crowded together in an information traffic-jam. It became stalled and moved fitfully, unable to travel smoothly from my brain. This pattern repeated and repeated so often, I wondered if I was ever going to pass. Each time I failed, enormous pain from shame rampaged through my entire body, and I felt like a humungous piece of shit. Saddened and burdened by the constriction, I held out Hope for the next time and the next time, if need be, and it was. When I confessed my shame and other self-deprecatory feelings to my friend Jennifer, she became annoyed at the content and intensity of my self-flagellation. "Ernest, that test does not makeup who you are and the work you do, you are already qualified."

Those last four words, "you are already qualified" served as a balm and mixed mightily with the four prior failures. It was true I was well respected at the NYPD for my clinical work by my supervisors, but more importantly by the cops I served. I was pleasantly surprised when I received a thank you card from a cop after I had to remove his guns;

most significantly, cops recommended other cops to me, including white cops. When I did pass, on my fifth attempt, my boundless joy and pride saturated my pores.

Now that I was legitimate, licensed by the State of New York, I opened a private practice in 1990. Sitting one-on-one or in a group helping people deal with psychological conflict is my métier, and I have never felt stymied or intimidated.

A white Jewish man, who was a CEO in a major corporation, became my client. He commuted by corporate jet twice a week to see me—he wanted to come three times a week. He began to praise me because he was making the kind of progress he sought but never had with prior therapists. "Some people find religion as the answer, well, I found you."

I was elated.

During a session as he talked about one of his ongoing concerns, in mid-sentence, an absolutely devastating non sequitur exploded from his lips with vitriol dressed in a white gown and white hood: "Niggerrrrrrrrr," rolled out of his mouth as if on an elongated raging welcome mat.

I froze. My survival system came to the fore in a flash; ready to thrust forward in either fight or flight.

"Motherfucker." He was just beginning.

I felt like I was sitting in an unbuckled seat in an airplane spiraling downward out of control; trying to keep from being tossed about like a rag doll, I gripped the sides of my chair.

"Big nose motherfucker." He spoke like he was exempt from prosecution.

"Martin Luther King big nose motherfucker." He was on a horrific roll.

"*You.*" Said with added emphasis.

I could not believe what I was hearing; did not want to believe what I was hearing; did not want to hear what I was hearing, as my ear drums beat back his incendiary invectives; an intense pressure filled my head.

"Nigger." My humanity was nonexistent.

With my sixth sense I began to take stock of what was happening.

"Martin Luther King, big nose motherfucker. You." The brisance of his verbal grenade completed its mission.

As a psychologist, I try to figure out the multiple levels on which a person operates and address the level or levels I think appropriate. In the common therapeutic situation I am objective. But in this situation, racial epithets were loaded, aimed, and fired at me, and my street survival patios kicked into gear, "Am I going to have to kick this motherfucker's ass?"

From my experience as a psychology intern on the inpatient service two lessons prevailed: 1) position myself to control the door to be able to exit when and if necessary, 2) With psychotic populations, if there was an uncontrollable person, the best solution was to summon help.

In my office there was only my client and me, and he was sitting in front of the door. I knew I had to assert control. But when I focused on him he was not out of control. He sat quietly, with a dependent penetrating gaze, relaxed face, anticipatory smile, not exceptionally different when he ordinarily sought answers from me.

But what was the question?

An absence of a scowl or even a furrowed brow made for a plaintive face seeking refocused attention and anticipatory reaction. There was no heavy breathing, no body churning, no repetitive nervous tics, no rage in his eyes, no threat to my safety, and he made no attempt to leave. He began unfolding gradually: "In all respect, I was always physically afraid of blacks." This from a man who was raised in a virtual lily-white neighborhood, primarily Jewish, and had little actual exposure to black people except in the form of "help" at times.

Once the "black ice," as it were, was broken, the following comments during the course of treatment followed. "You are black, you are an idiot…Cops are good, blacks are bad…this humidifier, this little black thing, thought of you…I am afraid of black people like the plague"

The white American fear of black Americans is primordial, rooted in the mythology of the nation's origins. African human beings were wrenched from their country, transported to America where survivors were sold at auctions, and kept under control by physical violence and intimidation. Africans had to learn to live under a democratic slave regime, mythologized as Southern hospitality, benevolent slave masters, and naturally docile slaves. White Americans never believed the latter. Subservience to the crown was oppressive: the shackles worn by the American colonies were shorn through violent assertion during the Revolutionary War. Aware of their own propensity for unfettered freedom, they understood that involuntary subservience of the African would elicit, at minimum, the same response they gave their British cousins.

After being in psychotherapy for an extended period, my white Jewish client's language changed. "My wife does not like black people; it upsets me, seeing you may have affected my view…I said something negative about black people in front of my son, I'm sorry…It would be okay if my daughter went out with you." He also reported his wife "fell in love with me all over again," and his children said he was no longer gratuitously angry.

One day in 1994 while riding the subway, I was engrossed in a Steven King novel, and looked up and saw eight black fingers gripping a book with bold black letters: **Bar Review Course**. A medium of exchange took place and my mind leapt to the idea of tackling the ghost of law school past. The painful truth be told, I could not admit to myself that I was too afraid to take the New York State Bar Exam in 1975 because I did not think I was smart enough to pass; not smart enough to be a lawyer.

Even though I graduated from law school I still experienced a dispirited inadequacy, because I graduated with a C average. I should have done better despite my debilitating anxiety. Then, in 2000, a perverse irony presented itself on the front page of the New York Times "Week in Review" section. Al Gore, a Harvard University graduate, did not want to be perceived as a policy wonk, for fear of being out of touch with the common voter he sought to identify with him; thus, the candidate to be President had his grades revealed: he was a C student, "bragging" about his grades. Then I later discovered he entered Vanderbilt University law school but did not graduate. President George W. Bush, in his commencement address at Yale University, acknowledged he was a C student while at Yale, stating: "Now you know you too can become President of the United States."

Ernest H. Adams Junior, for President of the United States?

I wonder if the American electorate would have elected Barack Obama President if he bragged about being a C student.

Putting the mettle to the pedal, I drove straight into the midst of my fears. I studied for the Bar Exams in New York and New Jersey. My brain began to hack and cough while being re-introduced to the law as the cobwebs and mounds of dust were roused from nineteen years of nonuse.

I sat down at my kitchen table to do a practice corporation exam, and the terror resumed, from whence it left off. My entire equilibrium was shattered. My body trembled and my mind quaked. I read and reread and reread over and over the sample exam without understanding the issues. I tried to calm myself by taking deep breaths while repeating positive mantras. "Just calm down, slow down, it's okay, you are intelligent, a smart man. You can do this, just take your time, you can do this." The warmth of the sun was shining through my window when I sat down at 9 a.m. I sat in my underwear and undershirt, now drenched with sweat, without moving from the chair. I gave up trying to answer the practice question. When I looked at the clock, it was 3 p.m.; I was stupefied. I did not get up for water or go to the bathroom; yet, I knew I traveled, even without leaving my seat. How could I travel without moving? Where did I go during this six-hour period? How could I travel and not be hungry or thirsty? Though I hungered for solace for my tortured soul, none was present in the sticky wetness of my skin.

During a break at the bar review class, a white woman went to the teacher and said she was having difficulty with the volume of work and all the time it consumed. The teacher testily said, "Stop complaining. Buckle down and get the job done."

Two students later, the teacher heard the same complaint from an African American woman and cajoled, "I know it's hard, it's not easy; just do the best you can."

"Did you hear that? That was some racist shit," Aldric, a black friend said bitterly. "He told the white girl to 'get the job done' and the sister, he indulged. He should have told her to 'get the job done.'"

"Perhaps he should have, I'm not certain. But he wasn't being a racist; he was trying to be sensitive, trying to encourage her while not discouraging her."

"True, but why didn't he expect the same of the sister?"

"I guess I am assuming he did expect the same."

"So why didn't he tell the sister the same thing?"

"He thinks he did." But, did he?

I failed the New York State Bar Exam six times, and each time I felt like a bigger and smellier pile of doo-doo; like in my childhood dream: I kept trying to cleanse myself and clean myself and cleanse myself until I received a phone call from Stan Futterman who said, "Congratulations, Ernest."

"What are you talking about?" I had no idea.

"I'm sitting here looking at the Law Journal and see your name, you have passed the New York State Bar. Congratulations."

I had stopped telling most people I was taking the exam because of my mortal shame, but Stan Futterman was always a supporter and he never made me feel like I was less of a person. I was surprised Stan called, but I was not totally surprised, this seventh time around. When I took the bar exam I saw multiple ways to answer some questions, and wrote longer and more comprehensive answers than on previous exams. Why my terror did not emerge that day, I have no freaking idea. I had passed the New Jersey Bar the second time, likely because I took it the day following the two days of the New York Bar; I surmise my terror had abated enough for successful completion.

Now law school was complete. But I was not.

Meeting the Goldstein's

> "For where you go, I will go; where you lodge, I will lodge; your people are my people, and your God is my God; where you die I will die, and there I will be buried."
>
> ***Ruth 1: 16-17***

> Men worship what they respect and what they consider to be fairly good imitations of themselves
>
> ***Amy Jacques Garvey***

Nothing distinguished Meyer Israel Goldstein from all the other potential lawyers at NYU. Then one cold blustery February day 1973, upon entering the warmth of the law school Meyer shook his body trying to shake off the chill that had attached itself uninvited. Not directed to anyone in particular he said uneventfully, "Brr...Brr...it is very cold outside."

"The hawk is out," I quipped in my Harlemesque style.

Meyer stopped, and he turned to see who greeted him. With a sense of humor at his lip he asked, "I beg your pardon, what does that mean?"

I explained that in Harlem it was an expression used to describe very cold weather. Meyer smiled a curious smile, and I matched him from ear to ear. Despite this pleasant cultural exchange we remained acquaintances until graduation two and one half years later. At the University wide graduation, I was surprised to see Meyer. We introduced our families to each other. Most saliently, we discovered a common bond about our law school experience; we both felt like "outsiders."

On the strength of that not-so-strong common bond I invited Meyer to a party I was giving. He was one of three whites that came of the eight I invited. He came alone to 141st street and Riverside Drive, a black and Latino neighborhood, to attend a party that began at 10 P.M. There were throngs of black folks chattering and drinking. I observed Meyer standing alone and looking out of place. He was uniquely visible, as black folks moved about and mingled with one another avoiding him like a huge pothole in the street.

I was not able to give Meyer sufficient attention because I was co-host and disc-jockey. Unable to rescue him because of my hosting responsibilities, I was starkly reminded why I avoided the party invitations offered to me by a white law student, Richard Marmaro. He tried to befriend me and when I did not attend the first party, he enthusiastically informed me that I missed a great party. "Ernie, you have to come to the next party."

"You bet, I will be glad to come," I said disingenuously. A white man had never invited me to a party with white women. Who was I to dance with? Remember Emmett Till and the Scottsboro boys.

A friend asked if his friend could bring his white girlfriend to my party.

"Of course he can bring her, that's fine with me," I said sincerely. Since he felt comfortable in public, so did I.

I spun the music and black bodies gyrated around Meyer without "seeing" him. He looked straight ahead with a blank stare unable to "see" the black bodies. Meyer did not bail out and remained at the party, stiffly posed for a couple of hours. When he left he came over to me composed, and thanked me for inviting him. I felt relieved.

The other two white folks who attended the party were Stanley Futterman and wife Linda. They were the first to arrive and leave. Being socially deft—Stan was also professor to some of the law students—they both talked to my black friends.

Clearly, I was important to Meyer, and his presence at my party inspired me to get to know him better. I called the next day and invited him to go with me to the movies, and he would later say, "I was shocked you called me. You had so many people at your party, I couldn't figure out why you called me."

I was most struck by how he did battle with himself while trying to be there for me.

After a fire in my apartment building in December 1976, I moved two floors below Meyer on 110th street. We instantly liked each other and got along rather famously, even as our different personalities emerged. We went to the theatre, movies, concerts, hung out in the neighborhood, read New York Magazine as guide to fine dining and ate our way through some of New York City's finest restaurants. We went to Yankee stadium, with my dad and nephew, to see the Yankees and Red Sox play. Meyer, from Worcester, Massachusetts was a Red Sox fan; my father, nephew, and me Yankee fans. Our loyalties were quite transparent as we jived each other. Meyer and I became boyhood chums: two ghetto boys, one white and Jewish, one black and atheist, had crossed the racial Rubicon of relationships.

Meyer spoke of his life as the child of a Holocaust survivor and lapsed Jew. Since Meyer was not religious, our penchant for dining in fine restaurants did not raise an eyebrow with me until I innocuously mentioned, in front of his father, about our eating delicious lobster and shrimp. Meyer's father, Baruch, an observant Conservative rabbi, looked up from the Moment Magazine he was reading, looked at me for confirmation that his hearing did not deceive him, then quickly turned toward Meyer, his eyebrows arched a notch, and gazed wondering, I imagined, if he was losing his son to the openness and freedom of America that had saved him and countless other Jews.

I shared my history as a black man, and described my parents as "survivors" of an American racist and lynch culture that would admit Jewish European immigrants in peril, subject to a biological theory of race, allow them to flourish, but not "admit" Negro Americans into the same American culture, failing to provide the same support and resources, as an American biological theory of race was perpetuated.

I listened to Meyer rightly laud America for accepting and permitting freedom and freedom of choice for Jews new to the American shores. When I contrasted the black American experience with Meyer, he was uncertain how to react to the imbalance of unfairness meted out to black folk by the selective sight of that allegedly blind woman called Justice. But Meyer was open and listened attentively to my story. His genuine openness allowed me to connect with him from beneath the hidden layers of my barbwire defenses. I was able to open up and let him through the defensive moat I had constructed.

Meyer invited me to his home in Worcester, Massachusetts. I gladly accepted the invitation, but then came the hard part, actually going to his home. I journeyed with hidden trepidation, my guard up and a tentative smile folded in my face. I had never slept overnight in a white person's home. Meyer's father, Baruch, was the rabbi at Beth Israel synagogue. I had never been to a white church and did not know how I would be received.

My experiences taught me that white people were white people were white people, were people not to be trusted. Memories of trying to get a hamburger, drink white water, four black girls blown to bits, black men as "strange fruit," riots born of frustration, ghosts of slavery and slave uprisings modern and otherwise galvanized. The ongoing struggle to live with dignity, integrity, humanity, and black manhood in a racist society left me with a rage that pressed the boundaries of my skull, and it took daily battles within myself to monitor and prevent a volcanic eruption.

I had to learn that unfettered rage was unproductive, most importantly, destructive, and if it went unchecked, I would be the first, and most egregiously injured victim. I then learned to effectively manage my rage: to avert inappropriate comments, conduct, and moderate paranoid thinking. Yet, simultaneously and in apparent contradiction, I had to maintain a hypervigilance, a healthy suspiciousness as an analytic tool—it is a survival necessity—as I struggled to keep from decompensating to a narrow view that identified all whites as the enemy.

The process of using this healthy suspiciousness as analytic tool is so ingrained, as if it is genetically encoded, that I never thought to have a critical conversation with myself regarding my racial perceptions, and without thinking, I never thought to seek a second opinion. Even if I had thought to talk to someone, what would I have said? That I am afraid to visit one of my most trusted friend's home and synagogue because of my fears?

What fears?

Fear of being attacked?

Yes.

By whom? Meyer?

No. His parents?

No, but rejection loomed large.

Synagogue congregants? Maybe...yes, for sure, damn right.

A sense of terror accompanied me as I jogged through the neighborhood; even though I had no knowledge then and have none now of Jews precipitating racially motivated attacks on black people.

Whenever black people enter white dominated environments, the way we will be received is a concern that registers automatically. Would the congregants be coldly polite and civil, yet look down at me in disgust? Or, was disgust anticipated in the lining of the defensive armor I wore everyday? Would they look down at me from their superior perch? Was the notion of superior perch based on my internalization of inferiority?

Rabbi Goldstein and wife Rebecca (Riva) were warm and welcoming. "I'll see how long this last," *I thought, without thinking*. The rustle and bustle of Riva in the kitchen, white table cloth, lighted candles with a soft glow, kiddish cup of wine, two loaves of challah with a beautiful cover, prayers, singing, and my curiosity and wonder at all this fuss for a Friday night dinner. My first Jewish Shabbat. Further, I was employed in a new role, "shabbos goy," which tickled my insides, made me smile gently as Riva exploited a rare Shabbat evening.

As a "shabbos goy" (a non Jew used to perform activities prohibited on Shabbat by Jewish law and custom) I turned lights on and off, lit the stove so Riva could cook overnight on a low flame, a dish called cholent. It was so delicious that when I returned to New York I went to a Jewish restaurant to have more. Two middle-aged women stood before me at the counter, one unreceptive, averted her eyes, and the other smiled and asked for my order, "Cholent, please." Both women looked at me in surprise then looked at each other incredulous. When I told Meyer he began to laugh and when I asked, "What's so funny?" He began to laugh louder.

Then came the hard part: Saturday morning Shabbat service, my first time in a synagogue. Seamlessly imprinted is the font of good feelings received as I listened to Rabbi Goldstein's sermon. I don't remember the content but distinctly recall that the teaching was universal, prescriptive, and applicable. Specifically, I felt this Jewish teaching was directed at me, applied to me and, most important, I could see my black self and locate my black manhood, in plain view.

The Torah offered a spiritual real estate that was welcoming, nurturing to my soul and was a mirror that reflected the black community: my parents, siblings, relatives, black neighbors, and black friends. The Hebrew language also resonated; though I did not understand what I was listening to, what I listened to understood me, and I, in turn, understood the spirit and spirituality of Hebrew prayer.

It provided solace, peace of mind and a safe place for my body and soul. The words traversed my bloodstream, nested in my cells, bound my body and inner being. It evoked and evinced a spiritual energy that was exhilarating, yet soothing, tranquil and enduring. The synchronicity of time, my past, present, future became linked to the Hebrew evocations and formed a primordial connection with my eternal spirituality. The possibility of becoming a Jew was based upon the light shown through the mirror of the Torah, and the reflections seen were people who looked like me, and people who did not.

How well I remember the feelings that flowed into and from my heart; the warm and firm embrace of the inclusiveness, a gentle swirling that coagulated and took root. That warm spot remains today and I believe it was the catalyst for altering my perceptions about the Jewish people and white Americans in general.

However, before I could become a Jew, I had to first come to trust my new experiences, the people that provided them, and my reaction time—my un-learning and re-learning to trust human beings who were white—was, oh so slow: to feel safe enough, it was twenty years in the making. All the centuries of white American ill will, duplicity and ostracism, never allowed me to genuinely perceive that the worship of the Creator of us all could be truly universal; that the Jewish faith and Jewish bible could and would be recognizable by me was not fathomable. Yet, the tieferet, the beauty and truth of the Shabbat service, dvar Torah, and resonance of Hebrew burst forth like orange blossoms of light, and I was exhilarated by ALL, of it. When I returned home I felt sure, "I ran into God over the weekend."

Then came the hard part: a dinner was held at the synagogue the next night. I had to meet the congregants, talk with those white faces up close and personal. Since I was in defensive mode it never occurred to me how I could look at and see *them* through a different lens, that is, how the Jewish congregants could be different from my prejudgments. It was easy and easier to have nondiscriminatory anger, morally righteous anger, and it was safe to be angry. To modulate my anger and change my pattern of responses that lumped all whites as "people not to be trusted," required *thought with thinking,* about my own fears, prejudices and how the decision-making process was influenced. Suppose, just suppose, *they* are not out to get you? How does one respond when not prepared to be veritably welcomed?

It is a difficult presumption to overcome when one is coiled in a position of fear, defensiveness, and coded to strike and protect. To simply relax in such circumstances is problematic, and maybe the most difficult result of growing up in a racist society is modifying the precautions and defenses one *must* develop in order to survive. Trust, the most significant element in any relationship, is never fully experienced by African Americans simply because the assault on trust begins in the womb for too many of us. Suspiciousness, hypervigilance and paranoia easily flow to and become embedded in the daily ritual called living one's life.

With this racial freight, I sat down at the synagogue dinner next to the president of Beth Israel, Nathan Sneiderman. He spoke with a quick homey cadence, a voice that sounded slightly grated, and looked me in the eye as we made innocuous chitchat. Nathan then spoke forthrightly about concern for his daughter's safety living in New York City. He said, "She lives in the nineties near Central Park, is it dangerous there, Ernie?" I told him it was a safe neighborhood. When we parted Nathan shook my hand vigorously, reached into his pocket and took out his business card and said, "Ernie, here is my card, if there is *anything* I can do for you, please call."

Nathan's sincerity was apparent, genuine, and credible, but it crashed head-on with my lifetime of accumulated survival mechanisms and techniques. Even though I was happy to be veritably well received, paralyzing disbelief set in. Overwhelmed, my mind activated, "What does he want from me? What is the hidden agenda?"

The warm and welcoming interactions I had with Baruch, Riva, and Nathan were unsettling, because I did not have a template to trust white people. Though white people are friendly, it does not mean they are capable of being friends that can be trusted. My new and differing experiences with these white folks had a paradoxical effect, instead of decreasing, my anxiety increased, because I had no place to put genuine feelings of acceptance. Unbeknownst to me, the sincere and genuine feelings I was experiencing were osmotically penetrating through my heretofore hermetically sealed defenses.

As I tried to moderate a lifetime of survival skills developed in the trenches of American reality, my inchoate feelings whirred willy-nilly. The plane I navigated had been safely steered my entire life, but now at age thirty-one, my fuel tank was leaking and wreaking havoc. I found myself flying with no safe airport to land.

Nathan Sneiderman, as human being, as president of Beth Israel Synagogue, with his receptive embrace of me as human being, provided a powerful counter to the white people who did not want me to drink water on my own terms, who did not want to sit next to me while I ate French fries; he also chipped away at the notion of superior perch because I felt he treated me with high regard.

One day while reading quietly, the phone rang and quite unexpectedly, Baruch's voice greeted me. Pleasantly surprised, I greeted him with warm affection. Baruch called seeking my counsel, sharing some of his Holocaust experiences and the emotional sequelae he was going through at the moment, forty years later. I listened as a friend and making use of my clinical skills, responded as needed, and Baruch was deeply appreciative.

I was utterly amazed that a rabbi had called Junebug from Harlem seeking counsel and support. Many years and conversations later, Baruch referred to me as, "You are my shoulder, Ernie," said with the deepest affection and smile that came from his soul and bridged his face.

From the first time I met Rabbi Baruch Goldstein and wife Riva, try as hard as I might, I could not come up with any words spoken or behavior that indicated I was not welcomed in their lives. And be sure, I looked and listened, politely, with an ingratiating smile, and palatable conversation coming from my mouth. I shared my experiences growing up in Harlem with Baruch, and he grievously related his shtetl life in Mlawa, Poland.

Baruch described life growing up with his mother Tirtza, younger sister Rachel, younger brother Samuel, and father Israel Meyer, who had an unshakable belief that Mosaich, the Messiah, was going to come to the rescue of the Jews. The Nazis invaded the Goldsteins shtetl and Baruch and Samuel were separated from the rest of their family.

When Baruch and Samuel arrived at Auschwitz the air was foul with the thick breath of death oozing in and out of the Nazi soldiers nostrils. While they stood in line Baruch and Samuel were touching and caressing each other, seeking comfort, desperate for the familiar, as their love mingled with brooding gloom. The angel of death hovered greedily; the safety and warmth of their fingertips steadied the quail arching through their exhausted souls and brought an anxious calm and malignant repose.

Baruch and Samuel moved forward when a Nazi soldier silently ordered terminal directions. When the Goldstein brothers arrived before this Nazi, he looked down on them with matter-of-fact evil blazing calmly in his eyes, and with the finger of god and with his finger mocking God, Josef Mengele, with a simple effortless motion, flicked his finger like a monitor in a school lunchroom and silently ordered Samuel left and Baruch right.

In panic, controlled by the uncertain but certain fear of imminent death, they looked deep into each other's eyes filled with fear, parting, uncertainty and love, imagining they would see each other again; they looked even deeper into each other's soul, not knowing but knowing, knowing and not knowing they would never see each other again. Mengele's hideous flick of his finger dictated their final moments together. Baruch never saw Samuel again.

Near the end of the war Baruch completed the march to Buchenwald from Auschwitz. His body was a sheath of skin and bones after three years in Auschwitz, his spirit was thinner yet, and his will moribund. Placed in a railroad car, too weak to go on, a final peace, though not peaceful, was upon him. Baruch laid down to rest for eternity, in absolute mental and physical weakness. The lights sprayed his closed eyes. He awoke in a white room, in a warm soft bed swathed in white sheets. Baruch thought he was in Olam HaBa, the world to come, not in an allied hospital, as the Germans were being vanquished, finally.

The miracle of being alive became coherent as Baruch lay motionless in exhaustive disbelief, astounding relief, cynical in religious belief.

As the miracle of being alive merged into the reality of living, the reality he now lived poured into his prostrate soul and spirit, the lethal memories of the total loss of his family and destruction of his way of life flooded his body and saturated his mind, weakening and depressing every fiber and cell.

Baruch entered a Displaced Persons camp in Italy where he was nursed back to full physical viability, but his mental health retained emotional scars, indelible to this very moment. With no family and only a decimated culture to return to, Baruch fled Europe and arrived in the proverbial "Land of the free, home of the brave" in 1948, to unlocked doors that opened a second chance to a full life proffered.

Despite the Holocaust murdered into the depths of his soul with the memories of his beloved family coursing through his veins, Baruch Goldstein, with 76303 etched on his left arm, became a schoolteacher and rabbi. His dispatched spirit resurrected when he married Rebecca Golinkin and Meyer was born. He rejoiced with flowing tears at the miracle of life he produced given his close encounter with death. Baruch has cherished Meyer every day of his life.

One day in conversation Baruch said, "Ernie, I am glad Meyer has you as a brother, someone he can talk to and rely on; if I had another son, I could not have done any better than you."

Whew! I began to shake; a foudroyant experience was upon me. A transcendent and transforming moment in time: I was not a Jew and not thinking about the possibility of becoming a Jew. Overwhelmed with humility, Baruch's spirit and language of pure love and reverent respect for my humanity, became the epitaph on the tombstone of my absolute and unyielding rational distrust of *all* whites, Jews, and hope in America. Rising up from the grave was Judaism in its natural incandescence, Jews in their humanity, in full panoramic view of my now rehabilitated capacity. The unexpected denouement: the ability to be in intimate audience with myself without anti-Semitic filters, and automated anti-white screens, alternately distorting and damning my vision.

Meyer met his wife Sue-Rita Silverman, single mom, at a party I gave. Sue-Rita adopted her sister's son Jonah when she was no longer able to take care of him, and she had a biological daughter, Liza Rachel, from a prior relationship. At the wedding I was nominally the best man, but I sincerely felt and said, "Today, Meyer is the best man, and I groomed him for this day."

For Liza Rachel and Ernest Adams it was "love at first sight." The first time I slept overnight at Meyer and Sue-Rita's home, Liza climbed out of her crib and crawled under the cover with me. One afternoon a group of friends were sitting around the kitchen table and Liza was comfortably cuddled in Sue-Rita's lap. Then Liza stirred, turned to me and crawled out of her mother's arms into mine. All of us, most of all me, sat with amazement as she so naturally moved around until she found a comfortable snuggle-spot. Sue-Rita said in a voice filled with wonder, "You two were made for each other."

Liza was two and a half when adopted by Meyer. She came to me when five years old and said, "I want to talk to you Uncle Ernie." (Meyer had all his children call me uncle "out of respect for you") She took me by the hand and led me to the kitchen, and we sat at the table. She looked perplexed and I was unsure what was gripping her. "I was adopted," she began haltingly, "adopted by Meyer." She was trying to bridge the chasm in her five year old head. "Meyer is my father now," her head was at an angle with the confusion tilting it to one side. Not privy to her motivation I simply said, "Meyer is your daddy. He loves you." Meyer also adopted Jonah. Jonah has a quick wit and sense of humor, which makes him the funniest among his siblings.

One day, Sue-Rita frantically called me. "Ernie, the *shit* has started."

"What happened?"

"Liza came home and said, 'I don't like brown people,' the *shit* has started." Liza was four years old. Another white Jewish friend told me the same story about her daughter, also four years old, who voiced the same sentiments. Both families were upset and confused as to how such ideas could be implanted when the parents in both households did not harbor negative racial sentiments. Sue-Rita reminded Liza, "Uncle Ernie is brown."

One evening it was time to prepare Liza for bed and Meyer said, "It's time for your bath Liza Rachel."

Liza answered, "I want Uncle Ernie to give me a bath."

I looked over at Meyer whose eyes perked up excitedly as he nodded his assent, with anticipation and relief from his parental duty. Liza showed me how to run the water and the proper amount of bubble bath used. We talked, played, and washed. She asked me to comb out her tangled hair and when I did not quite get it right Liza gently said, "No, Uncle Ernie, let me show you, like this." I learned quickly and as I was combing out her hair, Liza, representing God, asked in pristine innocence: "Uncle Ernie, can you make my hair like yours?"

Stunned into silence, initially; then with pure love, the words organized themselves, opened my mouth, and found their own order and path. "If I could, baby girl, I would. Believe me, baby girl, believe me, I would if I could."

And for those wondrous few moments I felt I had a deep resemblance to God, and I liked the way He looked.

I flashed back to the colored, Negro, black, Black, Afro, and African American community's cultural notion of "good" hair versus "bad" hair, straight hair versus wooly hair. "Junebug, you got a nice grade of hair…" The reserved compliment offered at the start of this sentence was welcomed but despoiled by its completion, "it ain't too bad." No mitigation and compliment was offered to the depth of ugly feelings I long possessed.

I dubbed Liza, "Princess." It became a "famous" name that characterized our special relationship. I took her to many theatre performances over the years including: Little Shop of Horrors, her first Nutcracker, Children's Theatre, Puppet Theatre, Jelly's Last Jam, Disneyland; we dined at fine restaurants like Tavern on the Green in Central Park and sat in the Crystal room as the waitress explained that the chandelier was used in the making of Gone With The Wind; rode a horse and carriage through Central Park, shopped at FAO Schwarz, and purchased her a Cabbage Patch doll which was only one of many presents given. Liza and I were enjoying an especially fun and memorable day at Disneyland when I humorously quipped, "Hey there Prince, how you doing Prince?

Liza exploded in panic and rage, "No! No!" She bellowed, "Don't call me prince, I'm no prince, don't ever call me prince, don't mess my name up." I was astonished. "I am the Princess," said with certitude. "*The Princess.*"

Liza and I were also viewed as the "odd couple," as people in the public tried to figure out our relationship. After a performance at the

Children's Theatre, we were eating at a restaurant and Liza suddenly did not feel well and she snuggled up in my lap until comfortable. The white woman and her three children in the adjacent booth were all staring at Liza and me with their curiosity agape, when her children observed, stated and asked simultaneously, "Her father is black and she is white..."

The mother began to answer before her children finished their inquiry, speaking softly she said, "When black and white people marry and have children, sometimes the children can look like the mother or the father, she looks like her mother."

While dining at Tavern on the Green, Liza and I were sitting at a table, and seated at another table across from us separated by a thin divider, a white woman, with her hands poised to cut the food on her plate, could not stop staring at Liza and me; her head swiveled back and forth, until finally, quite rudely, shaking her head, and looking past me to hone in on Liza, she said, quite audibly, "She is not his." And not satisfied with her observation, added, with anger I did not understand, "they don't belong together."

All I could do was to be pissed and internalize it.

But I was not the only one listening. Too young to know she had a right to be angry, Liza looked at me seemingly confused, but she expressed an understanding that surprised me: "We belong together, he's *my* Uncle Ernie; he takes me different places; he won't let anything happen to me. We belong together."

The woman blanched, then a crimson "tide" seeped onto her face; with her hands still poised to cut her food, she looked wanly at her husband. All I could do was grin and bear it, as I now fully understood the time-honored wisdom, that children are closer to the truth. As Psalms 8:3 reads: "Out of the mouths of babes and sucklings You have established strength..." The commentary explains: "Such uncorrupted intelligence is the strength God has established for man, so that he can refute and silence enemies of truth."

We were walking through Central Park and she lovingly asked, "Uncle Ernie, do you want a daughter?"

It was a sentiment I felt, and I felt it from Liza, but a statement that was unexpected. Liza wanted to know if she could come live with me. I told her, "Of course you can come live with me, I love you; my home is your home. But Liza, your mommy and daddy won't let you come live with me, but I will always be in contact with you and never lose touch."

Sarah, four years younger than Liza, was born in 1981. We lacked proximity to consistently get to know each other because the Goldsteins moved to California. Over time we developed a mutual loving relationship and I became her Uncle Ernie, and she shared some of her candid observations and secret wishes.

The Goldsteins California dreaming ended and moved to Portland, Oregon. One day I tagged along with Meyer to the Portland Jewish Academy and I was caught-off-guard when he introduced me as, "This is my brother, Ernest." A jolt of surprise went through me as I smiled and said, "Hello." The hoary headed matron froze in her seat for several seconds, then her eyes darted back and forth scanning us both, searching diligently; finally her eyes locked intensely onto Meyer as she scrutinized every micro millimeter of his face searching for the telltale signs that biologically linked us.

Then there is Daniel Aaron Samuel Goldstein, adopted in infancy by Meyer and Sue-Rita. Meyer longed to have another son, and Daniel, serving as catalyst, was unexpectedly presented among the many children considered for adoption. Daniel's father was black and his mother Japanese. My counsel was sought. I encouraged them to adopt Daniel if their love for him was genuine; that they would deal with the issues that arise uniquely for him just as they would for their three other children.

Though I was not a Jew at the time and had no thoughts about becoming a Jew, the Goldsteins acceptance of me as "son," "brother" and "uncle" was substantive proof they could be more than good-enough parents to a mixed race child who would be perceived as black. Among the black friends with whom I discussed the Goldsteins adoption plans, none agreed with me and vehemently disapproved, but I was not surprised, and cared less.

With frequent enough visits I managed to develop a relationship with Daniel with the same process used with his sisters. During one visit Meyer, Sue-Rita, Baruch, Riva and I were sitting at the dining room table discussing a race issue and I made a reference to myself as an African American. Unbeknownst to us Daniel had fallen asleep under the table and he woke us up asserting without equivocation, "I am an African American." Daniel was ten years old.

I lifted up the tablecloth and there was Mr. D, my affectionate name for Daniel, waking up from an impromptu nap. Sue-Rita reported that Daniel thinks he is only African American. She emphatically reminds Daniel he is half Japanese, "because I don't want him to forget." At times I do refer to Daniel as "little brother," and Meyer and I address each other as "brother" or "bro." My intimate involvement in Daniel's family life and my sense of ethnic pride was a contributing factor, but the "American School of Racial Reality" was a very good teacher. For example, when Liza and Sarah were adolescents their friends would come over and Daniel was introduced as "my brother." After a comfort level was reached one girl asked, with Daniel sitting near her, "If he is your brother, how come he is so dark?"

Sue-Rita and I differed on her referring to Daniel as a "little monkey" while watching him motorically flit about as a child. "I call all my children monkeys," she postured defensively. "I was only referring to their activity."

Though I understood her explanation, I thought it not appropriate to continue to make such reference. It certainly did not bother me that she referred to Liza and Sarah as little monkeys, though I don't remember her actually using the term, possibly because it was not offensive to me. Having been traduced by the American culture with pejorative descriptions, my sensitivity as an African American was acute; perhaps, I was being overly sensitive, but sensitive I was, however disproportionate. I vigorously disagreed with Sue-Rita refusing to back away from her use of the term little monkey. In lieu of arguing, I shut my mouth. Sue-Rita felt that since she did not mean it in a denigrating way, it was thus okay and no psychological harm would come to Daniel. My concern was that if Liza could come to say, "I don't like brown people," that Sue-Rita could not reasonably expect her child, of African American ancestry, still subject to the same American racial mythology as Liza, to make the distinction she made as a white sophisticated adult.

During the holiday of Purim, a carnival like atmosphere is created, costumes are worn, parodies are encouraged, and we are commanded to eat drink and be merry. I was intrigued as I watched Abby Miller, a synagogue mate dress up her young son Adam as a monkey. Observing the fun Abby and Adam were having as she put on his costume, I was loathe to imagine me dressing my son like a monkey.

I explained my concerns about Daniel, and Abby believed I was being overly sensitive and agreed with Sue-Rita. I felt a smidgen better. It is both the visceral and viscous historical experience of black folks being compared to apes and monkeys that Abby and Sue-Rita lacked to feel my alarm, though Sue-Rita said, "I always felt your pain and your influence, and I rarely referred to him as a monkey again."

The Goldsteins and I were in Jerusalem walking down Ben Jehuda Street on our way to the Old City. The sun was high on a cloudless hot July day. Baruch and Riva stopped to rest, and wisely decided that water and sunscreen were needed. As the sunscreen was passed around and folks lathered up, Liza said, "You're lucky to be dark so that you aren't as sensitive to the sun."

Sitting on a bench in the shade Daniel retorted, "I'm not the darkest. Uncle Ernie is darker than me!"

I casually sat next to Daniel and gently leaned into his side and said softly, "There is a saying where I come from that I want to teach you."

"What is it?"

I looked at him with loving scrutiny and buying a moment more, said nothing.

"So what is it? Tell me!" Mr. D said impatiently.

Assured that I now had his full attention, I leaned into his ear and said with all the loving truth of God I could muster, "The blacker the berry, the sweeter the juice."

Daniel's reaction to his dark skin as identifying marker and identity, is a familiar shame shared by many of African American descent. As I write these words, I experience at this very moment, with a grave and great intensity, that some of my own racial angst was due to my not being able to meet the standards of white beauty and buying into, in part, the white cultural parameters that continue to "enslave" many African American folk.

The paradox that makes a pancake landing, why does Daniel so readily identify as African American and not Japanese American? Why not say, "I'm a Jewish American?" Since I am not clairvoyant I am unable to glean the specifics of how Mr. D came through his own experiences and conclusion of identity, and no less how and if it will alter as he matures. I assume his statement was a positive affirmation about his choice of self-identification: that he feels proud, and wholesome, notwithstanding the negative barrage of the Whispers War already in progress.

It needs to be said that I and most other Americans with African ancestry are also proud and happy, and feel whole and wholesome, with our God given selves and souls; that we love who we are and we will never permit the campaign of the Whispers War to defeat our humanity. But I think African American heritage will weigh heavily in America for an indefinite time to come, for African Americans and all Americans.

Daniel had his Bar Mitzvah August 2002 and he leyned the Torah and Haftorah, gave a dvar Torah in both English and Hebrew. Baruch trained him as he did all his grandchildren and said, "Daniel was easier to work with in ways different from the other grandchildren."

It was a series of proud and profound moments for Daniel and the rest of the Goldsteins, and of course, his Uncle Ernie. And I most certainly rejoiced in being a part of the service as proud uncle, observing him blossoming before my very eyes, his enchanting coming of age, was magnificent for me to behold.

Despite my loving relationship with the Goldstein family, being "adopted" by Baruch, who filled me with the spirituality of his humanity and Jewish soul, and his unconditional acceptance of me, inspiring me, healing me, still, more than a sliver of mistrust and a hunk of uncertainty would not remain permanently buried, but kept resurrecting. My racial ghosts were haunting me. I went to Baruch and said, "I have to talk to you."

"Of course, Ernie." We sat down at the dining room table when becoming a Jew was a mere twinkle in the eye of my imagination. I felt awkward and clumsy with my racial ghosts chasing me, wearing me out, draining and drowning my energy, polluting the air I breathed and fogging the road I now traveled, while trying to sort out the racial raucous from the racial reality.

My face curled in hesitation. I stuttered; my words stumbled drunkenly over the surfeit of doubts regarding my acceptance of Baruch's acceptance of me. I breathed deeply. I said, "Baruch," the safest and easiest word to get out, "I am black, from Harlem. You are white,

Jewish." My throat was caught in a rush-hour of awkward feelings. Again, I breathed deeply, trying to compose myself, and I shook all over. "How do you, do you, you think?" Unable to go on, I paused, and looked at Baruch to gather the wherewithal I needed. "You are from Poland, I'm from Harlem. You treat me, accept me, and tell me I am like a son to you, but I am black, you are Jewish and white. You think it's okay for me to be Jewish. But I am black. I'm from Harlem. Africa. How does that affect you? How does it affect how you see me? I don't understand?"

Baruch sat motionless with his hands clasped, and patiently waited with concern in his eyes. A rabbi is a person of words, and I wanted words that would soothe and be an analgesic to my doubts. What words I wanted to hear I did not know but anything tranquil would do, something to ease the distress of my never-ending razor-edge doubt about being and feeling acceptable and accepted, even though I could not ask the question unless I felt both. The racial raucous was mushrooming its very big and very ugly head. I waited for some rabbinical wisdom.

Our eyes met, and I searched his countenance, for comfort and safety. He embraced my face with lines of wisdom and tradition, etched plainly for me to see: Abraham, Isaac, and Jacob forged deep indentations on his forehead; Sarah, Rebecca, Leah, and Rachel formed heavy lines around his eyes; Chassidic wisdom sat deep inside his eyes; Moses formed the curve in his mouth.

I tried to look away, but when I did, Baruch's gaze seized my attention, seized my soul and began to speak, his eyes soft, calm. Then when I was feeling safe, his eyes blazed with an x-ray vision of love that pierced to the deepest parts of me, the nadir of darkness where the Basement served as a pillar in my foundation; and spread his uncompromising and unconditional love. Saturating the darkness, the light of his love lit sparks of my hidden hope and humanity that was buried, a long, long, time ago.

Embers of my trust began to flicker, weakly at first, but his blazing gaze of love remained focused on my injured soul; the silent tears, the silent fears, that no one ever witnessed, wept with my trust and hope together. The tears of my tears slowly began to dry, and the fears of my fears began to smolder, become weak and crumbled as the trust of my trust and the hope of my hope began to solidify, melding from his blazing love. Baruch spoke with an overwhelming and convincing eloquence that brought a significant measure of healing, with his wordless touch. Through it all, Baruch never uttered a word.

Judaism, Jews, and becoming Jewish were now viable, part and parcel of my racial reality. Still, I had no realistic idea I was on the road to a new destiny-nation.

Change is a Coming…To Jew or Not to Jew That is The Answer To Be or Not to Be… You Know the Rest

> "It's uh known fact…you got tuh go there tuh know there. Yo' papa and yo' mama and nobody else can't tell yuh and show yuh. Two things everybody's got tuh do fuh theyselves. They got tuh go tuh God, and they got tuh find out about livin' fuh theyselves."
>
> ***Zora Neale Hurston***

> When someone says, "I believe," they are really saying: "I feel my soul and it's alive." Non-belief is a sense of detachment, not from G-d, but from our own soul. Our soul knows G-d already, because our soul is itself Divine, a fragment of G-d, as it were. Our soul sees G-d all the time, and needs no proof of G-d's reality.
>
> ***Rabbi Aaron Moss***

Hanging out with the Goldsteins I got to know members of the extended family and attended countless Shabbat dinners, lunches, Passover celebrations, Hanukkah parties and three of their children's bar and bat mitzvahs. After Sarah's bat mitzvah I was having a conversation with Meyer's uncle, Rabbi Noah Golinkin, who smiled a wizened smile and in the remnants of his Russian youth said, "Oernie, you should become Jewish."

Jolted by his gross and naked non sequitur and undisguised solicitation, I excused myself, ran to Meyer and excitedly told him what his uncle said, even mimicking his Russian accent. Chuckling and dismissing me with a wave of his hand, Meyer said, "He likes you. What do you want from me?"

Sitting on a high chair in the kitchen, I found myself surrounded in a semicircle of Jewish love. Standing around me was Rabbi Golinkin, wife Dotty, son Abe, a cantor, Baruch and Riva. The conversation turned to their desire to see me become a Jew. As they each smiled and cajoled, each one touched me as they formed a chorus with exquisite harmony, encouraging and supporting the notion of me converting to Judaism, stating softly but firmly, "It's not too late, Ernie."

I smiled appreciatively at the sincere emotion and ambition directed toward me, and concluded with thought without thinking, "They are nice, well-meaning, sincere, but crazy, definitely crazy. How could I be a black man and a Jew?" The concept seemed so intrinsically improbable, no, impossible; the idea was at loggerheads within itself, the ultimate oxymoron. Didn't *they* know there is a schism between blacks and Jews? Of course they did. But this moment, and all the moments they knew me, their collective focus was this specific black man who sat before them, Junebug, whom they most wanted to become like them: the ultimate expression of their collective Jewish spirit.

Why didn't the theory of black inferiority deter them? Why didn't the notion of my African blood make them cease and desist? Why didn't the notion of me marrying into their white family frighten them? Patently the pigmentation of my skin was not part of their equation. The lesson I packed and carried was that my dark hue was not a deterrent. For me it was a rare, rare time in America to experience a white person reacting, responding, reaching out to me, for me, without a selfish profit motive, to make me feel so plainly human because of who I really am, just an ordinary man, common man, everyday man, just a man.

Susan Markman, a Jewish friend, chuckled, "Of course, they want the PhD's."

When I told the story to a black friend, she said fearfully, "I'm glad they didn't get you."

I said, "Don't worry, they aren't going to get me. I have no desire to be a Jew."

I was at a Shabbat dinner at Meyer's home and there was an interfaith couple present, Ari Norman and Jenny Spraker. When Jenny, an Episcopalian woman, recited some of the prayers and sang some songs,

I attempted for the first time in my many years of Shabbat meals to do the same. Unable to recite the prayers and sing the songs, I, Ernest Henry Adams Jr., felt left out of an ancient Jewish ritual and was upset. My usual modus operandi was to tune out when the songs were sung and the prayers recited, and then resume mental contact when food was served. However, on this occasion, I felt a need, rumbling like a hungry stomach, to know. After the sumptuous meal, I felt sumptuously empty. The idea of, the possibility of, Ernest Henry Adams Jr. becoming a Jew became a conscious thought, and serious thought.

Initially they were intrusive thoughts, images, feelings that were disturbing, annoying and frightening. I was being challenged from within: my belief systems, social configurations, and religious identity were being called-in for questioning. The process of change began to demand more of my attention and time, pushing me, goading me, and shoving me around quite vigorously. How preternatural it all seemed, that first thought of Ernest Henry Adams Jr., the Jew. I don't look like a Jew so how could I be a Jew? While I loved and respected Meyer and Baruch, I would be betraying myself, family, friends, and black people. However, the life sustaining part of me felt, oh so different, so very very different. I went public with my conflict and told Meyer and Baruch of my newfound thoughts.

This conscious part of my struggle lasted about three years. I discussed my conflict in psychotherapy and neither resolution nor rest followed; my conflict remained dynamic and ongoing. Then in September 1996, I was invited by Ari Norman to attend with his daughter Elena, the Rosh Hashanah services at Jewish Theological Seminary in New York City. During the services, the warm feelings that I felt the first time at Baruch's synagogue stirred within. As we were leaving, I stopped and slowly looked around the room; the felt spiritual aura absorbed into my being and my life force. It felt familiar, yet long ago forgotten: Paleo-memories stirred steep. "This feels like home, this feels like home," I said to Ari and Elena.

I had no further conscious thoughts of conversion for three months until detonated out of my sleep in the middle of the night. Simultaneously, I experienced an implosion and explosion that sat me straight up in bed. I attempted to gather my diffuse thoughts and tried to figure out why my chest was heaving and my heart was galloping at 3:00 a.m.

As my thoughts coalesced and became more focused, I opened my eyes to the darkness and looked around; alone in the dark. Wet with the sheen of ethereal energy that gushed from my soul and swept through my body, I said: "Judaism, explore, go explore, I have to, must do this, explore Judaism." God's "big bang" fully awakened and re-authored my soul.

This was a life altering decision that I had to make alone. I did not want to be influenced by any close Jewish friends because I knew they would cheer me on. I chose to call Rabbi David Woznica, then of the 92nd Street YMHA, Director of the Bronfman Center for Jewish Life, and former neighbor to seek advice on how to proceed. Making minor chitchat, I asked David about his wife and son. He was his usual polite self, but a bit constrained, as he wondered why I was calling. Unsure of how I would be received, I took the risk: "I'm calling because I have been thinking about converting to Judaism."

A heart-stopping pause powered through the phone smacking my ears firmly, reverberating acceptance: my words landed safely. David's voice rose with controlled excitement, "Ernest, you should come talk to me. When can you come in?" A date and time was set and he reassured me, "Ernest, this will only be a preliminary discussion, there is no pressure," he emphasized with forced neutrality, "you don't have to make any commitments, any commitments. I just want you to come in and feel comfortable," his giddiness bubbled under his neutrality, "and we'll talk."

At David's office we spoke for ninety minutes about my personal, social, and religious histories, development of my atheism and my interest in Judaism. I told him about my relationships with Norm Brier, Mitchell Cohen, Meyer, Baruch, Rabbi Golinkin, Ari Norman, and Stanley Futterman—I attended the bar mitzvahs of his three sons—and other friends. David observed, "You have a lot of Jewish friends." I told him of the time I was driving home from an afternoon of shopping when news of Israel came over the radio just as I was about to get out of the car. Mesmerized, I was unable to move until I heard the complete story. I described how, in general, my ears and concern perked up when news of Israel came over the radio or television, and the angst I felt when the news wasn't good.

David said, "Religion must have been a good experience for you, so why not return to your religious roots?" Pausing to give thought to a question I never gave serious consideration, I felt the physical sensation of a silent snap, a tangible disconnect inside my head and body. I responded, "It was a good experience." The words that facilely fell from my lips startled me, because of my secret adoption of atheism when I was ten years old, and my denunciation of religion as the "opiate for the masses." The snap I experienced was no longer feeling obligated to return to religion as a Jehovah's Witness; that the sincere promise I made as a young dutiful son to his loving mother could not be honored honorably by the man I grew into: who developed and differentiated an identity based on the reality of my historical time, experiences, and resulting beliefs. I felt unfettered, free to choose Judaism without guilt.

David then asked, "Why at this time in your life do you want to return to religion?"

I was fifty years old and said, "I am fiercely independent and have always believed I don't need anyone or anything to get along in this world. Look, I have accomplished a lot in my life that I feel good about, but I don't feel connected to anything. I want, I need to belong to something larger than myself." Then I hesitantly raised an issue that I thought could possibly be a deal-breaker. "I don't how this would fit in, but I have been an atheist since childhood."

"You will be in good company," he replied. "Let me tell you the story of the Holocaust survivor who would point to the serial number on his arm and say, 'Where was God? Where was God?' Then he goes to pray with his congregation."

And then, there was Race, waiting patiently to be introduced and discussed. A serious tone emerged as Rabbi Woznica attempted to prepare me for how he thought I would be received as a black man. He said, "Let me warn you…"

"Uh oh," I thought, "here it comes"—as I braced myself internally and clutched the sides of my chair.

"…that some people are going to be solicitous of you because you are black. Some will want to be your friend because you are black. How do you feel about that?" Afraid he might have possibly alienated me, his face twisted with uncertainty.

Countenance unchanged, I thought with thinking but in stunned disbelief, "The rabbi is telling black me, white people are going to be nice to me *because* I'm black, that some will want to be my friend *because* I'm black, and I don't play basketball. I don't play football. I don't play baseball. I don't make movies. I'll take it."

Rabbi Woznica inquired about the reaction from my friends. I told him that I continued to hear negative reactions from many black friends. With my head moving from side to side I said, "I hear things you would never hear." His head jerked and eyes widened.

To calm the doubt that crept into his eyes I said, "I am prepared for the flak that will come. I can handle it." When we finished talking, I was invited back for another conversation.

The first black person I told about my interest in Judaism was my father, because one of his greatest assets was not to be judgmental. I spoke with him privately at a family gathering. "Pops, I am thinking about converting to Judaism and will start studying soon."

With brightened eyes he enthusiastically replied: "Congratulations son, on your latest endeavor. As long as you are happy, that's what matters most. It can't hurt you, son. If the Jews want my son, that's okay by me." There was a pause. Then a sly, jovial smile, and a palpable shift in mood: "Son, does that mean you're going to get one of those little Jewish girls now?"

I said, "Pops, been there done that, got the t-shirt too," and he broke out in a wide grin.

I informed mom and Audrey and both became immobilized. Visibly shaken, mom began spouting biblical verses that confirmed the "truth" of being a Jehovah's Witness. Audrey, taciturn by nature, had no apparent reaction. When I told Florita, also a Jehovah's Witness, she sat frozen. When the shock subsided, Florita—who had worked for the Council of Jewish Federations—began to discuss Jews waiting for the Messiah versus resurrection and Armageddon. Mom discussed with my sisters my adolescent promise, that if I were to return to religion it would be as a Jehovah's Witness. She lamented my failed promise and her promised hope, but she never said a word to me. When I ended a conversation because I was going to a Hebrew lesson, Mom smiled and said, "Shalom."

When I informed black friends of my intent, their smiles dropped when my words pierced the unexpected. Virtually all sat mute attempting to maintain a poker face, but their eyes and bodies became transfixed. A few responses: "So you are betraying the black man now, huh?" "I don't see it, how is it that you *now* trust white people?" "So Ernie is trying to become white." "You know, I have been a Catholic all my life, and I have been taught to be loyal to your religion, loyal to your country, loyal to your race, why aren't you?" One childhood friend asked, "Are you really going to become a dirty Jew?"

When I challenged his savage remark and threatened our relationship, he apologized profusely. "Look, I did not mean anything by it, you know as kids we used to get on each other like that, sounding on each other, playing the dozens. I'm sorry."

Elliott Burgess, a deacon in his church, said to me, "I'm glad you found God and spirituality, it's about time." When I told my Uncle Charlie, he said, "That's great, as long as you are happy." Then he said, "Junior, You need a Jewish name. Adamswich, I'm going to call you Adamswich," then he roared with loving laughter. The mellifluous way Uncle Charlie would sing my new name whenever we talked, "Hey Adamswich," made me feel completely accepted and protected.

White non-Jewish friends were equally shocked, but their initial responses were more demonstrative. One white woman's jaw dropped fast and low, eyes bulged and mouth widened. I was reminded of the "Scream" as she stood frozen in her doorway. Another white woman said, "I don't get it. I know you told me last month, but I still don't get it. Why do you want to be a Jew?" The irony, she lived with a Jewish man.

Virtually all my non-Jewish friends, white and black, warned, "They are not going to accept you, Ernie."

One Christian white woman had attended a Purim celebration and left in a huff when she overheard someone make a reference to the "goy who are here."

Robert Jekyll looked at me and said with conviction, "You know you aren't going to find anyone else like Meyer and his father. They like you because they are humanitarians, and you are not going to find other Jews like that."

I first attended B'nai Jeshurun in December 1996 for a Friday night Shabbat service at the invitation of a friend, Susan Margolies. Being the only black person, I was self-conscious, but it was also unexpected and awkward to be sitting in Saint Paul and Saint Andrew (SPSA) Methodist church—where Friday night's late service and Saturday morning service is held—with pieces of Christmas pine tree branches cut and laid out in wreaths spread across the front of the pulpit. Not expecting Christmas decorations at a Jewish service, I squirmed in discomfort and confusion at the Christian artifacts, looked around and saw there was no concern or upset by the congregants. SPSA was old drab and worn, but the B'nai Jeshurun service with its singing in Hebrew filtered a warmer emanation.

Rabbi Woznica informed me, during my second visit to his office in January 1997, that I could begin study of Judaism at the 92nd Street Y.

"It's too late to sign up. I called and was told the class was filled."

"No. No!" He said quickly, "We can get you in, don't worry."

I felt warm all over from this exercise of Jewish prerogative, this affirmative action taken on my behalf.

I began my formal study of Judaism in January 1997 taking the year long derek Torah (road/path to the Torah) class, learning the basics of Judaism. Going to my first class, I took the eighty-sixth street crosstown bus and noticed a woman who gave me a curious look when she observed I was reading a book about Jews. She kept looking but did her best not to stare, and we got off at the same stop. We ended up in the same elevator at the 92nd Street Y, and got off on the same floor. She stepped off first and was not sure where to go. I got off and knew where to go, so I turned right. Observing me, she turned left. I entered the class, sat down, and felt conspicuously out of place as I looked at all those strange white faces. Then the woman from the elevator walked in, and she paused ever so slightly. Her head jerked as if she had a mild tic and her face registered surprise to see me in the class. Perhaps, if I had been white she might have said at the elevator, "Are you in the Judaism class?" or, "Do you know where room number 602 is?"

Except for the son of a Protestant minister who was engaged to a woman in the class, and his parents knew of neither, the other ten people in the class were Jewish. I was expecting the entire class to be potential converts. It was surprising to see accomplished and high-powered professionals in the same rudimentary course as me. Despite feeling intimidated, I enjoyed the learning but what I liked most was giving a dvar Torah, a "talk" to the class. I volunteered to give a second one because the preparation was invigorating.

One month later, I began to learn Hebrew, starting with the alphabet. It was a return to first grade, matching vowels and letters to make coherent sounds; learning how to write Hebrew letters from where to place the pencil to how deep or short a line or curve of a letter should be.

A thirty-something lawyer in the class introduced himself and said, "You should come downtown to my synagogue for a Friday Shabbat meal, a group of us young professionals get together, men and women. I think you will enjoy it." My youthful appearance hid more than my age.

Even though gripped by an emotional full-nelson, I said disingenuously, "Sure, be glad to. Thank you." From then on I politely ignored him with nods of the head in class, and the back of my head after class. He was being too damn friendly for someone he did not know: too damn friendly for someone I did not know. This gentleman, already Jewish, perfectly Jewish, dislodged me from the perfect balance on the perfect tightrope; falling, I fell back on antiquated defenses, isolation from the enemy. Just perfect.

My atheism shifted from the center of belief to the periphery while studying Judaism and Hebrew. I don't know when a belief in God had insinuated itself back into my life, but I vividly recall the experience that shredded the last vestiges of my absolute non-belief in God. Dr. Trevor Forbes, friend, psychiatrist, and colleague came into my office and explained that his wife Liz had given premature birth at 5½ months to daughter Alexandra, and there was a high probability she could die. His eyes began to water, despair formed deep lines in his face, a tear bubbled, reluctant to take the plunge down his face and heart; yielding to the uncertainty, it tipped over and streaked down his face; now pierced, more tears slowly rolled down his cheeks.

"I will pray for your daughter, I will pray for Alexandra." I said spontaneously from a place I thought no longer existed. I had given up on God and prayer at age ten because my specific supplications went unfulfilled. After Trevor left my office, I resumed seeing my psychotherapy clients like any other day. I went to sleep that night having forgotten my promise, but awoke in the middle of night with the words,

"I will pray for your daughter, I will pray for Alexandra," reverberating in my head. In the darkness of my bedroom, the darkness in my soul, and from the night of my spirit, I prayed: "Dear God, I am not sure how to do this. I have not been here in a long time. I don't want anything for myself. I'm praying to You, Dear God, asking You, to help Alexandra, help her live. Please, please Dear God, let her live."

My soul began to come out from under, to open up gradually, as a mature faith moved to the center of my belief that God existed. And yes, Alexandra is alive and doing quite well.

I began a synagogue search keeping in mind Rabbi David Woznica's neutral info-mercial: to choose any branch of Judaism and any synagogue where I felt spiritually comfortable. I was given a choice of synagogues: Rodolph Shalom, Reform, B'nai Jeshurun and Ansched Chesed, Conservative, and Lincoln Square, Orthodox. He explained that each branch was "separate," that there was no hierarchy, and that one did not go from Reform, Conservative to Orthodox. Rabbi Woznica said, "It's like figuring out which is your favorite fruit, the one that taste the sweetest is the one for you."

My first foray into synagogue shopping was Rodolph Shalom. I entered the synagogue, and without external provocation, was immediately chilled by my racial fears. I stumbled to a seat near no one but close to someone. I felt stupid, awkward, and felt the chill of the gothic structure. It seemed all too familiar, like a Church, bare and empty in its grandiosity; it did not feel welcoming. How much of that feeling was related to the distress I was experiencing, I don't know, but it must be considered in the calculus. English dominated the service and was denuded of the Hebrew lyric, the linchpin I was hungry to hear. When I was leaving, I saw Norm Brier and I felt lighter after seeing a friendly face. Meyer came to New York on a visit and accompanied me to Ansched Chesed. He knew the rabbi, Michael Strassfeld, a childhood friend, and introduced me to him after the service. I felt safe, no distress, and enjoyed having Meyer explain the service.

I next called the Orthodox synagogue, Lincoln Square. A woman answered the phone and said, "The beginner's service starts at 8:30." I thought without thinking that the woman knew I was black and did not want me to show up. Orthodox Jews conjured black hats, black coats, long black beards: Crown Heights evoked turmoil, where racial tensions exploded after the death of a black boy and a visiting Chassidic scholar in 1991.

"Don't go to the Orthodox, they are rigid and racist," two Jewish friends warned. Genuinely frightened, I tossed and turned all week until I arose Saturday to attend Lincoln Square. When white Jews—especially when it is someone you trust—say with disdain and conviction that an entire "race" of fellow Jews are racists and to be avoided, it was both damning and credible. Overwhelmed with fear, I did not consult with Baruch or Meyer, and I did not attend Lincoln Square or explore Orthodox Judaism.

My friends inadvertently heightened my fears about being Jewish and Jews in general because, in my estimation, the same white skins were to be found in Reform and Conservative synagogues. My defense system made many appearances during my search for a synagogue.

I had to prepare myself, fortify myself, many a Shabbat morning with pep-talks, pep-thoughts, and use my prodigious capacity to absorb embarrassment, fear, and pain to push me when my resolve floundered and doubt rushed in. But slug it out I did, in an emotional internecine struggle, a heavyweight battle, with black blows flying every-which-way just to get out of the door. I could have returned to the religion of my mother, or to the gentle nest of Reverend Calvin Butts and the Abyssinian Baptist Church. I wanted more of myself and more for myself; want compelled, and composed. I was not about to ask Susan Margolies to accompany me to B'nai Jeshurun in broad daylight to the Saturday morning Shabbat service. This black man was not going to admit, "I'm terrified to go to a synagogue, alone." I began to wish, with excruciating discomfort, that I had someone to go with me, another wannabe, preferably black—so we could make a grand entrance together.

As I ascended the steps of St. Paul St. Andrews Church, my first Saturday morning Shabbat service, my heart rate also ascended. Each step left me with a sinking feeling, and I felt as if I was backing up while proceeding forward. Then two steps from the entrance, my viscera revved up and I felt the vibrations from the whirring. I took one more step, and a lattice field of energy unfolded before me, then engulfed me; it felt as if I was wrapped up securely, yet, it also positioned itself as a screening wall before me and seemed to be evaluating data;

I know not how. I felt the rhythm of prickly sensations moving rapidly across my entire body, probing, penetrating, and searching, exactly what and how, I am unsure. The persons ahead of me and behind me were scanned, ushers were scanned, the balcony was scanned, the lower level was scanned; how, I do not know. I ceased moving forward and stopped for an intense eon; three steps later I was inside: All Clear, No Present Danger. The energy field came down. The lattice structure folded, but my self-consciousness was acute

I was greeted by a welcoming face, soft eyes, puffy black beard, and gentle voice: Lenny Picker, the usher, said, "Shabbat Shalom." He spoke to me like I am a Jew, and I felt welcomed. Still on alert, I cross-over into the non-personal world of Jewish life.

There were neither unkind people nor unkind treatment, subtle or otherwise. Then one day, without notice or fanfare, my protective lattice simply failed to appear as I arrived for services. Yet, I did not feel accepted nor did I feel rejected. I realized I would not be lynched, physically injured, humiliated nor would I get killed. Why even consider Judaism if the process of "crossing-over" was torturous? By taking up permanent residence behind the racial wall of fear, the racial wall of fear would reside permanently inside me; my imagination and aspiration, forever truncated, dead on arrival, when attempting to live my life.

I settled on B'nai Jeshurun and began attending Friday night and Saturday morning Shabbat services. A typical excursion on Shabbat morning was getting dressed-up in my "Sunday-go-to- meetin' clothes." I always wore a shirt and tie, with a suit or sport jacket and pants, and fine dress shoes. I stood preening before my mirror trying to make sure my hair was combed just right, the colors matched, the knot in my tie wrapped and fell just so. I was surprised when someone said, "Why do you come *so* dressed up every week?" Soon I was dressing just as casual as everyone else.

As I met new people and began to feel welcomed at B'nai Jeshurun, I compared myself as resume qua resume to other members of the synagogue, while I was being compared. Trained and armed with a law degree and doctorate in psychology, I felt equal to the largely college educated and professionals at B'nai Jeshurun. A black friend with an alternate view worded sharply: "Nigger, you ain't black. Black folks ain't got what you got, most of the Jews in your synagogue ain't got what you got, you got a J.D. *and* PhD. Nigger, you ain't black."

But the unspoken comparison by me was: "Do they really think I am intelligent?"

The unspoken comparison by whites, I assumed: "Is he *really* qualified? *Really,* intelligent? Affirmative Action pretender?"

At B'nai Jeshurun, Susan Margolies, Irma Radus, and Joyce Rosenfeld had a Bat Torah—a Bat Mitzvah for adult women who did not have one. At the reception that followed, I walked over to the rabbi, who took one look at me, grabbed my hand and began shaking it like he was pumping for oil with a grin spread across his face. He kept repeating, as he kept turning his head, announcing to no one and anyone who was in the vicinity, "I've known this guy fifteen years, I've known this guy fifteen years." Roly Matalon, my former neighbor, now the rabbi at B'nai Jeshurun, was trying his very best to remember my name as he glad-handed me. I stood before him feeling naked, conspicuous, black, the token, with only my full-fledged smile to cover my embarrassment. "Ernest, I am Ernest," I spoke to his lapsed memory.

"Ernie, how are you?" The pumping of my hand slowed down.

"I'm doing well."

He dropped my hand and abruptly transitioned, "What are you doing here?" Roly had no plausible expectation of my presence in a Jewish setting, for a second time.

"Susan is a friend of mine. She invited me." There was no sign of surprise. "Also, I am taking the derek Torah class at the 92nd Street Y."

Roly's eyes widened, he took in a long suck of the stale basement air and it all rushed out excitedly, "Come talk to me." It was a command without being commanding. "You have to come see me." Nodding, I agreed.

My attendance at B'nai Jeshurun quickly became a routine that segued as indispensable core to my soul, identity, spirituality and wellspring of spirit. The Friday night Shabbat service with its singing was joyous and soul fulfilling. I looked at the prayer book, heard the Hebrew words and melody being sung. My ear, mouth, and vision coordinated as best they could, but by the time my pronunciation wrapped itself around a word or two, the congregation was a page away. The transliteration allowed me to sing along until my Hebrew knowledge increased.

The Saturday morning Shabbat service became my spiritual staple because it combined singing with the essential part of the service, the dvar Torah. Making the Torah come alive and applicable to daily living, was and is the sine qua non in shaping the connection to and through God, to leverage life and relationships; to struggle with both the light and the dark from its origins. Then there was the reading of the Torah, which manifested another link between God and me. Though I did not understand what was being read, what was being read *felt* understood. The holy synergy of Torah reading and the dvar Torah fused and infused a spiritual morphology that became the cornerstone for my love and learning of Judaism. The reason I could have this dynamic reception was because the B'nai Jeshurun community was welcoming of me as an African American man—with an emphasis on African and man.

After a Friday Shabbat service an acquaintance invited me to dinner. I politely refused. This time I informed Meyer, and he remarked, "Look, this is what people do on shabbos, it's part of being a Jew." Then he switched gears and spoke to his understanding of me, "I know you feel encroached upon and your space has been invaded, but let the paranoia go, dude. This is the Jewish world."

I first met with Rabbi Roly Matalon in May 1997. Here I was, sitting in the office of my former neighbor, now reputed to be "one of the most powerful rabbis in New York." When I first heard those words mentioned in the Westside home of Meyer's cousin, I wondered what "most powerful" meant in the Jewish world, and how a slender rabbinic student from South America could rise to such heights in New York City Jewish and political circles.

Roly—all the congregants called him by his first name—gazed at me for several moments as if I was a surreal portrait. I sat motionless not knowing the protocol and rules of engagement. He pressed both elbows to his side, his hands palms up, then raised them to his face. He cocked his head, and in veritable confusion, shaped my name in the form of a question with the virgin honesty of a child: "Ernie?" He waited for the rest of the sentence to form, "How did this happen?" It was rhetorical. He continued, "We were neighbors, lived on the same floor, had no idea that you would be sitting here before me...you never know," his voice trailed off. His astonishment obvious, his understanding gauzy, I provided some history and insight to the self-portrait that sat before him.

Roly directed the conversation to the Torah. I told him I thought the Israelites got a bad rap as "stiff neck people" that "they had been through traumatic times, were vulnerable and in a weakened state after four centuries of being slaves and fugitives. Aaron was an appeasement maker not a peace maker." A lull blanketed the room and Roly looked at me searching, for what I wondered and did not know. Pushing my way through the silence I said, "I'm trying to figure out Shabbat, I no longer work on Friday evenings, and I am unsure how to negotiate all that the tradition requires."

Roly's face brightened for a moment. I tried not to process his reactions, which is so unnatural for a clinical psychologist, but he seemed pleased. But was he really? Or did I just imagine it? I told Roly, "I am going to Israel for the first time this summer." I assumed he would be pleased.

Roly then asked a question I could not have anticipated, "How are you going to deal with the racism in the Jewish community?" The assumption was startling coming from the mouth of a white rabbi, notwithstanding his left-wing credentials. What Jews did he have in mind? Orthodox Jews? Reform Jews? Was he warning me about racist Jews at B'nai Jeshurun? Rabbi David Woznica warned that I would be inundated with Jews loving me, and now the opposite, Jews hating me.

I answered: "There will be people who like me and I will like them, and we will hang out. There will be people who don't like me, and I won't hang out with them."

Surprised at my simplistic response, Roly sat forward abruptly and raised his voice, "Is that all?"

What more was there for me to say or do? Racism was not new to me, and I would not place myself where I would be subject to undignified treatment carte blanche, and, would not tolerate it when and if it occurred. This was my life's credo and process, and also how I adapted to living in a culture where I was devalued. Simply ignoring some racist prick I anticipated dealing with on an infrequent basis was something I had long given thought to and had extensive practice, and I would deal with any such person as I would in any other situation outside the synagogue.

We finished talking, the first in a series of expected conversations to measure my progress on my journey to Judaism. Rabbi Matalon did not do the expected; instead, with his finger jabbing enthusiastically he pointed at me and said with increasing crescendo, "You're ready, you're ready, you're ready!" I was frozen in my unexpectedness and instinctively turned around to find whom that finger was pointing. He said I would be converted after the summer and before the High Holy Days, in September 1997. I walked into Roly's office nervous and not knowing what to expect, then walked out even more nervous, stunned, and not understanding what just took place.

What did Rabbi Matalon see that made him so certain that I was ready for conversion? It was May and I began my study in January. Were they desperate for black folks? Was this an Affirmative Action hire? When I told Baruch and Meyer they didn't seem surprised. Perplexed and pleased, I consulted with my black friend Robert Jekyll who said, "Look Ernie, I've known you for almost thirty years, when I think of you back then, see you now, I am not a rabbi, certainly not a Jew, but I see your commitment, you are committed to Judaism, committed to being a Jew. That's what they see."

Now that becoming a Jew was on the horizon, the first thing I considered was taking a Hebrew name. After looking in books and considering the names I read in Jewish texts, giving myself a new name required thought with thinking. Stan Futterman suggested "Aryeh, because you are like a lion." I sought Baruch's advice, and he also suggested Aryeh. I asked if I could take his name Baruch, and he said, "I don't own it." Out of love and respect, and to honor the way he accepted and treated me, I took the name Aryeh Baruch.

The beit din, court of three rabbis, evaluate one's knowledge, spirituality and commitment to Judaism and determine if one is ready to take on the commandments. When I was given a date for the "final exam" everything became heightened.

The anxiety was palpable, visible, flying all around me and flying all around inside me. I was preparing for a test, not an ordinary test, but "thee test" of my life and the possibility of failure was unacceptable, yet terrifyingly real, according to my frenzied perception. There are no guarantees when taking any test unless you pay off the examiners and there was no chance of that; not that I thought about it. Instead, the night before "thee test" I chose to cram; trying to anticipate all the questions I would be asked. I sat with Joseph Telushkin's book, *Jewish Literacy,* trying to osmotically absorb three thousand years of Jewish history into my memory bank.

There was no do-over that I was aware of which served only to heighten my anxiety: this was the ultimate test. Reporters asked Duane Thomas, halfback for the Dallas Cowboys in 1972 how it felt to play in the ultimate game, the Super Bowl. He answered, "If it is the ultimate, why are they playing it again next year?" Clearly, Duane Thomas had no reverence for "thee game" but I was in Awe and reverence of Judaism and God. Unlike the Super Bowl, there was no next year: what more faith, love of Judaism and the Jewish people could I bring next year that I did not have at this time?

Seated diagonal to me in my living room was Meyer. He had traveled from Oregon to witness when I would immerse myself in the mikvah to symbolically cleanse all manner of prior beliefs and emerge pure of soul and spirit, Jewish soul and Jewish spirit.

Meyer spoke hesitantly, "Ernie, that's not what they are going to be concerned about."

What did he know?

"You are worrying too much," he continued. He sounded banal. His father was a rabbi as was his grandfather. He had no conversion credentials so I ignored what he said. Ari Norman called while Meyer was trying to calm my nerves. He became furtive for no apparent reason when I asked where he was calling from. Ari wished me luck and said he would call after the beit din.

I was to appear, the next day, before a court of three rabbis who would either accept or reject my spiritual yearnings for a Jewish identity. I wanted to be a Jew and this was unlike any court I studied in law school. With a dissertation defense you may have revisions, major or minor, and still pass. How does one revise one's soul, spirit, commitment to Judaism and the Jewish people? What would I say to my family and friends if I was not accepted into the Jewish faith? I knew, however, very well what they would say to me. Something like, "racism and religious bigotry kept you out." But as a black man who grew up in America and felt the direct sting of racism, I would not have allowed myself to travel on the road to Judaism and the final destination, conversion, if the journey was littered with unwelcome signs and obstacles. The lens that focused the concern of my Christian friends, black and white, failed to see that it was a two-lane road and Judaism also had to come to me.

Studying intensely, I was unprepared for what should have been an obvious question about my human being, from Rabbi Marcelo Bronstein: "How did you resolve your conflict about being a black man and a Jew?"

Once I became wedded to the idea of becoming a Jew, my overarching concern was to be sure I was adding something wonderful to my life and not rejecting significant parts of my life. I consciously monitored and measured myself to make sure I was not running away from parts of myself: my black Africaness, by black Negroeness, my black history, my black inferiority, my black ugliness. But it became apparent I did have to jettison, a quiet, lurking, invisible, insidious part of me: Hate; My Hate. As I write these words I feel a numbness flash through my body that feels like an eclipse that blocked out the light and life sustaining parts of my soul and plunged it into despair and dread. It made me less human, less a member of the human race by incapacitating my ability and imagination to see myself as connected and related to America and Americans as a true American. A common result of being treated as the *other,* not just an N-word, but the Nigger, not fully human, has engendered bitterness that clouds clarity and transposes reason from rational to rancid: Like the time in my youth when I drove intentionally close to a white family prompting the father to shout, "Hey, take it easy," as I passed his wife and six year old daughter. As this loathsome memory regurgitated into my thought processes, I viscerally remembered my hate filled feelings.

Hate meant I did not have to experience my true lot in life; it anesthetized my ranking in the American hierarchy. Hate is hopelessness and hopelessness hates; hate is thinking without thinking, being without being, avoiding the complexities, blaming the white man, yet, blaming yourself for not understanding why you cannot do better, and afraid to look closely at the reasons why, because in reality, no simple solutions can be found today. Hate mask's pain, hurt, fear; yet, hate is a manifestation of pain, hurt, fear; hate organizes and hate disorganizes. As I sat before the beit din, all of the above and more rose within and I placed my right hand over my heart and said, "My hate had to wane, my hate had to die and then and only then could the conflicting parts meld, heal, bring resolution and allow me to become a Jew."

When the beit din was completed I went into the mikvah, a ritual bath. In anticipation, I lost a few pounds and made sure I looked good for God, and my ego. I recited the prayers required and dunked myself three times. On that third submersion in the water I went down without a religion but emerged with an ancient Tradition, assisted by the sages and guided by God, soaked into the pores of my soul.

Once I emerged out of the mikvah the wait was over: A Jew at last, a Jew at last, Baruch HaShem, (Thank God) a Jew at last. This was the holy rite of passage I treasured. To descend into the mikvah, longing to be a Jew, and to ascend being a Jew was the most profound experience of my life. A new addition to my identity, I became the Jewish people and the Jewish people became me. Shalom: peace with myself; Shalom: peace within myself; complete within myself: now, spiritually, I am whole.

Rabbi Bronstein said, "Welcome achi," (my brother) formally." Roly gave me a certificate certifying my conversion with a bit of humor, "Here is your diploma." Then added with an encouraging gleam in his eye, "Ernie, there are so many single women at BJ…," his voice trailed off but his message came through loud and clear. Rabbi Steve Moskowitz, my derek Torah teacher, gave me a hearty handshake and hug. I was greeted with flowers from friend, Jennifer. And there he stood, Ari Norman, grinning with joy and pride because I was now a Jew. He had fooled me when we spoke the night before. Ari Norman had flown from Oregon the day before to support and surprise me when I came out of the mikvah; he joined Jennifer, Stan Futterman, Meyer and me for a bite of celebration and food.

The Shabbat after I converted I had an aliya—to recite a prayer at the bema before the reading of the Torah—and was formally introduced to the community as a fellow Jew. Rabbi Matalon recalled how he, Rabbi Bronstein and I lived in the same apartment building as graduate students. As I stepped down from the bema, I was momentarily startled when I saw a few people rise from their seats and come in my direction, then in a blink of an eye a cascade of people rose out of their seats—as if they were a wave at a sporting event—and came out of every aisle and greeted me with "mazal tov." I struggled to keep from crying. This Jewish welcome mat was simultaneously an ending and beginning: Over the years and through my fears I grew apart of the Jewish people and now I was a part of a Tradition and a People that left no doubt that I was truly accepted as an ordinary man, everyday man, a common man, and yes, a black man, and, a Jewish man.

Triple Consciousness
American…African American…Jew
Being and Living as American Jew
With Emphasis on African

> Let us be clear: America is not a racial utopia. It can be painful to be black and love a country this difficult and that still gets so many things horribly wrong.
>
> ***Debra J. Dickerson***

> Conversions, whether they be…religious form another way in which bound energies are let loose. They unify, and put a stop to ancient mental interferences. The result is freedom and often a greater enlargement of power.
>
> ***William James***

One day on my way to work Rick Greenberg, a Jewish neighbor and fellow baby boomer told me the following story as we walked to the subway. When he was a college student at the University of Wisconsin at Madison, it was January, unseasonably mild, and Rick felt so exuberant he impulsively jumped into a nearby lake with all of his clothes on and took a swim. When he returned to his dormitory room he emptied his pockets, took out his wallet and the dollar bills were soaking wet. He setup the ironing board, plugged in the iron and proceeded to iron each dollar bill to dry them out.

Rick's roommate, a Christian young man from the Midwest, walked in and saw him ironing a dollar bill, and said to Rick, "I heard that you Jews are good with money, that you know how to take care of money, but I did not know you took care of it *like that*." I roared with laughter as did Rick reliving the story. He told me this story in 1989, long before being a Jew was on my identity radar.

When I got to work I immediately retold Rick's story to two Jewish co-workers, who not only did not laugh, but looked askance at me. I was flummoxed by their reaction. When I told Rick he said, "If I had told them the story they would have laughed."

"Why?" I asked.

"Because, I'm Jewish, and you're not."

There have been significant changes in the American racial culture since W. E. B. Dubois described in the early twentieth century the Negroes "two-ness," being an American and a Negro. Despite the social changes that have occurred since that time, today, in the twenty-first century, being both an American and black/African American still means having a dichotomized identity, a "forced choice." The "split personality" of the black person mirrors the enduring and deeply entrenched psycho-social pathology of the American culture.

When I became a Jew my fractured identity was enlarged, my two-ness grew to "three-ness," from American and African American to African American Jew, but simultaneously less fractured and less fractious I became: the world was now a larger place, and safer place. Notwithstanding my new peace and piece of mind, I found and still find myself, at times, in pointed disagreement with some fellow white Jews about issues involving race, because of the nature of the dual-purpose culture we live in; excuse me, I mean, duel-purpose culture, that we live in. Our origins and entry onto the American stage has historically been subject to a racial polarity that remains vigorously viable today.

America's first president, George Washington, came to Newport, Rhode Island in 1790, and responded to the epistle from the warden of the Touro Synagogue welcoming him to the city. President Washington wrote:

"It is no more that tolerance is spoken of, as if it was by indulgence of one class of people, that another enjoyed the exercise of their inherent natural rights. For happily the government of the United States, which gives to bigotry no sanction, to persecution no assistance, requires only that they who live under its protection should demean themselves as good citizens, in giving it on all occasions their effectual support."

The American Jewish community, then and now, views these few words as solidifying their safety and acceptance in a country derived of European and Christian traditions. Extolled as an example of the Age of Enlightenment, these trenchant words are legendary and bear repeating: "...the government of the United States gives to bigotry no sanction...to persecution no assistance," because they are moral life-boats that float the promise of America. Unequivocally decent by any standard, Washington's letter is read every year at Touro Synagogue because it is seen as welcoming and accepting, though conditionally, I hypothesize. The condition: unwavering and absolute support for the incipient nation's vile system of slavery and racial hierarchy, in return, for "protection" as long as "...in giving it on all occasions their effectual support." Plainly said, as long as the Jews condoned and maintained loyalty to the government and social order and not challenge the status quo, prior European and Christian ostracism and persecution would not be resurrected, again.

When the Jews complied with President Washington's eloquently veiled threat, they made a pragmatic deal with American Christianity, its devil and religious culture, and chose the morally indefensible New World American way, and the American racial heritage of "whiteness" became their cross to bear—adapting the common language and understandings of race and white supremacy. Nothing of their life style and existence was excluded from the fruit of this "poisonous tree." Aaron Lopez, one of the founders of Touro, was a slave trader. This was the founding and foundation of the white American Jewish heritage.

This "divided house" produced differing historical and personal histories for me and white Jewish friends from its inception—resulting in racial landmines activated by mere human fallibility or traditional maliciousness, in the twenty-first century. In order to embrace Judaism and permit it to embrace me, I needed to feel fundamentally safe; harbored and hugged, welcomed, protected and accepted by the greater Jewish community, unconditionally.

B'nai Jeshurun was a true sanctuary, as modeled by the Goldsteins, because when the doors closed behind me, I felt totally safe from physical harm and racial bigotry, while recognizing racial misunderstanding and racial disagreement *would occur*, even among the most racially mature of us; not easy words to conceive, to give life to, to nurture and think about; yet words easier to write but excruciatingly problematic *being* those words and *living* them. My way of being and living each morning I got up was grounded in vigilance born of daily rejection on America's black streets. Like Israeli pilots, I always sit in my "cockpit" and remain alert because the most insidious enemy is within—the struggle not to give up making the effort to differentiate individual whites, and within close proximity, white persons unknown to me who can strike and do harm in an instant.

Integrating into B'nai Jeshurun religiously was easy, as the major battle was merely showing up for services. Moreover, my thirst for knowledge led me to take classes and attend lectures and workshops, inside and outside the synagogue. Early on, I was uncomfortable in all classes because of the Jewish tradition of verbal exchange around the study of religious texts. I remained silent for fear that my questions, interpretations, and opinions would sound stupid and unintelligent. Privately, as friendships bloomed, I sought out and engaged in verbal exchange with some of my new Jewish sisters and brothers, who were more than happy to share their knowledge of Judaism, and very respectful in answering my questions.

While having a cordial Shabbat dinner with friends, Barbara was talking about her experiences as a principal in a local school. She said that a school in Harlem was advertising for a principal and encouraged Eleanor, an assistant principal, to apply. She said, "I am the wrong color." A catatonic chill engulfed the entire dinner table and everyone became embarrassingly aware I was the color Eleanor lacked. My heart rate catapulted as I digested the thick slice of silence that ensued. All seven white friends, all white liberals, none of whom are racist, all totally accepting of me, looked straight ahead with frozen eyeballs, until the initial catatonia wore off.

I was dismayed at the presumptive conclusion that the Harlem school would base its decision on discriminatory racial grounds—given the history of heavy Jewish representation in the New York City public school system. My dismay was sucked into the vortex of my rapidly beating heart, and I was lost for rational words as my annoyance rumbled.

For all the realpolitik of powerlessness and race, from George Washington to George W. Bush that black folks continue to endure, frankly,

I found that comment appalling. Jews have experienced the institutional lash of discrimination, but absent the continuous violence and discrimination in law and policy abuse based on their hue. It was their whiteness that got the welcome mat, initially unrolled, then rolled out to them. No doubt there has been and there still exists anti-Semitism, but nothing that *not being black* allowed them to work out and work their way up into the economic and policy power crevices of American life.

As the catatonic chill thawed awkwardly and the eyeballs relaxed and looked around, Barbara said she was the principal in a school district comprised largely of black and Latino students and when she was interviewed by the community board for the job, "They asked if I spoke another language and I said 'Hebrew'. There were those who wanted to hire a Latino person who applied, but I had the better experience."

At B'nai Jeshurun, Rabbis Bronstein and Matalon, invited Reverend Calvin Butts, the black minister at the Abyssinian Baptist Church in Harlem, to give the sermon on a Saturday morning Shabbat service. Reverend Butts received a standing ovation. Rabbis Bronstein and Matalon suggested a committee be formed to address black Jewish relations. Immediately I was onboard. Barbara also expressed an interest when I broached the subject with her.

Over coffee at Starbucks, we were strategizing when Affirmative Action, uninvited, wandered into the conversation. "I don't support Affirmative Action," Barbara said bluntly, looking me straight in the eye. In my next breathe, my heart rate accelerated to sprint speed as I looked her straight in the eye, battling not to allow the trauma to my system to show in my voice or face. My reaction was based on the firm belief that nonsupport of Affirmative Action was inimical to black people's interest, including mine. I was thoroughly surprised because Barbara unequivocally embraced the idea of improving the relationship between blacks and Jews, is a common Westside B'nai Jeshurun liberal democrat, so I assumed she was an advocate for Affirmative Action—I never give anyone an Affirmative Action litmus test.

This visceral emission from Barbara's mouth and heart, resulted in my feeling that I had no right to exist in my current form as psychologist, lawyer, and Jew; that I should be serving her Starbucks and relegated to the lower end of the privilege-chain. Despite our friendship and her being a liberal democrat, if in fifteen minutes of conversation and disagreement over one issue I was feeling uncomfortable, was she appropriate to be on such a committee? How was it possible for me to be on such a committee if the members premise were seen as inimical to African Americans and my personal interest? How could common ground be found and cultivated?

How was this issue not going to be divisive since Reverend Butts and his congregants supported Affirmative Action? How could healing take place? Notwithstanding, at the rabbis request I pushed forward. The coda: there was a lack of enthusiasm and reciprocity from my counterpart at Abyssinian Baptist Church. The potential for a progressive relationship died a quiet death, receding into another missed opportunity.

A grateful recipient of Affirmative Action, it has been good to me and for me, allowing me to develop my abilities and give life to my life giving yearnings, aspirations and goals. I am unabashed and proud because enough of me survived vexing white American racist attitudes, behaviors, policies and institutions that subsidized and franchised dual educations and expectations. When Affirmative Action was created after the 1960's urban rebellions, it was not easy to "qualify" and be successful. I *had to lack* the necessary educational background and experiences common to whites, yet have learned the minimum of educational fundamentals, to be intelligent enough to catch up and then keep up with my white counterparts with a "Head Start." Simultaneously, I had to have the minimum sense of "I can do" and a recognized sense of entitlement i.e. self-worth, and continue developing the necessary confidence and sophistication to live in and negotiate a "new world order" that was historically an exclusive "club" for whites that was both rejecting and hostile to me and those of my ilk.

While struggling with and attempting to hide my upset and agitation I said to Barbara, "Why don't you support Affirmative Action?"

"Because I don't like what it does."

"What does it do that you don't like?"

"I see it in the school system, children are promoted who shouldn't be promoted."

"This is how you see Affirmative Action?"

"Yes, the children are not prepared and they are passed on and it is a disservice to them."

I was incredulous hearing an intelligent person, well-trained, and respected education professional with an extensive knowledge of Judaism and Torah reduce Affirmative Action to social promotions, a practice I abhor. I thought her idea absurd but nary a peep of disagreement crossed my lips. We were good friends, but, with not a strong enough affinity that would withstand the vigorous challenge I would mount and the unavoidable entanglement of competition and verbal conflagration, surely to follow. I didn't think I could convey my rational reasons without exploding on her. I chose imploding, a common defense mechanism, as a safe alternative. Barbara then described how she facilitated the tutoring of a black student to help him reach his potential.

Surprisingly, Barbara and I became closer, and we learned to trust and support each other in very difficult times. I genuinely came to love, care about and respect her as we shared intimate aspects of our lives. Six months later, while walking home from synagogue one Shabbat day, I resurrected our conversation and disagreed with Barbara's characterization of Affirmative Action. As our disparate ideas were flailing and moving about, we both became agitated and heated in the discussion, she concluded by saying that: "Black people are there own worst enemy. They do it to themselves."

Stupefied, I looked at her in disbelief, saw the shimmering of her head, surge of energy in her eyes, and realized she really believed what she had just said: that this tired, tried-and-true canard, used and abused in various forms since slavery times, was common knowledge and irrefutable; so common, that many black folks have chastised their black brethren with the *exact same language*, but, albeit, a different spirit. When white people speak of black folks in this manner, they exclude or deny the impact of racism. When black folk criticize other black folk in this manner, they mean despite racism and its impact, African American citizenry must take responsibility for their behavior and attitudes; that racism cannot be used as a platitude not to do better.

I responded affirmatively to Barbara, "Black people never volunteered for slavery, never lynched themselves, never discriminated against themselves, never denied themselves employment or housing, did not invent or employ racism no more than Jews invented or employed anti-Semitism." There was a moment, a look of surprise, that flashed into her eyes and flushed over her face, a look of recognition that something was heard, taught, learned; something new, perhaps—perhaps, a figment of my imagination, or need to see some change, however minute.

Ellen is a partner in a law firm. I had been a guest at her home and she had been mine at the opera. Over many meals she began to tell me some of her intimate struggles in life and I did the same. Ellen invited me to be her escort to a law firm function, "because I can trust you." Her trust in me further informed my trust in her. That is, a white woman inviting a black man to a major function as her escort at the work place where she was a major player was astounding to me. We were friends, not lovers. I did not escort her because I felt inadequate as a lawyer—I told Ellen a black lie, that I had a prior commitment.

In a casual conversation, after the fact of our friendship, Ellen told me she had tutored black students at a New York City public school and had gotten some of the students placed in jobs at several law firms. "Righteous, righteous sister," I thought with a quiet smile.

I was about to turn off my television one early Friday evening when there was an interruption of the program and "Breaking News" flashed across the screen and the commentator said the cops were found not guilty in the Amadou Diallo case—shot forty-one times by New York City police officers who allegedly mistook his keys for a gun.

Frankly, I felt like I was shot forty-one times, again, and was in agony as I headed off to B'nai Jeshurun. I arrived for the Friday evening 6:45 service and the rabbi mentioned no word about Diallo—I don't know if she knew—and I was in an accentuated and active rage though my demeanor and expression were non-revealing. At the Saturday morning Shabbat service, I became increasingly overwrought as I listened to the dvar Torah and could no longer hear, because nothing was being said about the Diallo verdict (Rabbi Bronstein said he discussed Diallo at the Friday evening 6:00 o'clock service) and I drifted into reverie as self-medication to find some comfort, and wistfully began to fantasize what I would be saying: "The police department in New York City and anywhere in these United States should not be worshipped like a golden calf, that it is idolatrous to do so…"

After the service I felt raw and woozy as if from a cracked skull, as if I had been beaten with a black nightstick, again and again, again. I went over to Ellen and sought camaraderie, some solace, and placed my face close to hers in assumed solidarity and said, "The Diallo verdict has me fucked up?"

"Why, Ernie?" She asked, perplexed. "I thought the officer who cried was very credible?" Ellen's response measured fifteen on my emotional Richter scale, and my entire body cracked open. I retreated back to reverie—as I looked her straight in the eye—and the safety of the underground mental bunker of my youth that I had built to find some peace of mind, and to preserve a piece of my mind.

I thought, "Even if the police officer is genuinely remorseful, there are crimes committed that people sincerely regret, but remorse, despite how genuine it is, does not mitigate the reckless disregard taken, and the police officer should have served his time, notwithstanding." Unable to coherently gather my traumatized reaction, I dissembled while looking at this truly wonderful white person with like-mind, unlike mine. Though I felt invisible, I tried, my best, my very best, to disappear.

With Ellen's shocking statement of support for the verdict, I began to experience Post Traumatic Stress Disorder (PTSD), as described in the *Diagnostic and Statistical Manual of Mental Disorders, Fourth Edition: "the person…was confronted with an event or events that involved actual or threatened death or serious injury, or a threat to the physical integrity of self or others…the person's response involved intense fear, helplessness, or horror. The traumatic event is persistently re-experienced in one or more of the following ways: recurrent and intrusive recollections of the event, including images, thoughts, or perceptions…recurrent distressing dreams of the event…acting or feeling as if the traumatic event were recurring…intense psychological distress at exposure to internal or external cues that symbolize or resemble an aspect of the traumatic event."*

I naturally called to commiserate with Meyer, my brother and best friend, which I do about everything in my life. I was fuming along about the Diallo verdict and stopped to give him time for rejoinder. The father of an adopted black son, he responded with a technical and legal analysis of the case. I heard no outright dismay, angst, or pain so I launched into a verbal squall about his insensitivity, and he argued the case was lost on the lack of legal merit. Well, that is not what I wanted to hear and so I said accusingly, "The only reason you are not as angry and upset as I am is that you did not grow up black. You did not have to face the fear that police, in too many instances, engender in black folks, regardless of their station in life."

In a trembling voice, without hesitation or qualification, Meyer said, "Look, you are probably right, no, you are right. I did not grow up black and I did not experience what you experienced and the way you experienced it, and I am not as sensitive as you. And I don't have to go through it. But I do understand how you feel." Meyer spoke with genuine humility.

A swath of silence lay between us, as we each tried to gather ourselves. Because I believed him and believed in him, I did not feel invisible. Then, words formed in my gut, rolled up into my throat, got stuck, blocked my breathing, until necessity calmly discharged them. I said, "Meyer, you need to become more sensitive, because you have a black son, and Daniel could very well become the next Diallo."

Silence, now serving as an adhesive to keep our relationship from fraying, filled every communicative space between us. Meyer absorbed my words as a professional boxer absorbs the unexpected blows; my words, of knockout proportion, cut deep; I hurt him, and I could feel his hurt, because I could feel I hurt him, though that was not my intent. Stunned from my verbal battery, Meyer bled silently with love and, without remonstrating. I did and do believe Meyer is Daniel's father, and, the best, natural father Daniel could have.

I sought solace and nuanced wisdom from someone I knew steeped in the black church. When I explained my disappointment about Meyer and Ellen, he said, "Your friends are just being white." He spoke without anger or angst, talking softly with no hurry in his voice, like he was teaching a lesson. He followed up with a corollary with logical cynicism, "Ernie, since *we* have to be around *them* six days a week, why do you on your holy day, your Sabbath, want to spend it with *them*?"

After I returned from a trip to Israel, William Haden asked how I was received. I said, "I was welcomed and accepted in every place I visited. The people embraced me and being black was not an issue."

William Haden responded, "It was like that this time, but wait till the next time, it's not going to be like that, it's going to be different."

Astounded by the tenacity of his cynicism and distortion of reality, I challenged him. "I just told you the people treated me well, that I had no problems. So what's your problem?"

"You got a lot of problems, but your big one is…" William Haden stopped what he started to say, glared at me, paused, then continued, "You don't respect our leaders."

I did not understand his non sequitur and attempted to get off the irrational road being traveled. "What are you talking about? I just told you I was treated well in Israel, and you don't want to accept what *I experienced*."

"Man, you know you can't trust white people to always be in your corner, and when you get in trouble with them, you will need Sharpton and Farrakhan."

"Come on man, Farrakhan don't like Jews, and I am a Jew."

"Farrakhan is only trying to keep people off your back. Sharpton is in the mainstream of the democratic party, so what you got bad to say about him?"

"I don't have anything bad to say about him. I think he does some things well, but he could learn a lot from Congressman John Lewis, a genuine statesman." I related the following story to William Haden.

In April 2001, I attended a dialogue featuring Reverend Al Sharpton and Rabbi Shmuley Boteach, moderated by the academy award-winning actor William Hurt. The intent of the meeting was to help ease the tensions between the black and Jewish communities and further the healing process. The meeting became disagreeably unsettled when a black man—sitting among the supporters of Rev. Sharpton—serving as agitprop, stood up with an anti-Semitic tractate in his hand and searing words from his heart, confidently announced, "You Jews, you stole those peoples land," referring to the founding of Israel in 1948. Forthwith, the room temperature shot-up beyond the boiling point, and the black and white young Jewish men sitting next to and behind me became agitated. Mr. Hurt became flustered and did not know how to negotiate the divisive acrimony that followed, and with the power of the gavel he ended the conversation abruptly.

When this common and popular bromide, repeated by the agitprop black man, is tossed into a discussion like a hand grenade, most Jews, myself surely included, hear that we as a people do not have a moral right to exist as a nation. While the anti-Semitic black man was ranting, I watched Rev. Sharpton become like I have never seen him: speechless. As the vicious invectives spewed forth, the moment was pregnant for him to publicly build bridges by politically correcting the heinous bromide, and publicly state his stance on anti-Semitism and the State of Israel. Instead, Rev. Sharpton chose not to respond, and remained, loudly silent.

Yet, Rev. Sharpton said Jews should support black issues of fairness and justice because, "It is the right thing to do." Jews expect no less of black folks, especially influential black leaders.

As an African American, I firmly believe black American leadership has a moral responsibility to affirmatively and publicly address any distorted and misinformed notions about Jews and Judaism, and subtle or blatant anti-Semitic notions. As a Jew, in this specific instance, I wanted to know Rev. Sharpton's stance on the right of Israel to exist and anti-Semitic publications.

Among some prominent black folk, Rev. Sharpton has been criticized in private and public, as a divisive narcissistic gadfly. I believe Rev. Sharpton's merit is his unwavering support of members of the black community who have experienced racial injustice. When the police in Brooklyn killed Gideon Bush, a mentally disturbed Jewish man, Rev. Sharpton reminded the audience that he stood with the Jewish community because, "It was the right thing to do." Rev. Sharpton also admitted he was wrong for using the words "white interloper" outside the white Jewish owned store that burned down in Harlem.

Rev. Sharpton went to Israel in October 2001 with Rabbi Boteach to show support for recent victims of terrorism, "to bring their communities together." After four Israeli civilians died from terrorist attacks, both men met with several influential Jewish leaders in Israel, including Ehud Barak, Israel's immediate past Prime Minister and Rev. Sharpton said, "This is about restoring solidarity between two peoples who have historically been in the trenches, side by side, fighting discrimination." A very welcomed statement.

It may be argued, convincingly I say, that Rev. Sharpton's statement to the higher echelon in Israel serves little practical purpose on the ground in the New York City black community of his influence. I would like to believe that Rev. Sharpton actually meant every word that flowed from his mouth in Israel, rather than the alternative; that he was attempting, as a crass pragmatist, to burnish his image for purposes of "political cover" leading to political power in American domestic politics—to present as a moderate man of the world with international credentials.

So where was Rev. Sharpton's words of solidarity and refutation of anti-Semitism when he stood loudly silent as the agitprop black man stood up and launched his verbal fusillade? I hypothesize that Rev. Sharpton remained silent because it was one of his constituents, and he did not want to publicly rebuke him because he believed he would have lost credibility. Rev. Sharpton should have rebuked him, better still, he should have "re-educated" him at that moment, to send a public message to his constituency regarding the moral right of Jews to be in Israel. That is, Rev. Sharpton should have given the same message to his constituents that he gave to Ehud Barak and Israel.

It is not necessary to travel to Israel, "to bring their communities together." To help rid the festering sores of angst between the black American and Jewish communities, it will take black leaders in their own institutions educating and re-educating their constituents, in order to bring them to the point where they look at Israel and their fellow Jewish Americans and say, "This is about restoring solidarity between two peoples who have historically been in the trenches, side by side, fighting discrimination."

When I said Rev. Sharpton needed to be principled and flex his influence in his own "blackyard," neither William Haden's expression nor his cynicism abated.

One Shabbat morning I was listening intensely to the dvar Torah of the visiting rabbi and the person next to me leaned over and whispered, "Do you understand what she means?" I nodded affirmatively. The visiting rabbi was making an intricate argument and I was trying to grasp it all. The person next to me said, "Tell me what she means." I'm now annoyed because my concentration was interrupted, but I explained my understanding and in apparent surprise he said, "You got it."

I continued to listen but was distracted because my gut response, unspoken, why was he so surprised that I "got it?" Why did he think I did not understand what was being said? Why didn't he ask the Jew sitting to his left, or the Jews sitting in front and back of him? Why me?

For quite a while I replayed this scenario frequently in my head. This situation was complicated by the fact that this was someone supportive of me and not antagonistic to black people.

I was subsequently asked in an interview, published in the synagogue newsletter, if I had "experienced any racism at BJ?" I thought without thinking, recalled the above-mentioned scenario, and referred to it as a racist expression. Two white close friends of mine came to me—many other congregants went to the B'nai Jeshurun rabbis—and disagreed with my understanding. Barbara and Vivian thought me presumptuous and absolutely wrong. I was told by Vivian, "You are on a slippery slope. He could have meant something different...maybe he was trying to help you understand what the rabbi was saying." Vivian described how she tried to make black visitors to the synagogue feel comfortable by explaining the service.

I had been at B'nai Jeshurun two years as the person who queried me knew. Moreover, the sermon was in English and I said sarcastically, "Since English is my native language, so what should I not understand?" I then observed, "Let's keep in mind, I am not the one who did not understand."

In other conversations of this ilk I have been told, "You are too sensitive; you *should not* be so sensitive." But I am and don't apologize for it, because my so-called sensitivity—a chronically injured part of my personality due to the chronic American racial insults experienced—is a survival tool constructed in American reality.

White Americans do not experience chronic racial insult and the result is that too many white people do not perceive when they are being racially inappropriate or are insensitive; they remain ignorant and/or indifferent to the accumulative disappointment and hurt of their American brethren.

When I recounted the story to black friends they understood immediately; *none* questioned my perception and all gave that "we told you so" look; some gleefully verbalized it. It felt good to recount my tale of white woe and not have to go through laborious explanations and then be doubted upon completion. The simple fact that not one black person challenged my thinking or asked critical questions, limited my potential at having an alternative perspective, a larger vision, because we looked through the same black lens. The collusion was suffocating.

I believe the white congregants were being defensive, and I think their defensiveness turned on the word "racism" from the original newsletter interview. In retrospect I do not think that was a true racist incident. What is a true racist incident? How is racial maliciousness defined? Is intent necessary? Is racial insensitivity a valid category? Are there objective criteria? Who sets the criteria? The larger issue is how to distinguish between someone racially insensitive as opposed to someone racially malicious: a person may respond naively, insensitively, or out of stereotypical notions or ignorance, which does not necessarily equate with racism's venal intent and its accompanying behavior.

When one feels racially misunderstood or offended, he may ask a person what they mean when the statement is made, or to explain such conduct when exhibited. But people are afraid to have frank conversations about race, including the author of these words. Such discussions are difficult because of all the raw racial emotion stirred up internally, and with cultural and stereotypical images moving in uneven motion, each person believes they are correct and that the *other*, "really does not get it."

To help avoid compounding misunderstandings and reifying current attitudes, we may treat each other's perceived racial offense as landmines or landfill. The former means conflagration and no potential change. The latter means we try and dig up "garbage" that we have buried and make a conscious attempt, a sincere effort to understand the other, even if we really don't get it.

During a discussion of this incident, Barbara vigorously disagreed with me and entertained the possibility that my interlocutor queried me because he honestly did not understand what the rabbi was saying. The idea was far-fetched because he was an Ivy League graduate, successful businessman, and knowledgeable about Judaism. Was this my presumption of white superiority? That is, if I understood something complex that a white male, Yale man to boot, should also understand?

With a needed push from Barbara—which I accepted because I trusted her—I decided to explore the issue with him because I felt it would bring closure, and model for myself a way to discuss racial conflicts with whites. The Yale man, Jonathan, remembered the day and reported he made the inquiry because he did not know a lot about the topic, did not understand what point the rabbi was making, and was simply asking if I understood, and he concluded, "I thought what you said was so erudite that I just said, 'You got it.'"

I was more than surprised because I had carried around a misrepresentation in my head—of my own creation—that used up unnecessary energy and time, and published it in an interview. The good news is that I retained my friendship with Jonathan during this period, but I did feel a little foolish, actually a lot foolish, but a lot more humbled by my self-assuredness which was not assured. Notwithstanding, my suspiciousness told me for quite awhile that Jonathan only said what he said to hide his real feelings—black paranoia and thought without thinking, prevailed. One obvious lesson: I must be sensitive to my racial sensitivity, to review my presumptions, thoroughly evaluate and question them. Moreover, I must genuinely try to learn to be sensitive to a white person's insensitivity.

"No one ever said it was going to be easy," an attitude and fortitude I heard from both my mom and dad. Goodness knows they had a bull's-eye understanding of some of the greater aspects of life, and likely those words of hard-earned experience passed-down to me, contributed to my capacity to endure, mature and change.

Israel
The Good the Bad the Unexpected

> *Even if your outcasts are at the ends of the world, from there HaShem, your God will gather you, from there He will fetch you. And HaShem, your God, will bring you to the land which your fathers occupied, and you shall occupy it…*
>
> ***Prayer For The Welfare of The State of Israel***

"I'm going to the Holy Land," I said, with great anticipation to a black friend. "Israel."

"Have you been to Africa yet?" She asked with furrowed brow.

"No," I said.

I began to defensively question myself why I had not been to Africa, especially since I talked the talk of Africa and proudly proclaimed my *African* American identity. Yet, I did find my way to Amsterdam, Belgium, Switzerland, Sweden, and Paris twice, but that did not count, certainly not with my internal black critic squawking.

During the Black Power era, Marcus Garvey was admired as a beacon of black light. In the 1920's, Mr. Garvey observed that Africans and African descendants around the world were either colonized or not treated as full complementary citizens. He advocated one land, Africa, where an ingathering could occur of all its descendants dispersed throughout the world. The commerce of living would be under the auspices and control of the black man, where respect, dignity, economic opportunity and safety would be a universal right. While Mr. Garvey was trying to enact his dream of ingathering African descendants, Theodore Hertzel, the modern inspiration for Jews to return to Israel, was having more success with the same motivations. Mr. Garvey identified with and supported Zionism and the Jewish struggle for a homeland. Despite the similarities, many black Americans do not identify with Jews and Zionism.

"Then why are you going to Israel?" My inquisitor honed in. "I don't understand black folks who travel all over the world but don't go to Africa. I've traveled abroad to Europe, even gone to Jerusalem and the Wailing Wall, but I have been to Africa. You are still black, or whatever is left. You aren't even Jewish yet."

Baruch and Meyer, going to a cousin's Bar Mitzvah in Israel, had invited me to join them. On July 2 1997, I arrived at Kennedy Airport to take my maiden voyage. I was exhilarated waiting on line, pushing my bags forward with an unexpected experience in place to greet me: an interview. There were several podiums separated by a few feet with young men and women interviewers behind each one. A young man, no more than twenty-something, asked to see my passport and why I was visiting Israel. My answers were just not good enough. He was looking for danger, and the presumption that I was the potential danger was obvious.

I told the interviewer of my plan to convert, that Rabbi Baruch Goldstein invited me to Israel, and gave him my itinerary. He wanted to know about Rabbi Goldstein. I gave him a brief biography. He asked how I knew Rabbi Goldstein, and I explained that Meyer and I had become friends when we were students. I was asked and told him I was a clinical psychologist, and described the clinical populations I worked with and the treatment provided. He asked to see my professional card, which I gave to him, and he asked what the "J.D." meant on my card. I explained I was also a lawyer. He asked for my driver's license, and then without excusing himself, the young man walked away with my passport, driver's license, professional card, and disappeared behind a column. Another young man joined him, and I imagined they were calling my office to make sure I had not manufactured an identity to sneak into Israel.

I was pissed off at the one constant in the interview, his doubt about my veracity. I certainly knew of no history of middle-aged African American men coming to Israel to make trouble. I looked around and saw that just about everyone had completed their interviews. I felt like a black suspect in a criminal lineup with only whites.

I tried to catch glimpses of my interviewer, whose head darted out from behind the column, seemingly trying to observe my behavior. He returned and then returned my passport, driver's license, and professional card. Then he asked, "Do you have a letter to prove that Rabbi Goldstein invited you to Israel?"

Deeply offended, I angrily said, "You want what from me? I don't have to show you a letter, and you don't have the right to ask me"

Startled, the interviewer said, "Sir. Please, please just cooperate."

I took note that everyone had finished the interview process, except black me.

I inhaled attempting to calm myself. I thought, "Ernest, play the game, play the game brother, *play the fucking game*." I exhaled outrage, and, played the fucking game.

"No." I don't have a letter, said with suppressed contempt. I hated him and Israel at that moment and didn't want to go, but I really wanted to go and did not hate Israel, but I did hate the interviewer.

So very weary: The Fatigue set in.

The Fatigue is a natural reaction to the chronic racial assault; it smacked me in the face with the force of a shoulder-fired rocket; numbness absorbs the impact, then comes the very tired very empty feeling, filling the cavernous wound with nauseous feelings, and the message to cope is delivered medicinally, like an intravenous drip of morphine in a hospital bed..

Finally, I boarded.

But wait, one cautious minute. I experienced the interview as a racial assault, but was I racially assaulted? Did the interviewer intentionally provoke, humiliate and embarrass me with racial intent?

I sat observing the varying stripes of Jews ranging from young Orthodox women with wigs, headscarves, loose long dark dresses to women with tight pants, short skirts and cleavage available for all to see. The young women looked as if they lived in different eras. The Fatigue began to give way to the clashing mundane world of Jewry, and I dozed off with the contretemps behind and Israel ahead.

The touch-down of the plane lifted my spirits and excitement pushed me forward. After I passed through the exit interview, I took about seven steps when a man sidled up to me and asked about my coming to Israel and wanted to see my passport. The Fatigue joked that Israel wanted me to feel like I was in America, where I had been stopped for being a BMW, a Black Man Walking.

I went on a bus tour and visited Caesarea, Tel Aviv, Safed, Tiberias, the Golan Heights, Bethlehem, Jerusalem and Haifa. Looking from the Golan Heights and seeing Syria in close proximity, was like looking from Manhattan to New Jersey. Listening to the guide tell stories of battles that were fought to preserve and protect Israel, the reality of why Israeli air force pilots must sit in their cockpits twenty-four hours became apparent. We were told the story of Eli Cohen, a Jew born in Syria who was an intelligence officer in the Syrian army. He was caught spying for Israel and was killed by the Syrians; his body was not returned despite Israel's repeated requests. The sun reflected off the dark brown memorial that bore his honor, the mortal danger he had placed himself in, mourned his sacrifice and hailed his self-less courage.

I broke off from the group and wandered about, pondering the magnitude of what I just learned. As I walked through the brown shrubs and parched dirt, where ferocious battles had been fought, the sound of battles, bullets and blood whispered. I returned to the group and suddenly felt an ineffable rumbling of emotions swelling my lungs, expanding my chest, constricting my throat, and my eyes served as a dam to hold back the tears. I turned and rushed down the incline, embarrassed, and stood behind the tour bus, crying a muted cry, battling not to break out in sobs of pain, for hurt I knew not. I was baffled because I could not recall the last time I cried. Yet, the groundswell felt familiar, but how and when it came to reside in the depths of my soul, I have no idea. I was not a Jew.

One frequent question I received regarding my conversion, exclusively from black Americans: "How do you deal with the *politics* of your conversion?" During the Black Power era the assumption was that the Palestinians were morally right, and Israel morally wrong, for creating a nation and winning the War of Independence in 1948—this too was my opinion.

The question was answered while walking alone on a plaza in Jerusalem, in a location I had never been. The next stride I took thrust me into an epochal moment. Standing still, I watched parading before me, men with black hats, men with and men without yarmulkes, white Israelis and black Israelis, women dressed in pants and shorts and women in modest dress. They looked disparate and unrelated, not able to see their commonality, leaving each vulnerable to vociferously disagree with each other about how to be—as if mortal enemies—and not how to be, in the commonness of their commonality. As this panorama passed before me, scrolled onto my soul was the epiphany: "Jews have a right to have a nation of their own, to be, to live, to create, to do, in a self-protected environment: Israel must be."

Returning from Israel, I was in the airport standing behind Meyer and Daniel. A female employee walked down the passenger line casually asking questions and pressing stickers of approval on their bags. She looked at me and her eyes instantaneously registered a determination that I was the ultimate suspect, a well-defined potential danger—as if we were in the wild and I was a natural predator. Why was my black skin such an instant and guttural provocation? I was pulled out of line and my suitcase was patted down. Meyer was embarrassed that I had to be subjected to the additional search.

My second trip to Israel was in the summer of 1998 and I took a six week Hebrew ulpan. I gave a friend eight thousand dollars to bury me if I were to be killed by a suicide bomber.

I arrived at Kennedy Airport June1998 and knew what to expect from the interview; but this time I said, "I am a Jew," since I converted September 1997. The interviewer was startled, but he smiled when it sank in. It led to a new round of conversation as to how and why I made the leap to the faith. I was still held longer than most but the hostile edge was absent.

Shortly after arriving in Jerusalem, I went walking. A sign with blurred lettering hazily appeared. When I got closer, the letters solidified into English, and the shape they took caused me to become frozen in place under the broiling sun. Trying to elucidate my obvious hallucination, I asked and answered myself. "I'm in Israel, right? Right." But the sign, in bold black letters did not fade. It read: Afro Hair Products.

I sought out the mirage and met Leah, an African originally from Ghana, now Orthodox Jew who converted in Israel. She grew up in Ghana thinking she was Jewish because her family celebrated Shabbat.

Leah did not know the origin of the practice, but knew it was handed down through the generations. When she arrived in Israel, Leah was told she would have to have a formal conversion since there was no recognized Jewish life in Ghana. She loves Israel and encouraged me to make aliyah—to move to Israel. She said, "You would do very well here."

The uneasy relationship between African Americans and Jews was nonexistent in Israel. Every Israeli I spoke to became exuberant at my becoming a Jew, and when dining out free desserts and appetizers sometimes followed. I was affected by this unrestrained acceptance: I cannot ever take for granted that white people will treat me as an equal and be genuinely happy to see me become a member of their "country" and "club."

A new fear greeted me. I was sitting in the front of a bus when a brown skinned man juggling three large boxes struggled to get on. I became agitated at the mere sight of the boxes and vigorously scrutinized this religiously dressed man with black hat, black suit, and white shirt. Was he a Palestinian in disguise? I looked around and none of the other passengers registered any alarm. I was not allayed. He sat directly across from me and placed one of the boxes on the seat next to me.

The box seemed to have eyes and was looking at me, and I tried to look through the box with x-ray anxiety to ascertain if a bomb was set to go off. Listening intently, I heard no sounds except the rumbling of the bus and my accelerated heart rate. The box became the BOX, the center of my universe, time and movement slowed to a crawl as my fear increased exponentially. I wanted to be calm, but I also wanted to scream.

When I looked into the eyes of the man whose BOX commanded my attention, they revealed the frustration of a man clumsily trying to get his new purchases home. Now able to relax a heartbeat slower, my eyes remained on guard duty as if my intense stare could deactivate the BOX from exploding. I did not feel safe until I got off the BOX and left the bus.

I was walking around Ben Judah Street and had passed two adolescents that soldiers stopped, demanded identification, then asked, "What are you doing here?"

My African American sense of indignation ignited without thinking. Words from Gill Scott Heron's song played in my head: "Let me see your I-D." The two youths were Palestinians, and the Israeli reality made me aware of the potential danger in the young men with no facial hair or hardened looks; they passed by me, "invisible."

"Ernest, you better mind your own damn business, this ain't America," I counseled myself.

I conversed with Ethiopian soldiers, wanting to know about their life in Israel, and there were no racial complaints. Further, there was no sense of Ethiopian men and women embracing me as their brother, in the historical sense created by American slavery and Jim Crow. They perceived me only as an American tourist: these Israelis of African descent were not "black," and identified as Israelis and not, African Israelis.

The Bad: The Israeli police followed me while I was in Israel. The biggest problem in telling this part of my story is the issue of creditability. I cannot provide direct evidence. I used my clinical judgment, innate sentience, and hyper-vigilant personality.

Let me begin with what sparked my concern about being the subject of a boring spy novel. After arriving in Israel, I discovered that I had forgotten my nutritional supplements. I called my neighbor Carolyn and she promised to ship them forthwith. A week and a half later I had not received my supplements. I inquired and Carolyn confirmed they had been shipped express mail. I called the Israeli airport, and was told that my package was being held; no explanation was offered. Since I was going to meet a friend, I instructed the official to have my package delivered to my next-door neighbor, Tertzia.

"Where are you going?" the official asked, as if he had a right to know.

"I'm going out," I said, as my radar picked up his unlikely interest. Upon my return, I retrieved my package from Tertzia. I was taking-stock when the doorbell rang and I assumed it was Tertzia. I opened the door and there was a tousled man with dark brown complexion. He greeted me in English and I began to churn inside as he inquired about a specific individual. I told him no such person lived here. Something in my gut did not feel right. I connected the airport official's inquiry and the dark man at my door.

I was living in a fifth floor apartment with a voice and buzzer system in place. I may have overlooked his unlikely arrival but he made a fatal error: he spoke to me in English. Everyone in Israel spoke to me in Hebrew.

Observation: This was my second trip to Israel. I assumed Israeli authorities spoke to Baruch Goldstein, rabbi and Holocaust survivor. Since they knew of my twenty-six year history with the Goldsteins and that I converted, why was it impossible in the minds and hearts of Israeli intelligence for a middle-aged black man to convert and come to study in Israel?

I was leaving the Western Wall area intending to take a leisurely stroll to the Cardio, a shopping area in the Old City. A young white American Jewish woman stopped me and began a conversation. She lived and worked in Manhattan, and I confirmed her story upon my return. A poised and attractive woman, she was easy to converse with, and after she excused herself to use the bathroom, she returned and accompanied me to the Cardio.

She asked, "What has your racial experience been like in Israel?" Certainly an impertinent question from a white American, and even more surreal because she knew me all of twenty minutes, and thirteen of them she reportedly spent in the bathroom. The invisible man syndrome includes whites not being either aware or tuned-in to the African American experience. Moreover, even among the best of interracial friendships, such discussions are wrought with the fear of hidden minefields—offending the other or being offended—that make such conversations difficult to broach. Baruch and Meyer never made such an inquiry, likely because there are no laws, formal or informal, against Israeli's of Ethiopian descent, nor denial of employment or housing based on race.

I had no racial angst to share because I was made to feel welcome everyplace I visited. This peculiar question put me on notice that I was under surveillance; because she did what I was trained not to do in law school, "Never ask the one question too many." I knew that private citizens were used by the mosad, Israeli secret service, to detail people. Notwithstanding, I continued to charm her as she charmed me.

She directed me to a store in the Cardio, and as we entered the owner looked at me with wary eyes and his wife showed severe caution on her face. My American escort signed-off on my boring spy thriller suspicions when she answered their concern by prefacing my introduction, "He is a friend," said reassuringly. The fears of the merchant and his wife faded and warm greetings followed.

Five years later in New York, I was invited to a Shabbat lunch, and as soon as I entered, someone said, "I know you from Israel."

I did not know who this person was because I had been to Israel five times at that point. When I narrowed down the time frames and images from my memory, I recognized the same young woman I met at the Western Wall. No, I did not question her about our interlude because she was doing necessary work and may be needed again.

At the airport, queued up to return to America, I was pulled out of line again, no surprise. Taken to an area where no one could see me, I was asked to open my suitcases—and I refused. Instead, I gave the Israeli security guard a piece of my legal mind. "There is a fourth amendment right that prohibits unreasonable searches and seizures; at international borders, there is a lower standard, but that lower threshold has not been met, and you and Israel are violating my constitutional rights."

When he dispassionately said, "We don't have a constitution in Israel," I was embarrassed because I assumed the lone democratic government in the Middle East had a constitution. I opened my suitcases and all my luggage was taken away. Upon return I had to verify that nothing was missing. I assumed they looked for drugs because no bombs could be hidden in shorts and t-shirts.

Then I was taken into an enclosed private area where I had to "assume the position," with my hands up on the wall and my legs spread, but I only heard the voices of white cops in America, "Up against the wall motherfucker." I was patted down after removing my shoes, socks, jacket, and scanned with a hand held device. This unnecessary search was offensive. What did I do during my two months in Israel that warranted such humiliating treatment that led to neither arrest nor detainment?

When I returned to my seat, I noticed what looked like a Palestinian family, a mother and child sitting opposite me. She said, "I thought it was only *us* who got pulled out of line." I did not respond because, one, I had no affinity with her. Two, I did not believe she was an Arab though her phenotype was suggestive. I assumed it was another case of the Israeli security playing 007 games. It did not make sense for a shabbily dressed Arab woman who had command of the English language to be able to afford to take her family abroad. I did not see her on the airplane. Did Israeli security presume that I became a Jew at age fifty-one in order to be a latent mole for Hamas?

Once I got through the rigmarole of Israeli security, I walked around the airport to unwind, did some stretches to loosen the tight muscles knotted in my stomach and chest, then sat down to rest. I observed a woman with fine facial features and when she got up to board, she was beautiful. She wore a print dress that rested right above the knee, revealing shapely legs and the curves of the dress outlined a statuesque figure.

On the plane we talked. I told her about my being harassed at the international borders when entering and exiting Israel. Born in Yemen, raised in Israel, she was forty-five, and living in New York. With a gripping intensity, she defended Israel's rigorous security measures; her personal fear ran deep, and as it bubbled over and spilled on me, it produced a cord of awareness and understanding not previously felt. I inquired about her transition to life in Israel from Yemen.

She was Sephardic, and attended Ashkenazi schools because they provided a better education. This was in the early years of Israel's independence, and Odette reported the Ashkenazi, European Jews, looked down on the Sephardim, Jews from the Middle East. She fell into childhood memory and said, "I felt so unattractive. The Ashkenazi children always teased me."

"Unattractive, what do you mean?" I was astonished.

"I was so black and ugly," she said.

I was shocked at her self-assessment, because in America she passed for white. This revelation served to magnify a similar story I heard two weeks prior.

I visited a married couple of an American friend in Haifa and was taken aback to see that African art was the motif that adorned every room in their home. A native of Morocco, she spoke five languages, including English and Arabic, so I asked, "Are you ever mistaken for an Arab?"

"Why do you ask? "Is it because I look black?" She sounded devalued.

Sitting in the living room of an Israeli family, I thought I was the only one who looked black. She was attractive with Middle East features. Meeting two Israeli women with contrasting phenotypes, and both felt black, resulted in a head-on collision that shattered my world of racial self-perception.

In addition to ordinary terms of physical debasement, this drop-dead gorgeous woman described how her elementary school classmates derogatorily referred to her as "Black Sambo." I was beyond stunned, because Black Sambo, written in 1899 by Scottish woman Helen Bannerman, published in America in the 1920's and 1930's, was considered by many to be a stereotypical racist putdown of the Negro. This now grieving woman recalled a disparaging refrain that was recited by her peers: "Billy, Billy Sambo, Billy, Billy Black, Billy, Billy Sambo, stay back."

My immediate association was to an oft repeated refrain from my childhood in Harlem: "If you are white, you are all right; if you are yellow, you are mellow; if you are brown, stick around; if you are black, stay back." The travel of this insidious adage is something to marvel at for its sheer endurance to reach foreign shores (Was this book published in Israel?) and to proliferate where black Africans and their descendants were not part of the original cultural fabric.

Both Sephardic women had a sense of *looking* black, but their *being* black, was likely different from my being black, given the different historical roots. The Sephardim in early Israeli society experienced class discrimination from the Ashkenazim but there was no violence and hatred directed at them.

Listening to these two women, devoid of Negroid features, altered the state of my American sensibilities, and sparked further recasting of the American aesthetic. From the deepest part of my emotional wellspring, that white is alright and black stay back, there was further excavation; the newly freed space enhanced the connection between my intellectual foundation, my thoughts, which already knew the black truth verse the white lies, and my emotional foundation, which did not. This literal "meeting of the minds," combined for a more cohesive self-perception and revolutionary outlook: It is not about the texture of hair or skin color—the subjectivity of beauty—which makes one feel inferior, unintelligent, and ugly, it is the coercive force of the dominant power and authority to impose its arbitrary and immoral will—as universal, and the truth. The plane ride home from Israel took me to a destination that was not on my itinerary.

When I returned to B'nai Jeshurun I greeted Sandee Brawarsky. She said, "Ernie, I'm sure you have lots of good stories to tell."

"I do," and proceeded to tell my most memorable anecdote. Shortly after I had arrived in Israel, I was returning from purchasing yarmulkes, when I saw a man begging for money in the street. When I reached the beggar he asked in Hebrew, "Are you a Jew?" Not understanding, I shrugged and kept walking. He asked in English with a thick Israeli accent, "Are you a Jew?" In my second week of classes I answered in Hebrew, "Yes."

In Hebrew he said, "You are number ten."

I understood what he said and deduced, "Minyan, you need a minyan," and his head bobbed up and down.

"Come with me," he said in Hebrew as he gestured. We walked two blocks to his Orthodox synagogue, which was on the top floor of a two-story structure. A long staircase led to the second floor, and he indicated I should walk ahead of him. I bowed graciously and gestured that he should walk first, and I would follow. I was not about to go up a staircase leading I knew not where in a foreign country because a white man I did not know, said he needed a minyan. He insisted, and I relented, cautiously walking up the stairs. When I stepped into the room, there were eight men waiting to start the afternoon prayer service; all turned and looked at me in relief. I put on a new yarmulke and the service began. Ten men are needed, a minyan, to start a prayer service, and nine Israeli Jews were waiting for number ten. This was quintessential Israel, because they were waiting for an ordinary man, a common man, a Jewish man. I was that man.

Also greeting me, I overheard two men, one a familiar face at B'nai Jeshurun, and the other I did not know. "He's here every week," said the familiar face.

"Are you sure?" said the other.

"Every week, every week, I see him here, every week," the familiar face sounded exasperated.

Both men stood in front of me, as if I was invisible. I merely looked and never said a word.

Shortly thereafter, I noticed an unfamiliar man sitting in the section of the shul I usually sat. He was "strange" because he had a penetrating stare, and was scrutinizing more than interacting with people. The calmness of his face as his fingers confidently turned the pages in the prayer book indicated he understood Hebrew. He had no friends, was not interested in making any, evidenced by his lack of contact with those around him. He seized my attention with his intense gaze boring down on me, patting me down with doubt in his eyes.

This man showed up at a class at the synagogue. No one knew him and he did not try to get to know anyone. I had my camera that night to take pictures of the class. At the last moment he tilted his head away but the camera captured him in easily recognizable pose. He never returned to class and services.

My third trip to Israel included a visit to Ethiopia to visit the Falasha Mora, Ethiopians of Jewish descent, who desire to return to Israel. As a child I did not experience Africa as positive. In the 1950's television world, Tarzan was "King" of the African jungle and Sheena was "Queen of the Jungle." Africa was born-again during the Black Power era as, *"the motherland."* Yet, as I headed for Africa, I felt guilty and confused, because *the motherland* no longer resonated as powerfully as it once had. Clarity was not on the horizon, but it would make its appearance as I rose to the heavens.

From Tel Aviv, I boarded a plane bound for Addis Abba aboard an Ethiopian Airline with Ethiopian pilots. For the first time in my life, I was a passenger with black men flying an airplane where previously, only porters and baggage handlers were allowed to tread. I was proud but wondered why in the twenty-first century I had never seen a black airline pilot in America.

I stayed in a Hotel palatial by any western standard. A sentry was posted to monitor those attempting to enter. I began walking up the hill to the street, to blend in anonymously, and make unfiltered observations. After only twenty steps, a young man said, "Good morning, how are you? Can I help you?" I was perplexed how he knew I spoke English. In Paris, Parisians spoke to me in French, in Israel, Israeli's spoke to me in Hebrew, but in Africa I was "outted" in twenty steps. Earlier at the Hotel, as I was about to be introduced to an Israeli, he said, "You are an American," with absolute certainty, as I stood between an Ethiopian born Israeli who looked like your typical Ethiopian, and another Ethiopian man, who looked West African.

"How did you know I was American?"

With a big friendly grin, he said, "You look like a typical American."

Typical American, riveted in my brain. I always thought I was not a typical American because of my African features and hue. Now that I am in Africa, I look like I'm a typical American.

The young Ethiopian offered to be my tour guide for a fee, and I politely declined. On another occasion, walking up the same hill, a boy of about fourteen engaged me in conversation, and when I told him I was an American, his eyes widened, and he said in disbelief: "I thought you were A freak."

In disbelief I responded, "A freak?"

There was only a sincere expression on his young face with no hint of sarcasm.

"A freak?" I repeated.

"You look A freak," his scrunched up face emphasized that my incredulity was incredulous to him.

Nevertheless, his meaning slowly made its way through his Ethiopian accent and sunk into my awareness. Then I felt good that I was mistaken for an African. Finally, I looked "Afrique." How much of a mistake was it? Really? When my mom was in West Africa, indigenous folks told her what tribe she likely came from.

Traveling by car within Addis Ababa was shocking. The paucity of stoplights, the absence of someone directing traffic, I found heart stopping and appalling. The cars and trucks and people crossing the intersections, resulted in a negotiated chaos that somehow seemed to work, however precariously. When we stopped at an intersection, young children came off the sidewalks to beg for money. A boy of about eight bounced onto the roadway before the cars halted. The dust was dry and swirling as the traffic slowed down and the boy had layers of dust smoothly painted on his determined face. Like the pancake makeup of a minstrel it accented the vapid and glazed look in his eyes. But he walked with authority, and I gasped as he came close to the car, giving the illusion he was going to be hit but he deliberately swerved left, dipping his right shoulder parallel to the car and walked quickly to the front. At the exact moment it appeared he would be hit, he crossed in front of the car as it stopped, made a right turn, and stood between two cars, holding out his dusty palms and facing me for money. Hypnotized by the surreal scene, I sat motionless as our eyes met and I cried silently because the light in his life-bulb shone dark.

"Don't give them any money," said Andy Goldman, North American Conference for Ethiopian Jewry (NACOEJ) employee. The boy then spun around to the next car, moved down the line of traffic until the common chaos began to flow again.

I followed the rapid movements of this eight-year-old boy, a seasoned professional in the art of survival. He had no fear of getting hit; had he ever, I wondered. He moved like he had been taught to "hunt" the traffic, the way tiger cubs are taught to hunt by their mothers. Another boy of about twelve came up to the window and flaunted his severely deformed arm and face, flush against my humanity. I wanted with all the power I did not have, to tend to these desperate and needy children.

I visited the NACOEJ sponsored compounds in Addis Ababa and Gondar for pregnant women and children; they provided food and nutritious meals to the poor and hungry Ethiopians of Jewish descent, and medical care was provided by the American Jewish Joint Distribution Committee. Bulk packages of grains and flour were distributed directly to children, to be assured they and their families actually received the food. NACOEJ also provided educational, religious and cultural Jewish connections—schools taught the children Hebrew, math and reading.

In the countryside, children swarmed to me like mosquitoes, cloyingly, to "feed" on me; they followed me around as if I was the pied piper from Israel who could grant their wish: The Wizard of Aliya. Hemmed in, I had difficulty moving in any direction, which was a sad metaphor for their impoverished lives. There were one-room dung roof huts with dirt floors that housed entire families, some mocking modernity with one light bulb. A seven-year-old boy, whose mouth remained slightly parted, was a gathering place for flies to touch down, as if his mouth was a natural part of their habitat. He seemed oblivious, with fetching bright eyes, redundant stare and fly strewn smile.

Compared to this African story, the Basement I grew up in was a castle by any other name; we were never hungry, played checkers, monopoly, tag, raced each other for fun, played stickball, told corny jokes, laughed cornier laughs, and when all else failed we had Edgar Clark, to soothe our wretched souls with the magic of his medicinal story telling.

To attend Saturday morning Shabbat services, Lisa and I walked with Abraham Negusi, an Ethiopian Israeli, through the streets of Addis Ababa, for ninety minutes. People stared at me and gawked at Lisa, who wore a traditional Ethiopian long white dress and big black boots for the long trek.

I observed that Ethiopia was the land of oversized suits, wrinkled clothing, faded and dusty, but no offensive body odors. Then what was not obvious became obvious. No one wore eyeglasses! I then realized that wearing glasses helped to identify me as a tourist, as well as my jeans.

We arrived safely at the Ethiopian Synagogue, an open-air house of worship that consisted of rows of backless wooden benches covered with corrugated tin. An earthen floor pock-marked with rocks created an uneven surface.

I attended the children's service briefly and spent most of my time at the adult service. The men and women were separated by a machitza (a divider) made of cloth, and, the sight of rows and rows and rows of black men in tallis and yarmulkes was glorious to behold. The women were dressed in traditional white dresses with white head wraps and Byzantium crosses on their foreheads, a sign of beauty in Ethiopian culture, but not permitted under Jewish Law.

When we returned to Israel, I had a chance to visit an absorption center for Ethiopian immigrants, visited the homes of some who made successful transitions, and visited a school where Ethiopian children attended. But the leap to the twenty-first century is fraught with problems for the Ethiopians.

Returning to America was relatively smooth for me this time. As I left the interview area, a southern drawl bellowed, "What do you people want? You keep asking the same questions over and over and over again. What's wrong with you people?"

I turned to see a man yelling at the interviewer.

"You want to know why people don't want to come here? *This* is the reason why!" He made a pirouette, and his blond hair rose and swirled around in anger.

Gleefully, I said: "Yes!"

My fourth trip to Israel was to celebrate Baruch Goldstein's eightieth birthday. This Holocaust survivor longed to be only in Israel to celebrate his survival and pay homage to his family. He was born in April, thus I spent my first Passover in Tel Aviv, in 2003.

The Goldsteins and I traveled to Tel Aviv and the hotel we stayed in provided spiritually fulfilling Seders. To my dismay Tel Aviv was bustling with business as usual. The stores sold sandwiches made with bread, and Israelis were buying them with no visible sign that Passover had any significance. The inability to refrain from selling and eating bread for eight days out of the year was symbolic of a deep disconnect with modern Israelis from the not so ancient past of 1948, and the struggle with Palestinians for the right of Israel to exist.

I walked on the crowded boardwalk, warily concerned about the possibility of a suicide bomber which became heightened in bottle-necked areas. The deep disconnect: these Jews in Israel did not seem to make a connection between their freedom to eat bread on Passover, and the frenzied desire of Arabs to blow them back out to sea, straight to ancient Egypt. It broke my heart and rankled my understanding. My argument is not that all Israelis should practice an Orthodox religious life style, but to simply acknowledge that the defining history of Israel and Jews is sacred, extraordinary, and unique. Of course, it may be rightfully argued that as a democratic nation, Israelis have the right to eat bread and not practice any religion, which is true, and I support without reservation. And if it is true that democracy requires the partnership of its citizens, what is the rationale in the mind of the individual Israeli, and the historical understanding for his or her existence, as suicide bombers with baby faces blow them up because they exist?

Preparing to return to New York, I arrived at the airport with Meyer, Sue-Rita and Daniel. A female security guard, turned around, saw me, and her eyes widened. She pointed her finger, and shouted as if she just discovered a wanted criminal: "You." and every person who heard her shrill cry turned to see me pulled from the line. When I said that the Goldstein's were traveling with me, she also pulled them from the line and gave them the extra scrutiny I routinely received. When we finally got near to being checked-in, I felt the energy and observed the man behind us steadily eavesdropping on our conversation. I remembered him when we first got on the line. Then he quietly faded away, and I took note and saw that he returned to the back of the first line we were on. I pointed him out to Sue-Rita, "He is an undercover security agent," I said.

"This has never happened to me before," she said.

"When you hangout with a BMW that is the price you pay," I responded.

Sue-Rita said, "What is a BMW?"

"Black Man Walking."

Safely aboard the plane, I was struck by the humiliation and vulnerability I was experiencing. This time I focused less on my personal emotional insult and injury at always being stopped and profiled. I still don't like it, find it rather distasteful and it taste bad, and I like to think a better procedure can be found, but now accept Israel's prudent right to be safe, and not sorry.

The plane taxied down the runway and took off, and as it rose, I now realized—notwithstanding the deepest depths of pride and self-love of my African heritage coursing through my veins—why I feel challenged by the concept of Africa as motherland. Being a Jew in the present and future, now: Israel *is my motherland.*

Ernest Sex and the Single Man
Life and Love
In Black and White

> But to be perfectly honest, we are all shipwrecked... Start thinking of the mess we so frequently make of our lives, and words fail; no words seem to express exactly the deep regrets we want to feel and all the heartache we must learn to put up with.
>
> ***Judah Goldin***

I was working at the entrance to the law school library checking student identifications for admittance, when a white Jewish woman I had seen briefly in a professor's office stopped and introduced herself and we engaged in polite conversation. When I remarked I had to switch duties, she casually said, "I want to finish this conversation in my living room."

All the aplomb I thought I had with women shattered. Her request collided with my expectations; my poise floundered. I tried my best to play-it-off and said, "Sure." She gave me her address, apartment number, and phone number. Of course, I thought about the invitation and felt good about my crossover appeal. Of course, I did not follow-up, given the consternation-blues of Black Power. The 1960's "high" was intoxicating, with ambitions and dreams apparent, deservingly and righteously, on the next horizon, right over the rainbow. When the reality of the high set-in, the rapid descent of unrealized hope, crushed many and reinforced cynicism in others. Retreat into the safe bosom of blackness was an analgesic. Dating white women was a no-no: it was betraying black women and the black community.

Though I would have loved to have added a notch on my sexual belt, I became resigned to my inability to publicly cross the interracial date line. Everything was everything until Joan showed up again as I sat at my post in the law school library. She wanted to know why I had not called and come over, "because I still want to finish the conversation in my living room."

"Meet me in front of the law school during my break, and we will talk," I said.

Joan returned and we strolled around the law school. Her eyes focused directly on me. I met her gaze and saw she really liked me. "Look," I began in Ernest, "I'm from Harlem. I'm black. I have not dated white women, all this," and I swept my arm around to include her and the school, "all this is new to me."

We walked slowly, because I wanted to be finished after one rotation around the building. "Look, I'm sorry, I can't handle the pressure."

"What pressure?" She inquired.

"Folks, the brothers and sisters, black folks won't appreciate me dating white women; especially black women. Dating you is not acceptable."

"But, I don't harbor any prejudice. If I am not prejudiced, why would black people be angry?" Such a naïf.

I explained as best I could in that single rotation around the block—she was pregnant with questions that could have sustained a conference if I entertained them all, but there was no time or need.

Returning to work, I passed Reggie, a black man with a white girlfriend and white friends, who felt free to join in and hangout with black folks. There were a few comments made about Reggie but no one spent any significant negative energy on him, including me. Though I did wonder how he pulled it off with such grace. Moreover, I admired his individualism and integrity. Feeling good about being honest with my white classmate and successfully maintaining the American cultural paradigm, I went to a party that weekend on Strivers Row in Harlem, a block of brownstones owned and occupied by black professionals.

I arrived at midnight with friends and the place was "jumpin'". There were black women everywhere, outnumbering the brothers, the music was blasting, and the folks were dancing with a rhythmic edge that exhilarated me. It was the kind of party with so many women that not getting two phone numbers qualified as unmitigated failure. I scanned the dimly lit room, talked and danced with a few women, but no bells went off. Ron Alexis, a friend, pointed to the other side of the room, and there she was, dancing up a storm, the best dancer in the party. The girl knew how to get down. She knew how to shake that fine round behind. Ron had the "right of first refusal" since he saw her first, but said, "You check the sister out, I can't dance like that."

Being a good dancer, I offered myself the challenge knowing I could compete with her. We danced several times and worked up a good sweat, having unmitigated fun. When a slow record was played, we danced, and I found her to be equally engaging. She gave me her phone number and I was feeling the white debacle earlier in the week was now moot.

On our first date, we walked around the West Village. I showed her the law school, and introduced her to a black male friend who smiled approvingly. I took Esther to an Indian restaurant, and then to a play at the Negro Ensemble Company. We did the usual routine of getting to know each other, and we expressed a mutual sense of humor, laughing good naturedly and naturally. We sat down in the restaurant, dined, and continued our vibrant conversation. I made a reference to the party where we met, "I had a really good time. You know how to move. You out danced everybody at the party, except me of course." We both laughed. "We use partying sometimes as a great escape from racism, where we can be physically and culturally free, even superior, false though it may be, but we black folks know how to get down," I was attempting to amuse.

Esther then waxed the mother of all waxing: "I am not black. I am white."

Shocked, stunned, frozen, mortified, jolted, mesmerized, hypnotized, all combined are not enough to describe how I felt. I lifted my chin from the table, and my vision was blurred, because my eyeballs bulged out so far that they touched my eyeglasses. I started to say something, but could only shake my head, since the gears in my brain were spinning wildly.

"My girlfriends told me you thought I was black. They told me to tell you."

"I just thought you were a high-yellow black girl."

"I know; that's what my girlfriends told me."

"Where did you learn to dance like that? Where did you grow up?" I fired in rapid succession.

She perked up proudly, "I have always been a good dancer."

Again I asked, "But where did you learn to dance like *that*?" I had never seen an ordinary white woman move like that.

"I grew up in Brooklyn. I'm Jewish. I learned the same way you did, watching and adding my own touch."

"Jewish," I thought, there must be a misplaced gene or a mutation, Jews don't dance like *that*. Now, the hard part was just beginning: I had to go out in public with a white girl, and possibly be seen by black friends. "Oh my God!" I panicked at the thought that we were going to the Negro Ensemble Company, and walking from the West Village to the East Village. This was my first date with a white girl, but there was no mens rea. How could I be so stupid? True the lights were low, she had a round behind, and out danced everyone, but now she looked unmistakably white.

My heart beat rapidly as we walked to the theatre; I felt naked with my betrayal. We arrived at the Negro Ensemble Company, a small theatre, and we sat in the top row. No one seemed to notice us, that is, all the black folks glanced over us, but no lasting stares.

I began to feel a bit more comfortable until I glanced down, and two young black women were staring intently at Esther and chattering as if she were a rare bird out of her environment and they were trying to identify the species. The two black women were talking back and forth with each other, gesturing with their hands. They would alternately look up at Esther, then turn to consult with each other about their findings. Then both heads turned up and honed in on Esther, extensively studying her with their telescopic curiosity, a conclusion was reached and one woman said while still staring straight up at Esther, "She's not black, it's a white girl." Her girlfriend's head bobbed up and down in concurring opinion. The lights dimmed as if on cue, and my critics faded to black, so to speak. I was willing to see Esther behind closed doors and closed minds, but she was not.

Mary was a voluptuous white woman who professed her love for me, but terminated our relationship despite saying, "There is nothing wrong with you." Not understanding why, I sat in the Harvard Club with Stan Futterman telling my story. He gazed at me steadily, as if the answer was never blowing in the wind, and said, "It's because you are black, Ernest." His reason was a ground ball I easily caught. I became impervious to commitment until I lived with someone ten years later.

I was at a small dinner party with three African American friends, two were women. During the evening amidst the laughter and companionship, I said, "Gail is going to move in with me." After we dispensed with the mundane of how we met and got to know each other, a good friend spoke from the well of her discontent.

"I know you have a lot of choices as a black man," Shelia began in an attempt at objective presentation. "But this!" It was lost just that quickly. Her face contorted, her eyes focused on me and her voice was low and husky. Her prosecutorial tone indicted me for treason: because Gail was white, I betrayed her and all black women. "Look, you can move in with any type of black woman, with any complexion. You can move in with a black woman who had a black black complexion, or a woman with a black brown complexion. You can move in with a black woman with a dark brown complexion, chocolate complexion, or light brown complexion. You can move in with a black woman who was light skinned, or high-yellow. You can move in with a black woman who had white skin and could pass for white," she took a deep breath to bring the core of her argument, "but, you do *not* have to move in with a *white girl*."

I felt overwhelmed and unable to move, as the verbal hurricane that passed through the room left a belligerent silence. The winds of hate blew the life out of everyone, and only our desecrated souls remained. Because of her unvarnished vitriol, Shelia's controlled rant highlighted her varnished hypocrisy. When I was dating a professional black woman, whose company I kept for an extended period, Sheila mocked me, literally laughed at me, openly questioning, "Why are you going out with such a fat girl? Everybody is talking about it. She is not even pretty."

"What else are people saying?" I certainly wanted to know. It had never dawned on me that black women would speak harshly about another black woman dating within the race, or laughing at a black man for dating a black woman.

As we collectively tried to re-focus, the vicious tongue of my prosecutor was not finished and the coup de grace leapt from her demented spirit: "It is bad enough she is a white girl, just don't tell me, *she is a Jew.*"

With her case successfully concluded, Shelia's prosecutorial demeanor dropped, she sucked her teeth, her eyes shrunk to a squint, and her neck snapped her head around, as she stared into her own hate and self-hate.

We all sat motionless, stunned by this H bomb of Hate that precipitously dropped out of her mouth, exploding into the room, the brisance devastating us all. We sat limp, lame, lethargic, leaden, for how long I am unsure. I knew some part of me was no longer alive. I was merely trying to be as human as possible with whatever I had left; for whatever lacerated my friend, penetrated and lacerated me, and so lacerated us all.

The hostess looked bewildered and privately said to me as I left, "I apologize to you, for her, on her behalf."

Though race offered no impediment to our involvement—I got along well with her father, a conservative republican—my relationship with Gail failed, because I was unable to bring the trust and intimacy needed. I returned to drifting in and out of relationships.

I met a dynamic black woman attorney at a legal forum, and I was immediately smitten. She responded to my overtures, and I invited her to dinner. She arrived first at the restaurant and when I arrived the maitre'd' said, "This way to your table Dr. Adams." I was duly impressed, and sat down with this thoughtful woman to an evening of good dining and conversation. We talked politics, education, and healthcare. Then we got lighter, and spoke about theatre and movies, and I was riding a wave of euphoria and saw nothing but good written on the wall of this now likely romantic reality. She was bright, charming, sophisticated, and attractive. She told me what movies she had seen and the ones she wanted to see. I did the same and said I really was looking forward to seeing *Schindler's List.*

She responded, "I don't want to see *Schindler's List.* I am tired of hearing about the Holocaust. I want to hear and see people talk about the African Holocaust. Jews and their Holocaust, black people don't need to see that. They talk about six million, the Jews do. But what about the twenty million who were killed in the African Holocaust? The Africans who died avoiding capture, or after capture, and transported to America. We as a people, black people, are still feeling the effects today."

All the charm and light she shone on me turned into an angry diatribe; the bitterness in her analysis was startling. "I hear you, I think you have made some good points, and I agree with some of them, but can't there be room for two horrific events?"

"I am *not* interested in the Jewish tragedy. This is not about a mere two tragedies. Jews have gone on and recovered and are doing quite well. Look at the state we are in, we were just talking about it. Our Holocaust has not ended; their Holocaust has. So until they make a movie about the African Holocaust, I don't want anything to do with any Jewish movie about a Holocaust."

Her anger roiled and rolled on, until it became a rage that would engage any person when she walked down the street of life.

I now looked past this woman, staring straight into the faces of Baruch and Samuel Goldstein, standing before Mengele, pointing the finger of death at their entire family. As their faces formed and scrolled across the relationships written on the wall of my reality, I could not imagine taking this woman to meet Baruch, Riva, Meyer and other Jewish friends. She saw my mood change, and the distance between us was irrevocable. We sat in mutual understanding, trying to gracefully depart the company we no longer enjoyed.

When I told black friends, they thought I was unnecessarily harsh. "You should see the sister, she was only expressing her opinion."

When I told three male Jewish friends, at different times, all of them thought I was being impulsive. "It was a rush to judgment…I don't think you should stop seeing her because of *that*."

I was taken aback to hear the similarity of their responses. Still, I did not waver. I understood that the logic of her thinking and emotional locus was not inclusive but exclusive, and laden with unremitting and unforgiving anger. I dated another black woman, and when I invited her to a play at Stan Futterman's synagogue, she refused to go because, "I don't want to be around them." I did not see her again.

I went out with a black woman who was an Ivy League graduate and corporate lawyer. It was a blind date setup by a mutual friend. I knew from her educational pedigree that I would have to present myself in a particular way, so I dressed "armed" for the occasion: snappy custom made blazer, pleated pants with crisp crease, designer socks, and Ferragamo shoes. On our first date, I was watching the McNeill-Lehrer news hour in her living room as she prepared to go out with me. When she was ready, she sat next to me on the couch and asked about the guest being interviewed, "Do you know who that is?" She asked as if it was part of a current events test.

"He is President Clinton's secretary of the treasury, Robert Rubin," I said. I was incensed because I had been watching the News Hour for twenty minutes. Her "Affirmative Action" question pissed me off, but I let it slide.

Then she got up and beckoned me over to her glass-enclosed curio that housed a vase, bowls, glasses and other interesting items she had collected in her travels. As she unlocked the curio, I tried to figure out why it was locked in her apartment. She took out a vase and began to speak to me slowly, as if I was mentally deficient: "This is a crystal vase. Pure crystal. From the Fortunoff store. It is not like regular glass, it's special."

"You snobby little so and so," I thought, more amused than anything. I did not bother to tell her that I had recently purchased a Waterford crystal vase. Well, I was a little peeved, but only a tad. I felt I had passed the test. Now, I wanted to get to know this woman, who I still found intelligent, attractive and charming.

I went out with a white woman who I also found to be charming. She was a model, down-to- earth, and I enjoyed her company. We were on the phone making plans and decided to go to a movie on the Eastside of Manhattan—she lived in a suburb of New York.

"Do you know how to get to the movie theatre?" She asked.

Having lived in New York City my entire life, her question was offensive and a put-down. Indignant, I slid into implosive mode and said, "I will get back to you about the specifics of when we will meet." I never called her back. She called me several times, but I did not take her calls; instead, I listened to the sincere apology that she had not intended to insult me, as my answering machine took her messages.

Both women had given me the "Affirmative Action" treatment; both had insulted my intelligence—or so it sounded to me. I anticipated the black woman, with her Ivy League credentials and prestigious position, to test me. Underneath the impressive resume, lay a woman who had doubts about her own intellectual capacity and station in life. I was aware she was projecting her inferior feelings while measuring me as a social companion. I surmised the white woman thought and treated me like I was a stupid black man, and I felt disrespected and violated. In reality, it was my own feeling that I was a stupid black man underneath my resume.

Conversion expanded my dating pool and introduced me to a new category of competition, mainly white men, where I could now compete equally with them, at least on paper, my conversion paper. When my beit din was completed, Rabbi Matalon encouraged me, "Ernie, there are so many single women at BJ, go find one." He was so enthused he wrote "single" on my conversion certificate, and he had to cross it out. And, white Jewish men introduced me to white Jewish women.

After a Friday Shabbat service, I was schmoozing with Mark, when a woman I knew casually came over and began to talk with me. Mark, quickly and without explanation, excused himself. The woman pointed to an attractive young woman and said, "Ernest, that is my daughter. I want you to talk to her."

Stunned. I had never even fantasized that a Jewish mother would recruit me for her daughter. Lovely as she was, I had an interest in someone else. Mark returned and said, "I knew what she was about to say, that is why I left."

"I had no idea what was coming."

"You didn't know?" Mark looked at me as if I was from another planet, and I was. "Welcome, to the Jewish world, Ernie."

On another occasion, I was having a conversation with a rabbi when he leaned into me and said, "My daughter is available." Junebug and Ernest Henry Adams Jr., felt good about the invitation, while recognizing the invitation was addressed to Aryeh Baruch.

Riding the Broadway bus, I sat next to a woman who was looking over law materials. She told me she was teaching a law course at a local college. My heart pounded, because this woman possessed the ineffable magic, non-quantifiable attraction, bee pollen magnetism that sent me into, "I need to know this woman" mode. She was not Jewish so my enthusiasm tempered, but the flow of energy from her had me convinced this was a black woman I desired to know. I informed her I was Jewish, and she told me that she had been to Israel, describing the trip as a wonderful experience. Thus began my dating a non-Jewish black woman.

I brought her to B'nai Jeshurun and was impressed by two things. One, she eagerly joined the dancing during the Friday night Shabbat service. Moreover, when Kaddish, a prayer for the dead was recited, she stood up to honor her sister who had recently died. Both exchanges told me she was a "player," someone who could readily fit in a Jewish environment.

I liked her so much I sought rabbinic counseling. I told Rabbi Bronstein of my budding feelings toward Cynthia. He said he would not perform an interfaith wedding, but we would be welcomed as an interfaith couple.

I said, "You are telling me my rabbi will not marry me, but if I got married outside the synagogue my wife and I would be welcomed at BJ?"

"Yes."

"That is a gross contradiction, welcoming interfaith couples but not performing the marriage ceremony."

"Yes." He looked me in the eye, assured and conflict free about his position.

I continued to push, "So what's your reasoning, how do you make sense of this?"

He continued his intense gaze but remained silent. Rabbi Bronstein let me sit in the chamber of his wordless defense until I figured out that he had "rested his case." Yet, there seemed to be a burgeoning oddity at the B'nai Jeshurun rabbis willingness to perform "commitment" ceremonies with gay couples, albeit Jewish only. Despite being a liberal synagogue that may be aptly described as, "a ghetto within a ghetto," when two gay men were on the bema having their aufruf, (synagogue pre-wedding acknowledgment) Rabbi Bronstein nervously voiced support for their upcoming commitment ceremony. The congregation became tense, stirring uncomfortably, as they observed two anxious effeminate young men standing stiffly, unsure of how they should comport themselves, and even less certain how they were being received.

As I got to know Cynthia I liked her even more, but there was one crucial impediment. She was an active member of her Episcopalian church. My simple strategy was to let her indicate if she was satisfied with her religion. It was not my place to broach such a redefining issue. I assumed it arrogant to ask a woman to give up her religion to be in a relationship with me. Even if she had said "yes," I would have said "no," because she would need to have a personal relationship with the God of the Jews for us to be in the same edition of the bible, even if not on the same page. There was a conspicuous silence as neither of us broached the subject.

When Cynthia said that a woman who served with her on the same Episcopalian church board had converted from Judaism, a Big Red Interfaith Flag waved briskly. As lovely a person as she was, I took note, a supremely cautious note, and let our relationship lapse into a genuine and respectful friendship.

When a black woman friend asked about my relationship with Cynthia, I repeated the above scenario. She was incredulous, "Are you telling me that a black woman would have to convert to Judaism to marry a black man?" She looked at me as if I was from another planet, and I was.

"Yes. That's right."

"Now, you are talking Bellevue Hospital's mental ward."

Marriages require a tremendous amount of work, and I have had more difficulty than the average person in negotiating the intimacy and compromises that naturally occur. Moreover, having grown up in an interfaith household—my mom was a Jehovah's Witness and my dad was irreligious in my youth and a Baptist in his later years—it was excruciating for me to not have my father participate in my religious learning and practice; it was a significant missing piece in the puzzle of pain I went through and, it was one more thing we did not have in common. I do not wish that for my children.

Amidst my first Simchat Torah celebration, the Torah and I embraced with sacred congruity, dancing together, spiritual and holy partners, as people danced around us in merriment. I grew tired from whirling about with the Torah, and approached another reveler who happily embraced it. Among the throngs of partying people, all of whom were in motion or about to be in motion, I stood catching my breath as revelers whizzed by me in long conga lines of frolicking fun. As the blur of the last person passed me, I suddenly found myself looking upon the lovely face of a woman I had never seen, and she returned a steady gaze of interest. The loud music and loud people prevented facile flirtatious exchange, with only our eyes in mutual conversation. We dared not look away for fear we would lose each other in the madcap scene. She exuded an intense energy that rushed over me like a waterfall, and I was wet with desire to know this most intriguing woman. She stood motionless, grasped by my impassioned curiosity. She seemed to harbor a rare magic that mesmerized me. I moved close to her so that no one could get between us; and as we continued to transfix each other, stardust gained entry. Common words breathed uncommon excitement,

"What's your name?"

"Jacqueline."

"I'm Ernest, Ernest Adams." I could feel the magic. "Quite a simcha tonight," I made sure to sound authentically Jewish. "Do you belong to BJ?"

She recently moved from New Jersey, was separated from her husband, and her divorce was due soon. Struck by the avalanche of pain that danced horas inside her as conga lines of hurt snaked through her voice, Jacqueline's surprising honesty blocked out the noise of the revelers, and I comfortably stepped into familiar territory as sincere listener, as her sadness seeped out in the midst of the surrounding joy.

On our first date, we sat in Edgar's Café and getting-to-know-you talk flowed naturally, with smiles and laughs. The commonality we shared: humor, athleticism, and political outlook, was elevated when Jacqueline asked, "Have you read, *Time and Again?*"

"Yes, I loved that book, hated the movie, but I certainly don't want to go back in time, no thank you." We basked in the mutual discovery. I was at full throttle, joyously engaged, sparks flying everywhere.

Jacqueline took her left hand, placed all her fingers together, slowly waved it back and forth between us and said, "We click with each other."

I nodded in assent.

"How old are you?"

"Fifty-one."

"You wear it very well," she said in surprise.

"Thank You. How old are you?"

"Thirty-seven."

"You make thirty-seven look good."

After another date, we returned to her new apartment, which had little furniture. I sat on a cushiony leather recliner chair, the only chair in the living room. She went to her bedroom and returned with a chair and sat in it. We chatted amiably for a while, and Jacqueline offered me something to drink. She brought back the water I requested, and the nervous sexual tension between us was not quenched. Then, Jacqueline stood up and looked down at me with questioning eyes, her contemplation was apparent. She finally dived in, "Do you mind if I join you?"

"No," I said. I sat back in the chair and it reclined oh so smoothly, squeezed to my right, flush against the side, and Jacqueline sat on the chair and me, laid her head on my chest, while my left hand played with her hair. We sat silently for a while. Then Jacqueline abruptly raised her head, lifted her torso up, and looked at me and exclaimed in amazement, "I feel comfortable with you."

Listening with the third ear, I heard her say that it was not only physical comfort, but that we were connecting on a level reserved for people who had developed trust and intimacy. Coordinating with my thoughts Jacqueline said, "I don't just mean I feel comfortable laying on your chest, I feel comfortable *with you.*" I acknowledged I felt the same. To seal this startling moment of discovery, as Jacqueline laid her head back on my chest her mouth took a detour and she brushed her lips against mine, then parted my lips with her tongue and kissed me a kiss that set my soul on fire. Jacqueline's empty apartment cried out for fulfillment, as did the emptiness in her heart.

As a subscription holder to the Metropolitan Opera I extended an invitation to Jacqueline. In the taxi returning from our first opera she quipped: "Don't think you are going to *get any* because you took me to the opera," said with a smile and sexual bluster. I simply lowered my head and peered at her over the top of my eyeglasses.

She repeated, "Well, you're not going to get *any.*"

I knew it was a matter of time. The taxi pulled up to her building. I kissed her on the cheek, and said, "Good night."

The following weekend, we dined out and returned to her apartment. She hung up our coats, rushed to me and started kissing me passionately. We went to her bedroom and the fire works of bumping and grinding continued as we rolled around, pulling and tugging on each other. Then Jacqueline lifted her butt into the air, and began to wiggle out of her jeans. I followed the path taken by the jeans, looked at those delicious thighs and the sweet spot, as the jeans came to rest at her knees. I grabbed her jeans, and to her utter shock, I pulled them back up, over the delicious thighs and sweet spot, back to her waist. Perplexed at my behavior, she looked for the obvious marks of insanity engraved on my skin.

"What are you doing?" I said. "We don't know each other well enough for that. I don't know you well enough and you don't know me well enough. Let's talk and get to know each other better. Besides, we have not talked about our sexual histories. You don't know who I have been sleeping with."

Jacqueline was dumbfounded as I continued, "I don't know who you have been sleeping with." I propped myself up on my elbow and said, "Let's talk," and thus began some Ernest conversations, some Ernest sex.

The sexual tug of war within myself was no easy matter. It was hard and harder and at times, literally the hardest temptation to overcome. But as I oozed and dripped sexual desire, the relationship I lusted after and needed did not require sexual penetration. My single male confidants thought I was masochistic, and married confidants thought I should simply, "Stick it in there. Then get to know her."

I was in a new place, having moved from the old address of My Sexual Drive and Dick Thing Boulevard. I wasn't by any means perfect, but I was trying to achieve a healthy connection in an amorous relationship, in as healthy a manner as possible.

Jacqueline and I developed a sexual relationship, and it quickly became evident she was not another woman passing through the night of my loneliness and distrust of commitment. Moreover, I began to see that she was really starting to like me, and I liked her and saw potential for a long-term relationship. But I did bring to Jacqueline's attention that her initial intent as recent divorcee was, "…to just have some fun, nothing serious," while crossing the great American racial and sexual divide. She readily agreed.

Jacqueline said I was the first black man she had slept with, and defensively added, "And if you weren't Jewish you would not be here now." I made a mental note that the first man she slept with, who was white, was not Jewish.

"How has our sleeping together affected your attitude toward other black men?"

"Nothing has changed." She fired back at me.

"Impossible!" I shot back. "There is no way your breaking the great American taboo has not impacted how you see black men on the street. Look, I am not saying that something is wrong, but you look at black men differently now, you have to."

She remained silent, and the passive demeanor clouding her face told it all, for I had never seen her in passive mode.

On the surface, Jacqueline appeared very outgoing and not affected by race. I met her friends, one of her sisters, was introduced to her parents when they came to synagogue (I did not hang out with them), was invited to meals at her home with friends, to parties with me in tow; she even bragged that her division at work looked like a "little United Nations" because she hired "minorities" from Asia and South Asia.

"Oh," she exclaimed, "I hired someone from Jamaica too."

Everything seemed just honky dory, so to speak.

Jacqueline reenacted how she told her mom, "I'm going out with a new guy, he is Jewish," she paused, "and he is black," came out of her mouth as if discharged from a shotgun. Her smile, unwittingly, was stoic, and her personal doubts made their way to the front page of the story being told.

"How did she react? What did she say?" I asked impatiently.

"She was okay about it."

"But what did your mother say?" I wanted some hard truth dished up, whether it was too hot, too cold, or just not right.

"She said my father 'was okay about it' when a cousin married a black man."

Jacqueline was not convinced as she swallowed in tepid resignation.

"He was '*okay*' about it?" I said.

"He accepted him." She did not sound a tad surer.

"Accepted him?" I repeated. "Is that like you get a diagnosis of terminal cancer and you have accepted it? Or, is it like there is a new member in the family and you choose to dissemble, to appear politically correct, and then you say you have accepted the black person?"

Jacqueline invited me to spend a week with her in the Dominican Republic, scuba diving. She became ambivalent and rescinded her invitation, then reissued it, then rescinded; this went on for some time. When Jacqueline told her father that she was going to the Dominican Republic, she reported, "He asked if you were going with me, and when I told him no, he was relieved."

Her father's attitude was important but not dispositive. Her usual effervescent wide mouth smile, subtly melted into an unctuous grin of self-doubt, and unmasked her own racial qualms.

Jacqueline and I were in bed engaged in pillow talk as she held my penis in her hand. The warm, sensual mood abruptly turned 180 degrees when she said in a throaty voice and caressing fingertips, "This is not a Jewish dick."

The sudden change in temperature sent a chill through me as I tried to hear what I just heard.

"What the? What did I just hear?" My thoughts culled every crevice of my clinical capability. I did not move as I tried to decipher the words. Uncertain, I leaned on my clinical experience to gain clarity, "What did you say?"

"You heard what I said," She replied amused.

Conceding the obvious I asked, "What do you mean by that?"

"You know what I mean," said with a smirk.

"No, no I don't know what you mean," though I knew what she was driving at from the ridicule in her voice.

With a handheld smile she said, "*They* have little dicks." She paused, oblivious to the chill that enveloped me. "*All* of them. *Jewish men have little dicks.*" She was enjoying her verbal frenzy.

Hearing it made me quiver. However, at the same instant, a smile began to form, but before my thoughts could gather, she squeezed my penis emphatically and repeated, "*This* is not a Jewish dick."

I knew she had issues with her father, from listening to her describe how her brother was always favored, and she always felt like a second-class citizen vying for attention. When her brother, a scribe in Israel, came home for visits, she often raged because, "My parents let him have his way for every ridiculous thing. They had to undo the light in the refrigerator so it would not come on during Shabbat, so fucking ridiculous."

Intellectually, I knew she was speaking from her rage at her father, Jewish men, and men qua men, and obviously some anger was directed at me. Moreover, I could hear the stereotypical aspersions she cast had "the ring of truth," yet it was slander, and not rooted in the reality of the bell curve.

But my ego spoke to me like the serpent in the Garden of Eden, and I heard and saw myself as powerful and superior with the bigger dick. I felt triumphant. I was in macho heaven. I was thee man! I was now every white woman's dream and every white man's nightmare.

I told a black woman friend who sucked her teeth with disgust, "What do *they* know?" She exclaimed, "*They* haven't fucked a lot of black men. *They don't know* what black penises are like. She only fucked you? What does she know?"

Good question.

Better question: What did she want to know?

Nancy Friday claimed in her 1973 book, *In My Secret Garden: Women's Sexual Fantasies*, that the most provocative question about being in the bedroom was: "Have you made it with a black man/woman?" She asserts that most white women have only engaged in fantasized sexual relations with black men as some of her correspondents confirm. Speaking in the first person she said: "…size is the real power of the black man fantasy…In fantasy, the 'big' black man promises to take us to that final exploration of sex, the most absolute orgasmic time it is humanly possible to experience. And then, forever after, at least we'll have known what "it" is "all about." Possibly, this is what Jacqueline wanted to know.

(Query: Why did a white male dominated racist society that defined black people as slaves and intellectually inferior create the myth of black men as sexually endowed and "superior?" What was the social function?)

When I told black male friends they chortled in vicarious triumph,

"If any of *them* want some *real dick* they can come here." This collusion based on a cultural myth, a toxic myth created by white men, was indicative and an indictment of the irrelevant image *not* needed by colored Negro black Black Afro African American men. Thus, I missed the most important meaning behind Jacqueline's revelation, while attaching myself to the false positive that my parched ego absorbed.

When I told this story to Carrie Harris, a white Jewish woman confidant, she threw her hands up in disgust and said, "Ugh, what a racist bitch. She was telling you Ernie, that you are not Jewish. Ugh! Yccch!"

When I did allow myself to examine the truth of Jacqueline's assertion, my thoughts were mitigated when she proffered a guilt-ridden mea culpa: "I know I treat you like a boy-toy, but I don't mean to… but, you are the first man I have been orgasmic with when you are inside me."

She continued to insist that her father's racial predisposition had no influence upon her.

"Let's see each other exclusively and see if we can develop into a long-term relationship. I love-"

She interrupted, "I don't need this now." She sounded frustrated. "I'm not seeing anybody else and don't want to see anyone else. But I don't want to commit to you right now.

"Then it has to end. I can't carry on like this. It has to end now." And it did.

A couple of weeks later she called, "It's a nice April evening, and I want to see you. Come over now."

She sat on the couch with her legs extended onto my lap. Still in her stockings, she asked why I had to end the relationship. When I failed to respond, she wriggled her feet, which meant she wanted them rubbed. I rubbed them in silence.

She said, "Why can't we stay like this?"

"You know why," I said. "Tell me, who else is going to rub your stinky feet?"

"Nobody rubs my feet better than you. So why can't we stay like this?"

"I agree, 'so why can't we stay like this?'" Turning her patent self-evident desire into a mirror, she took a quick look at herself, sighed, and rolled her head.

I looked at her, wondering, considering, rethinking my strict demand. Since I had been through enough hurts in love, I was not about to subject myself, again, to her irrational whims. I thought about addressing the issue of her racial ambivalence, of which we had not spoken directly. My gut, prior experience, and clinical skills told me that if her overt displays and declarations of affection were not strong enough to challenge her own racial doubts, and her need to feel accepted by her father, or, just not disappoint him one more damn time—after all she was only a girl—then my becoming a bad psychologist and shoving her conflicts down her throat would not yield anything favorable.

We said goodbye for one long last night together, wrapped in the embrace and grip of a dying love that never came to life; an abortion on the idolatrous alter of interracial love. Amid all the conflicting declarations that plaintively poured forth, in the morning I got up to leave, and she got up to escort me to the door, with my Dignity and Integrity intact.

The next time I saw Jacqueline was five months later during Rosh Hashanah, when she sought me out in Riverside Park next to the Hudson River during tashlich—a ritual of casting away our sins and to be forgiven by God. The first thing I noticed was her weight gain. Her breasts were enlarged and her upper body was now broad and thick. I chuckled to myself, "She really misses me." We left Riverside Park together, chatted amiably, and when we arrived at Whole Foods on 89th Street, I said, "This is where I get off," and our interlude ended.

The next substantive conversation I had with her was on the first day of Rosh Hashanah, 2001. As the Torah was carried around the B'nai Jeshurun synagogue, I marched in the procession. When I passed by, Jacqueline smiled and waved. At the end of services, I helped Freddy, the gabai, roll the Torah to the next scheduled reading. When we finished, only a handful of stragglers lingered at the back of the sanctuary. Jacqueline was one of them. I knew she was waiting for me, but did not understand why. I walked by, stopped and turned, our eyes met and exchanged doubtful greetings; she remained in place with arms folded and fingers clutching the sides of her arms, as if she were trying to give herself some tactile comfort. Now fully engaged, our eyes silently reminisced, and when I turned to leave, on cue, she followed me—without a word spoken. We reached the steps, and the sun shone brightly on us. "Let's take a walk," I said. She followed and we began walking down Central Park West.

"Look, I don't understand you. Sometimes you blow hot and speak to me; sometimes you blow cold and pass without saying a word, like last month at shul. I don't get it. Have I offended you in some way?"

"Can I be honest?"

"Of course you can."

"You sure?"

"So what is it you want to say?"

"Remember when I stopped going out with you, the reason I did was because you were such an angry person. You had a lot of anger I could not deal with."

I was shocked at what I was hearing. "Why do you speak to me sometimes, and other times you don't," I persisted.

Instead of answering, she began to address why we broke up three years earlier.

"Remember that time we went to the movies about those young lovers?" She did not wait for an answer. "It was your attitude about them that was so off, so angry…" She began to describe in detail as if we had just seen the movie last night. I listened to every word she said, but I was trying to understand why she was saying this now, three years later. I remembered going to that movie, but it wasn't particularly memorable. She never mentioned any of this when we stopped seeing each other. But she told a mutual friend who informed me that she said, "'Ernest was way too serious,' "Jacqueline said she couldn't handle it at the time because it was too soon after her divorce."

Now Jacqueline said something that jolted both of us. "I loved you so much, loved you so much. Really loved you."

The force of her words, from the center of her suppressed emotions, caused her to become immobile. Her eyes widened in shock at her self-revelation; she rocked back and forth in place, as if a volcanic explosion was shaking her. She was aware of what she said but the shock, I surmised, was her non-conflicted soul and desire being set free, however briefly, but at last, free. Detached from all the barriers and defenses she had so ably erected, more deep words of truth bubbled up. "I love you, so much I love you."

"So it wasn't my imagination or projection," I thought. As a psychologist it was obvious that she spoke "involuntarily," that she did not consciously seek me out to confess her deep and long-term love for me. But I was cool, because I was not convinced. We reached the corner of Ninety-Third Street and she waved her hand toward Central Park. "Do you want to walk in the park?" she asked.

"Sure."

She began to sing my praises as we strolled. "When I saw you marching around the synagogue today, you looked like you were in sync, one with yourself, there was no separation. This is you. Judaism is you. This is your home. I could see that you were no longer angry, that you are at peace with yourself. I'm not there yet, not like you are. I want to be where you are, at peace with myself."

I am now stone-cold flabbergasted at all this lauding of my character and conversion from angry man to man at peace. When I informed her that my father died in December 2000, she responded, "If I would have known, I would have come to the funeral," and offered as part of her condolence a question that rocked me.

"Did your father's death have something to do with your becoming less angry?"

"No," I said, but something inside was stirring that was saying, "Yes."

As my thoughts coalesced, I realized, surprisingly, that when I had eulogized my father, I discovered that I was more like him than my mother—I interviewed friends and relatives about him and I had always thought I was more like my mom because she was not a drinker, and was a consistent presence at home. I asked my cousin Ronnie how he saw me, "You were always more like him, never like her."

The truth never rang so loudly. Every part of me was in agreement. I realized that my being ignored by my father when I was a child had made me so angry that I was unable to see a significant part of myself, how much I was like my dad. It is frightening to think I could have gone through my entire life misperceiving a core part of my identity.

Jacqueline agreed to go to Kol Nidre with me. I was exuberant, and the power of "fairy dust" began to take shape as a fairy tale; however, I retained some "skeptical dust," because the specter of her father's disapproval cast a long white shadow. I decided now was the proper time to broach the issue of her father's approval. I called to discuss it, but when her answering machine picked up, I left the following message: "I'm glad we are going to Kol Nidre together. Don't worry, your father will approve."

She called me back and exploded, "What are you talking about? Why did you say that? Why? Now *you* have ruined everything, ruined everything; *Everything*!" She was livid with disappointment. "Now, I'm not going to Kol Nidre with you. I'm going to go with *him*," referring to her current boyfriend.

"If that's what you want, that's what you want, it's okay by me," I said. When I see you at Kol Nidre introduce me to him."

I saw Jacqueline as she left Kol Nidre and walked toward her. She saw me and began to back up, her eyes wide with fright, as if I was Dracula. I turned and went on my way. Currently, I intermittently see her on the Upper Westside

It would be three years later when genuine love would knock on the door of my intimacy.

Becoming a Bar Mitzvah Boy
The Merging
Black/African American & Jewish Experience
The Emerging
Black/African American Jewish Voice

> Hence the victims of the great sin of slavery became, in this subtle psychological inversion, the embodiment of sin, exemplified in the Negro's… failings, indignities, and mistakes. For some two hundred years African Americans have struggled against accepting or above all internalizing this prescribed identity, this psychological curse.
>
> ***David Brion Davis***

More than anything, I wanted to be a Bar Mitzvah boy, a black man's desire after a half century of living. For reasons I still don't fully understand, a spiritual hole, settled into an elegiac sadness that had to be filled, to rest my spiritual yearning.

My Hebrew teacher Michal asked, "How are you going to control your anxiety on the bema?" I had not given it much thought but I began to doubt myself. After making confidence-building statements to myself about my oratorical skills, my fears were not allayed. I telephoned my mom and reluctantly admitted, "Ma, I'm nervous about getting up in front of all those people and giving my sermon."

"Boy, what you got to be nervous about?" She retorted without equivocation. Sucking her teeth when annoyed, I could "hear" mom turn her head away from me in disbelief. She could not conceive that I had any doubts about my speaking ability, or any ability.

Mom reminded, "You've done this before. Don't you remember? I used to get you ready for your talks at the Kingdom Hall."

I began giving talks, readings from the scriptures and relating my understanding, when I was nine.

"You don't remember, Junior? I gave you the broomstick. I had you rehearse your talks with the broomstick as the microphone in your nine year old hands."

Now I could hear her smiling and I vaguely recalled practicing with the broomstick. I felt a little stupid for raising the issue of self-doubt since there was no discussion or room for discussion. Not even, "You can do it son, I have faith in you." Mom's absolute confidence led me to say, "Yeah, I have done this before, I can do it, I will do it."

I rehearsed my dvar Torah with Robin Reif. As I began to read Robin's eyes slowly widened then retracted in surprise as if she had heard a new discovery. I was comforted by the soft pastel colors and soft light in Robin's living room juxtaposed to her keen attention, incisive questions and observations. I would read a few paragraphs and she would hold up her hand signaling me to stop; her eyes rolled as she analytically dissected what I said. Nodding ever so slowly Robin said, "The straw, the straw, people will respond to the straw." She also said I had a natural delivery that was effective, "You cannot teach that to people, either you have it or you don't." And she added emphatically: "You have it."

With my mother's imprimatur, I was able to crystallize Robin's comments and internalized them without distortion. When Robin was a Bat Torah and gave her dvar Torah, she found it comforting to look out into the congregation to see a friendly face nodding affirmatively, and she promised me the same. And when I looked down from the bema during my dvar Torah, there was the beautiful face and beautiful soul of Robin, smiling support and encouragement. Thank you very much, Robin Reif.

When I met with Rabbi Bronstein he said, "Your speech should be no more than fifteen minutes, it's a lot of time, twenty minutes at the most, more than that people become restless, distracted, we lose them." He had me read my dvar Torah. When I expressed concern it may last more than twenty minutes, Rabbi Bronstein shrugged: "So it is longer than twenty minutes, it's going to be great." I knew it was hyperbole, but I appreciated it. Then he said, "Since you speak a lot about what white people have done, what about putting in what black people can do to make things better between the races, to balance it out?"

"No," I snapped, "this isn't a political speech, this is a dvar Torah." I bristled. "Balance. There is not anything that a black person can do to balance the history of injustice we have suffered. Black people did not create racism and discrimination; white people have to balance out racism and discrimination by stopping it. The onus is not on black people, it is on white people and the institutions they control."

"It can be difficult to get to know black people, they aren't always open."

"That's true, but it wasn't black people who destroyed the trust."

Rabbi Bronstein nodded slowly with a tentative overlay in his eyes that failed to hide his thorough surprise at my "blacklash" and its intensity. He blandly mouthed the words, "I understand." His rabbinic posture of certainty and control dropped. I thought Rabbi Bronstein "got it." That he understood that white people have to own their racial attitudes and behaviors.

I recounted this exchange with Barbara, and she also said I should include what black folks can do to make things better. When I said that Rabbi Bronstein understood my criticism and agreed with me, she looked at me incredulously, smiled a bland smile with a tentative overlay in her eyes. I realized she did not believe he agreed with me. Rather, I now knew Rabbi Bronstein attempted to appease me, and in the process *we* merely became another failed statistic in the difficult world of honest racial talk. Rabbi Bronstein had been sitting three feet from me, but at that moment, we inhabited different worlds and worldviews.

But as the days passed, and as I wrote and re-wrote, honing my dvar Torah, my blacklash lessened and I replayed Rabbi Bronstein's suggestion and heard his deeper message. This led me to write: *"So how do black people find redemption in the twenty-first century? We can open ourselves up, however cautiously, but open we must, to meet and greet any human being of good will, regardless of race, sex, ethnic origin or sexual orientation, to gain the necessary strength, together, to fight racism and all the Pharaohs that present themselves. We only have control over our internal Pharaoh, that is, if you want to change the world, change yourself. The real power of free will is to be able to see the holiness in the other, to be able to freely choose those we love and the reasons why."*

I raised another concern with Rabbi Bronstein that I found vexing, whether to invite Shelia, a friend of twenty-five years to my Bar Mitzvah. I recalled the incident that occurred at a dinner party eight years earlier that left me bereft of trust, but whose disturbing comments now loomed lethal. Shelia was not only critical of my living with a white woman, but was outraged at the possibility that she could have been a Jew. Our friendship was not the same after that, and we only saw each other intermittently.

While preparing for my Bar Mitzvah, this conversation resurfaced, but a more recent memory screamed forth. When I literally bumped into Sheila while food shopping, I told her of my conversion even though I knew the grapevine had already informed her. In Hebrew I said, "I am a Jew," then said it in English.

"Congratulations, that is very nice, as long as you are happy, I'm happy for you."

"I didn't think you would be."

"Why?" She asked surprised. "It may not be for me, but if you are happy, it's okay."

I could have left well enough alone, but I knew something sinister was lurking. So I pushed, but not much. "I know you and you know me, so tell me what you *really think*."

"Are you sure? *You really want to hear*?"

"Yes. You know me, give me the truth."

Countenance unchanged, she spewed, "I understand black people having notions of equality, we are susceptible to the notion that we are all the same. I can see black people joining the Moonies, even joining Jim Jones' cult and taking the poison; that I can see, but a black person becoming a Jew, now that's bizarre."

I got what I wished for.

Pointing the finger of responsibility at me, Rabbi Bronstein said, "That is your decision."

After the Bar Mitzvah, he asked if I had invited Shelia and I said, "No." I concluded that Shelia's unmitigated anti-Semitism left no room for us to have a viable relationship; that my hard-earned joy, comfort, and newly found ease at being in an expanding world, would be compromised.

As the Bar Mitzvah drew near, to tamp down my increasing anxiety, I rehearsed ad nauseam; it was the only way for me to feel confident. I did not want to "think" while reading from the Torah and Haftorah and giving my dvar Torah. The weekly Torah reading is read every Monday and Thursday at the morning minyan.

I read Torah Thursday morning before my Bar Mitzvah. The custom at B'nai Jeshurun is for the Bar Mitzvah to briefly highlight his dvar Torah when the morning service is concluded. After the Thursday morning minyan was finished, I was waiting to be asked to highlight my dvar Torah. I looked in anticipation to the rabbinic student who led the morning minyan. The regulars at the morning minyan often times make the initial inquiry. This day, only the usual friendly chatter was forthcoming. I searched their faces and there seemed to be a "conspiracy" of silence.

I have no recollection when a young Bar Mitzvah was not asked to highlight his dvar Torah. My observations told me this was the time when rehearsal took place, and all potential errors and anxiety could be exercised, and if lucky, exorcised. I believed it was decided that I would not be asked because of how I had shown some anxiety on prior occasions. Only the rabbis would have that much influence. I believe it was Rabbi Bronstein who made the decision, since he was working with me.

I was also present on a few occasions when Bat Torah groups—adult women who did not have a Bat Mitzvah—read the Torah at the morning minyan and were asked to highlight their dvrei Torahs. I witnessed the cantor, Ari Priven, say to a woman who had one foot on the bema and about to go up to read the Torah, "I know you are a little nervous, but it is okay. It is not that hard." So as I was waiting to be asked about my dvar Torah, the conspiracy of silence was commentary, as it grew deafening. The thinking, I believe, was that the less anxiety I experienced in the synagogue prior to my Bar Mitzvah, the better.

At first glance, it may have seemed like a nice gesture, but I asked myself if patently nervous thirteen-year-olds were asked to highlight their dvrei Torahs, why not ask someone forty years older? Despite my anxiety, I am not a fragile person, nor do I come across as one. The fact that I volunteered to be a Bar Mitzvah—let alone a Jew—and embraced doing it alone, was conclusive of my being treated no differently than a thirteen-year-old child.

I am unsure what the collective thinking or specific individual thinking was, but race was a factor, but not racism qua racism, but race as a benign intervening variable, that is, no malicious intent and no malicious results, on this occasion. *What if I was a student or employee of my white synagogue mates? Would their expectations impact my learning? Would it impact their teaching? Would their perceptions impact my ability to being hired? Fired? Receiving a promotion or raise?*

These are people I prayed, laughed, and cried with, and shared holy experiences. They welcomed me into their arms and homes lovingly. However, if I were not black they would have asked me to highlight my dvar Torah. I was not asked because as white people, they had felt, I hypothesized, uncomfortable acknowledging my anxiety, because it may signal self-recognition of their struggling notions of black inferiority.

Ari Priven could freely acknowledge the Bat Torah woman's palpable anxiety because of the *felt underlying belief* that they were equals. However, during prior morning minyans, the rabbinic intern critiqued my Torah reading. She was not afraid to offer criticism, and I welcomed it. Rabbi Bronstein could have suggested that I prepare a brief summary.

... most American institutions and most Americans deny racial feelings of any kind. As a psychologist, I would label it denial, a form of darkness, plague number nine. You cannot have racism in institutions and yet have people who do not have racial feelings and attitudes. It does not mean you are a racist because you have racial feelings... but it does mean your internal Pharaoh will not allow you to own the complexity of your feelings.

Parenthetically, I am struck by my having been annoyed when white people were asking too many questions about my dvar Torah; then I became annoyed because no questions were asked. Ironically, I would have felt more like a man if they had treated me like a regular boy, but the unintended result was that I felt more like a "boy" because I was not treated like an ordinary man, a Jewish man, but a black man.

But how do I know this happened the way I perceived it? I don't know if it happened in total that way, but something like it happened. One comment was made that suggested my perception was accurate.

The next day at the Sunday morning minyan, Mark, who has always been genuinely kind and helpful to me said, "I'm glad *we* did not ask you to tell us about your dvar Torah at Thursday's morning minyan, because it was so complex and rich *you could not have been able to summarize it.*"

Excuse me, but wasn't that a condescending attitude?

Mark's projection? Rationalization? Honest Assessment? Guilt? Maybe all of the above, but the latter for sure. I think Mark's "guilt offering" was clearly an insult. If the insult was not clear, let me clarify: it was the presumption I could not summarize *my* dvar Torah, the one *I wrote* without the rabbi's help; that reflected "*my*" story that I "discovered" in the Torah. Most importantly, I was not given the opportunity to fail or succeed and stereotypical presumption gained more life force.

Moreover, Mark had no idea that he had insulted me; he had a beaming smile as he continued, "What I loved about your dvar Ernie..."

We stood face-to face, but he could not hear or see himself, therefore, he could not hear or see me. This blind spot, this "white hole" from which white people think, see and hear, is their Mount Sinai to climb. When black Americans experience this whiteness, this "friendly fire," it is potentially destructive, especially to mutual trust, which is the cornerstone of a healthy relationship.

Sometimes, I become enmeshed in the maelstrom of my racial sensitive spots. This leaves me in a quandary, because with no internal platform to stand on, and absent a language, such conversation is rarely addressed. And I retreat because I feel misunderstood, angry, unsafe, and believe my racial concerns cannot be knowable; consequently, I hide my true feelings and a lock-down mode follows. The white person does not have a clue, and if he did, his parallel deficits don't permit him to begin to address the issues. Thus, the racial gulf is both widened and reinforced, even among friends.

I knew that most of my black friends would feel uncomfortable entering a synagogue. One Shabbat morning I saw a black friend as I headed to shul. I wore a hat and was carrying my talit bag. We greeted each other and he asked, "Where are you going?"

"I'm going to synagogue," I said.

"Where are you going?" He sounded perplexed.

I reiterated, "I'm going to synagogue."

Pointing to my talit bag he asked, "How are you traveling to Africa with that little bag?"

Now I am puzzled. "What are you talking about? Africa? I'm going to synagogue."

"How are you going to Senegal with only that little bag?"

Masking my incredulity, I took off my cap so he could see my yarmulke and explained, "I am going to services to worship."

While sitting with an invited African American friend, Ivan, at a Friday night Shabbat service, he poked me in my ribs and whispered, "Ernest, is my hat on right?"

"It looks just fine," I said, referring to his yarmulke.

Several minutes later he looked around and poked me again. "Are we the only black people here?"

I tried to relax him and replied with what I thought was a sense of humor, "If you look to your left and three rows back, there is one, and if you look five rows in front and to your right there is another one." He craned his neck to find some solace. I returned to praying.

A few minutes later, I received another poke, "Ernest, Ernest, Ernest," he whispered in utter amazement, "I don't detect any hostility!"

"You are right," I confirmed.

William Haden, a friend of thirty years was a no-show to the Bar Mitzvah. Two years later he called and asked, "How can you be a black Jew and not be with the black Jews? I thought you went off, I ain't gon lie, thought you went way off. I felt like you betrayed your people, if you wanted to be a Jew, a black Jew, you could have gone to a black synagogue. I felt like you were separating yourself from your people, you left your people."

"I did not separate myself from anyone. *You left me.* I did not leave you."

His head jerked from the force of the logic but he continued, "How many black people belong to your synagogue? Two, maybe? I couldn't be a token. I wanna be some place where people look like me. I applaud you because you are doing what will be done in the future. You always did things differently. You did not let people define you. If you look at it like that, that is the way it should be, people should be able to belong to any group and race should not be a factor. I believe in the universal ideal, but I couldn't be no token."

"I am not a token. You can come join if you want to. If not, you can come to a service to see what it is really like."

"You think you did something," he said angrily. He leaned forward with a smirk. "You ain't did nothin'. How could you change to what you already were? Ethiopia, Solomon, Bath Sheba, Africans! Look at the Lembas in Africa. We're the original Jews. How could you become what you already were?" The smirk grew larger, as he grew smaller in my eyes.

I had three interactions with family members that provided profound insight to my compromised confidence. Two occurred while I prepared for my Bar Mitzvah, and the third happened earlier in my life, but its meaning crystallized during this period.

One evening I came home from classes at Bronx Community College and found my dad sitting at my desk with the lamp shining on his reading materials. He had propped his elbow on the desk as he read preparatory materials for a promotional exam. He looked rather odd, so focused, studying at my desk. Never in my life had I seen him study for anything or even mention studying for anything. The scene jolted me.

"Pops, what cha doin' man?" I said with humor.

He rubbed his hand over his face and when he met my eyes I saw something in the soul of my dad I had never seen before or since: the look of terror and self-doubt, the look of "whiteness." I walked over to him, placed my hand on his shoulder and he looked up seeking comfort. In a transparent reversal of roles, I spoke to his unspoken concern: "You are going to do okay, Pop. You are going to pass," I said like a father.

"Thanks son," he said like a son.

While preparing for my Bar Mitzvah, Uncle Charlie at age eighty sought to have his will written and asked my advice. I sent him to a synagogue mate Stanley Futterman, who said to me, "Your uncle is very intelligent and has a great memory for detail. He would have made a good lawyer."

Uncle Charlie had been taken out of high school to work on his father's farm and he did not graduate. Filled with pride, I rushed to relay Stan's assessment.

"Your lawyer, Stan Futterman, a Harvard law school graduate, thought you would have made a good lawyer," I said, beaming.

Shocked. His face contorted with disgust and he said with gargoyle conviction, "What! A dumb nigger like me? A lawyer? Get out of here!"

His words rocked me. I staggered as the squeamishness bloated me. My soul, given to me by God, felt fouled by Uncle Charlie's absolute exclusion of an intelligent sign of life in his body. I often wonder how such a seed gets planted in the soul of a person, and burrows deep, where there is no water, no light, yet it not only grows but flourishes as it envelops and develops into the human core. Was there resistance? What can resist such an insidious cauterization?

Uncle Charlie's deep belief was the result of a racial cancer that was created by "whiteness" and propagated throughout the American culture until it became as axiomatic as, "All men are created equal." He lived his entire life with this deep belief. Shortly after his will was completed, Uncle Charlie laid down for an afternoon nap, and it stretched into eternity. He died peacefully, though he was not afforded a peaceful life. The racial cancer obliterated his positive belief system, and he was not able to have a minimal awareness of his natural abilities. Although it did not kill him, it maimed him critically and he lived and died fully believing, "What! A dumb nigger like me? A lawyer? Get out of here!"

One thing I have come to fully understand, from having lived it, is that most black people want and expect to produce like white Americans, notwithstanding the disparity of allotments of straw. And we suffer, in part, because we alternate between exclusive self-blame, to exclusively blaming whites and racism. No peace is found in either place, and neither is the absolute truth, which is not absolute.

What a waste in American life. Whiteness: Detrimental to us All.

This racial sotto voce has accompanied me all my life, whispering loudly in one ear how utterly dumb and stupid I am, while the other ear has struggled mightily, desperately, to hear the voice of my true natural intelligence and humanity. This ongoing Whispers War has wreaked emotional havoc that has penetrated every strand, every fragment, and every crevice of my life.

In the here and the now, the deadly Whispers transudes with horrendous results: confidence impaired, ambitions challenged, vision of self narrowed; perception of the environment as suspicious, uncertainty in how to negotiate the world, slowing down every task I undertake, making me feel feeble and more than inept, which causes more pain that I cannot remember and sometimes resulting in failures temporary and permanent.

During a conversation about my Bar Mitzvah, Mom said, "Junior, is your synagogue called the shul?"

"My synagogue is a shul, it is another name for a synagogue. Why do you ask?"

Mom said when she first came to New York she lived with her Aunt Alonya, who was the superintendent for a building in the Bronx and the domestic for a synagogue in the same block. Mom used to help Aunt Alonya in the shul. On Friday nights, at the start of the Jewish Sabbath, mom and Aunt Alonya served as paid shabbos goys—non Jews who perform duties prohibited on the Sabbath, like turning lights on and off.

Aunt Alonya placed an advertisement in the local newspaper, the Bronx News, and an Irish woman, Mrs. Fitzpatrick, who lived on the Grand Concourse, hired Mom as a domestic. "It was just about what everybody could get in those days," Mom needlessly defended. She earned ten dollars a week for four years with Mrs. Fitzpatrick, "That was good money Junior, a lot of folks weren't gettin that," she recalled with pride.

Black women would gather on a Bronx street corner waiting to be picked up for daily domestic work at fifty cents an hour. They learned to bring their own clocks because their employers were notorious for setting back the clocks in their homes, to extract more work for less pay. "Mostly it was the Jews who picked up, but it was everybody too, it was the Irish and Jews who lived there," Mom said.

She recalled cleaning the home of a Jewish woman for eight hours who did not want to pay her the four dollars. The woman complained to Aunt Alonya, who asked if her home was thoroughly cleaned. She reported it was a good job, so Aunt Alonya exhorted, "Pay her then if it was a good job." Mom got paid.

"Junior, I remember cleaning that woman's house, the base boards were filthy, she had a dirty ole house. I took my time and cleaned everything. *I wasn't going nowhere.*"

Indeed. "*Nowhere.*" This was my mom's window to the world, and this is what she saw when she looked out into the future. My mom already resided in the Basement, indeed. When she moved in is anybody's guess.

It was this mind-set, this view from the window-pain, that prohibited mom from attending college, not the anticipated inadequate wardrobe from her father H.C., I conjecture.

My mom's Weltanschauung, her self-perception, was a "message," a "sign," typed out in large bold subtle behavior that complemented the rejecting signs in the American windows of both our youth. This was my psychological heritage, handed down to my sisters and me; it became a fundamental part of my makeup and outlook on life, and co-sponsored my anxiety to wreak havoc: to pummel and punish me each and every time, for each and every thought, for each and every step, for each and every breath I took that would lead me out of the Basement. In reality, my chances for leaving the Basement were dead on arrival when I was born.

The heart and soul of America was purposely constructed by the intellectually gifted and morally deficient, to house the African slave in the American Basement. Defined as subhuman and its natural corollary inferior, the master and slave lived in their proper places. The Civil War violently liquidated that relationship, and for a momentous moment, Hope was still, breathless, as the now Americanized African slave, silently sang in prayer, "Go Down Moses," in repose for a land of Milk and Honey to ascend to America.

The world's best known Redeemer failed to appear as urged in the Negro spiritual classic: "Let My People Go." For sure, the slaves were set free, but there is no doubt, my people were not let go. The opaque window opened in 1865, let out the suffocating slave air, providing a hairsbreadth of unprecedented opportunity for the "new" Americans to begin life as fully endowed human beings and citizens. The end of the short-lived Reconstruction period saw the restructure and reinvigoration of an altered but deadly Southern hierarchy, and the "new" Americans were redefined and reified as inferior to whites, yet again. In the white Christian spirit of the times, the individuals who helped rejigger the South were, in a profane hoax, known as, the "Redeemers."

This horrific redemption of American life set the historical menu from which all Americans currently choose; it was and is this split redemption, this "unfinished American revolution," that set the moral and spiritual table from which all Americans dine. With this tainted nineteenth century meal remaining on our plates, it has poisoned us all, leaving our sight and hearing severely damaged and judgment convoluted, while remaining self-righteous and damn right in how we perceive the *other*. The passing down of the Redeemers inferior prescription by mom, even as she loved, nurtured and protected me in the nest, made the imbibing of this [white] social poison invisible, odorless, but not colorless—Negro, colored, black, Black, Afro, African American fingerprints were and are everywhere.

I was weakened, severely compromised, down, but not out. I wanted to be different. And yes, I became different. With the spirit and courage of my Grandmother Hattie, I stole Hope, Perseverance, Self-Confidence and smuggled them across the psychic border past the signs that loudly warned: No Admittance to Colored Children.

With paper-thin confidence as long as a shoestring, the world was daunting as it dangled the American dream just out of my reach. Unable to turn inward to my family for support, my furtive ambitions, like fresh fruit not harvested, began to bruise and soften. If I did not rewrite the American script, the American nightmare I found as I entered into the greatest and darkest game of all, Existence, an anonymous implosion would have occurred, and I would have been another dead nigger with good riddance from the American scene.

As I looked through the sliver of light in the Basement, I snatched a glimpse of everything I wanted and needed to do, saw and knew everything I wanted out of life, what I was capable of, if given only half a chance, any chance—so I determined, made a promise to myself, long before I had the words, that I wanted **to be**, that I would not tell the world, again and again and again.

I kept my promise to myself to myself, hid my dreams within my dreams as I crawled, then stood, wavered, then walked, however crippled, through the Harlem corridors of America. No one was hearing my very audible cry, no one was seeing my transparent dreams, they only looked and looked and looked, again.

The shred of confidence in my possession I grasped tightly lest I disappear. Palpitations of my ambitions beat so rapidly, everything I read was difficult to understand; everything I understood was blurred as I read, and words fumbled out of my mouth. I moved in slow motion. I had to. I had no direction. I had no directions. I had to create and direct my directions, as I paved the roadway then walked it: Alone.

My mom's off-the-cuff comment was a revelation that was tantamount to an "admission" of her feeling inferior and acceptance of the American racial status quo. It was now transparent why she moved into and stayed in a Basement apartment that she found debilitating; why she did not support Florita entering a school for gifted children; why she steered Florita to be a secretary for the City of New York; why she wanted me to get a "good job" as a supermarket clerk after high school; why she did not know that the City College of New York, two blocks from our home, was a tuition free institution; why she argued so intensely against me going to college. Now I understood why my father and Uncle Charlie became taxi drivers after successfully completing training as automobile mechanics; why my father had terror in his eyes when he prepared for a New York City promotional exam; why it took me multiple times to pass two New York State licensing exams. It also provided "structure" for my amorphous and prodigious feelings of inferiority, incompetence and resulting anxiety; the Whispers War origin was now in plain sight. Mom was blind and deaf to the possibilities and potentials of herself, my dad and her children; it was a terrifying world in which to be a black mother, a black father, a black child, the terrifying world of America; to be unable to support and provide the necessities for living as any loving mother would like, she possessed the passive energy to only dream fragmented dreams, while being a strong mother who kept the Adams household intact. Though she felt inferior, Mom carried herself with Dignity and Self-Respect, and her Integrity was inviolable.

Mom, Dad, and Uncle Charlie were not unique. They were ordinary and extra-ordinary black folks—truly, the greatest generation. Due to Mom's unintended revelation, which sparked a comprehensive understanding of disparate situations, the darkness that shaded my Existence began to lift even further, and the morning light that rose lessened my confusion, and made my convoluted self-image, less so.

An Orthodox Conversion
It Was So Nice I Had To Do It Up Twice
Redundant? Redux? Ridiculous?

Ernie, you had two conversions to become one Jew?

Anonymous

Due to the warning that "Orthodox Jews are rigid and racist," I was reluctant to associate with them. At B'nai Jeshurun Orthodox rabbis were invited as guest speakers and none presented with any racist credentials—words or actions. Their Torah teachings were inspiring and learned, especially Orthodox Rabbi Chaim Seidler Fedler of UCLA Hillel.

When I began studying Judaism, I purchased books primarily from Westside Judiaca on Broadway and Eighty-Eighth Street, owned by the Selczer family. One day I walked into the store and Shlmo Selczer, lyrically said, "Hey brother, how are you?" It was so natural, like the intrinsic song and greeting call of a bird, and sung with such soulful good will, it immediately resonated in my black safety zone and, I felt safe. His mother's lovely grace, easy charm, and pleasing smile, were front door signs that I was welcomed. Courteous treatment is all I know from all the employees after eleven years of shopping at West Side Judiaca. Fortunately, I did not know the Selczers were an Orthodox family, because I may have missed out on some wonderful people.

Feeling less unnerved, I went to hear Rabbi Ephraim Buchwald—Director of National Jewish Outreach at Lincoln Square Synagogue—speak at the Chabad center in midtown Manhattan. I arrived early, sat down, looked around and men in black were plentiful.

A man with a yarmulke greeted me and said, "Are you Jewish?"

"Yes," I answered.

"Are you single?" He asked.

"Yes, I am."

He stated: "Go to Lincoln Square, there are a lot of single women at that shul. You will be well received."

I clung to my seat as my head seemed to spin, "Do you belong to Lincoln Square?" I asked.

"I used to, but I moved to Westchester."

The lecture began and Rabbi Buchwald did not present like a racist. A few years later, I sat next to Rabbi Buchwald at the wedding of Mark Shapiro and Miyuki Yussa—he converted her—and told him of the slanderous language that frightened me into not attending Lincoln Square. "Really," he said with curious surprise. "Who said such a thing?" He was unruffled.

Marty Radburd, a friend at B'nai Jeshurun, joined the Orthodox Carlebach Synagogue. He encouraged me to visit Carlebach. Reluctantly, I accepted Marty's invitation. Rabbi Sammy Intrator led his enthusiastic congregation from the bema. The service was spiritually kinetic, the clapping, singing and dancing aroused me but I felt constrained being the only Jew who was black. Rabbi Intrator stepped off the bema, came down the aisle greeting people, and when he reached the row where I sat, he reached out to me, shook my hand and pulled me into the aisle encouraging me to dance; we danced a duet, then another person joined us for a trio: I have not stopped dancing at Carlebach.

Rabbi Naphtali Cintron became the new leader of Carlebach. An intrinsically warm and personable man, he has always made me feel welcomed. I began attending Carlebach and hanging out in Orthodox circles.

Rabbi Baruch Goldstein said, "Ernie, if you hangout with the Orthodox, you will become Orthodox." I resisted his statement, saying that it was the Torah learning that held my attention. But my continuing association led me to consider becoming Orthodox.

One Friday Shabbat Rabbi Fund was the guest speaker at Carlebach and I was so thoroughly impressed by his dvar Torah, I returned Shabbat morning to experience another helping of his teaching. I decided to try this Orthodox rabbi's weekly parasha class, the weekly bible reading. Six years later, I am still engaged as Rabbi Fund unpacks the Torah during his weekly class.

Rabbi Fund invited me to attend The Flatbush Minyan, his synagogue in Brooklyn. After the service I went to his home for a Shabbos meal. Present was his wife, his mother, two of his married children and their spouses, an adolescent daughter, and a few grandchildren. With a friendly smile Rabbi Fund's mother said, "Shalom, you've been here before haven't you?" She was trying to make me feel comfortable and it worked. I felt relaxed, readily joined in the conversation, and, it was oh so normal. The next time I saw Rabbi Fund he had a broad grin and said, "You were a big hit at my house, everybody liked you." And, I liked everybody.

I visited the Flatbush Minyan several times and stayed in the homes of people in the community. Everyone made me feel welcomed. I was surprised to meet a black woman who had been converted by Rabbi Fund. Despite his affection for me, Rabbi Fund said, "You are not a real Jew," because I did not have an Orthodox conversion.

Michael Sholomovitch suggested I attend the class of Rabbi Simon Jacobson. He is a brilliant teacher, who teaches the Torah from a psycho-social-spiritual perspective, and applies his teachings to everyday life. Sometimes I got so intensely involved in the learning that a few times I wore my yarmulke home unaware, until it fell off when I got ready for bed. I made an appointment to talk to him.

When I informed synagogue friends they all said, "You're going to 770." When I surfaced from the subway, I began to look around and the bustling commerce of black hats black beards and black suits in front of 770 Nostrand Avenue was an address in itself. Rabbi Jacobson and I discussed my journey to Judaism, and my developing interest in Orthodoxy. I said, "I am considering becoming Orthodox. I don't know, but I don't think I can do it *all*."

He said, "*No one*," there was the slightest pause, "*does it all*."

During my second visit I told Rabbi Jacobson of an Orthodox woman I was going out with who stopped dating me because, "You are not observant enough, you don't know enough."

"She was scared and used that as a reason to stop seeing you," he said. "If you are still interested in going out with her, this is what you can say."

"I'm not interested in seeing her anymore," I said nodding my head. I discovered dating in the Orthodox world was like dating anyplace else.

I began attending Congregation Ramath Orah, a modern Orthodox synagogue in the same block where I lived. Carlebach was a mile from my home so it was a no-brainer to merely walk across the street in cold weather. Though I knew a couple of people at Ramath Orah, I was somewhat anxious walking through the doors alone. Now my anxiety was about being the new kid on the block, not the black kid nor the non-Orthodox kid, precisely because most Orthodox Jews I met made me feel accepted, racially that is, despite my Conservative conversion; it did not take long to feel comfortable.

Ramath Orah is located a few blocks from Columbia University and the Jewish Theological Seminary. The mixture of faculty, administrators, students from both institutions and local residents made for a heimish community, a down-to-earth environment.

Returning from synagogue one Shabbat afternoon, I opened the elevator door, started to step in when my body jerked backwards; startled, I immediately withdrew as if I were about to step in quicksand, and walked up the seven flights to my apartment. I was amazed how my association with the Orthodox influenced me, and recalled Rabbi Baruch Goldstein's prediction, "You are going to become Orthodox." No one monitors your behavior, point of fact: it is inappropriate for rabbis to ask you about your level of observance. There is not an expectation upon conversion that a convert will be completely observant, but that over time, one will continue to grow and embrace more observant behaviors. Motivated internally, I purchased two sets of dishes and silverware and had my kitchen koshered.

When Rabbi Fried koshered my kitchen, he said, "Food should not only be healthy, it should be holy." I informed Rabbi Fund of my purchases and he said, "You can't use them until you are Jewish," until I had an Orthodox conversion, "otherwise they won't be kosher." I parked my new purchases next to my couch until I became a "real Jew." I had no idea it would be two years later.

The rationale of Shabbat: ceasing the mundane orientation of the week, letting go of our material agendas, and turning one's attention over to God, to be able to connect, communicate, and integrate on another level of Existence. Shabbat came to be a true day of comforting rest; the day of the week I came to feel the most at ease and experience the least angst. Freed from the weekday goal of maximizing my power in the material world, reading, which I enjoy, went from satisfaction to succulent.

An unexpected jolt came when an Orthodox rabbi said, "I miss eating shrimp." I was surprised at his honesty and amused that his longing for unholy food was still active. I imagined it was intrinsic curiosity that led him to experience the forbidden. Then, seemingly without paradox, he decried Orthodox Jews who eat fish at non-kosher restaurants. He continued to right himself, "I don't permit non-Jews in my home," he said with certitude.

Viscerally, I ejected this idea as soon as I heard it: I learned to separate the myths about Jews when exposed to both the religion and the people at the feet of friendships with Jews, participating in the rituals and celebrations in the homes of Rabbi Baruch Goldstein and son Meyer.

"My children could get interested in their children, and that would not be acceptable," the Rabbi's certitude tightened.

Layered in his even tone was fear, juxtaposed the recognition of the attractiveness and vitality of the other, any other not a Jew. The fear of competition, that his beliefs, faith, and wisdom proffered, may not measure up to his children's personal standards—after all, and after all these years, if he still longed for, or worse, lusted for shrimp, no telling how weak and vulnerable his children could be or become.

Returning home from Carlebach one Shabbat afternoon I warmly greeted Sherry, a friend from B'nai Jeshurun. As we walked up Broadway, I began discussing my entry into the Orthodox world and studying with Rabbi Fund, and she said, "Be careful with Rabbi Fund..."

"Why do you say that," I interrupted.

"Rabbi Fund is a racist."

This racial bombshell left me in confused astonishment. I regrouped and my commonsense led me to further inquiry. I chose to feign ignorance, not informing Sherry that I had been to Rabbi Fund's home for several meals; that he suggested I move to Brooklyn and become a member of his synagogue; that he would find me a wife, and suggested I study Torah in a Brooklyn Yeshiva.

"How is he a racist?"

Sherry said, "I heard him give a talk once, and he referred to non-Jews as 'goyim.'"

Even though I knew goyim referred to non-Jews, and it could be used to denigrate if projected as such, in my six years of study with Rabbi Fund he never used the word and never made derogatory comments about non-Jews. "So how is Rabbi Fund a racist?"

"When he said 'goyim' he was talking about your family."

"My family are goyim," I asserted, "so how is Rabbi Fund a racist?" It wasn't rhetorical but she was so surprised at my response that she had none. Another friend, Elizabeth Koltun said, "I know how the Orthodox are, they are seductive, not telling you what they *really believe*, they are just trying to suck you in, trying to get you to become one of them. Don't let them *get you*."

Several friends from B'nai Jeshurun made denigrating comments, "You went to the bad side," "Ernie went to the dark side," "How can you adhere to all the nonsense *they* do?"

Being unable to participate fully in Orthodox synagogue life, disqualified from reading Torah, Haftorah and giving a dvar Torah—essentially not recognized as a Jew—felt discriminatory because I was qualified to read Torah, Haftorah, and give a dvar Torah; this felt similar to being denied the right to drink water at a public fountain, as in the Jim Crow days of my youth.

I felt like a Jew after my Conservative conversion. How could I not? Developing friendships with Orthodox men and women, I could not phantom a discernible difference in the emotional locus of our identities as Jews. Having placed myself in the not so holy, holy war between Orthodox and non-Orthodox Jews, triboluminescence followed: I decided on an Orthodox conversion because I desired to participate fully in Orthodox synagogue life, and be recognized by all official bodies of Judaism.

I had the privilege to meet Rabbi Elie Weinstock of Congregation Kehilath Jeshurun attending High Holiday services at the suggestion of Irene Susmano. I was invited to a Shabbat meal at Rabbi Weinstock's home where, during conversation, we got to see each other up Torah close and Torah personal. I felt at home in Rabbi Weinstock's home, and freely joined in the Torah discussion. I returned for other Shabbats and classes offered.

In his office, I told him of my desire for an Orthodox conversion. He asked a series of questions to test my knowledge and commitment to Judaism. He said I was ready for conversion but we had to meet with Rabbi Haskel Lookstein, the senior rabbi, to gain final approval.

Rabbi Lookstein's questions included my commitment to observance. I said, "I don't know if I can be perfect in my observance."

He said, "No one is perfect, that is why we have Yom Kippur." At the end of our meeting he said I would be converted in three weeks. Rabbis' Lookstein and Weinstock had investigated my Jewish past, which allowed them to make a relatively quick decision.

My first thought: "Will I know enough to pass?" Still, I was excited. Rabbi Lookstein led the beit din, and pass I did, January 30, 2005. Accompanied by my girlfriend Karen, we then went to celebrate with a handful of friends.

My first Shabbat at Ramath Orah as an Orthodox Jew, I was given an aliyah, reciting the prayer before the reading of the Torah. It was an honor to come before the Torah as an Orthodox Jew. However, being Orthodox contributed a new level of complexity when I fell in love with a non-Orthodox woman.

Karen's Love

We have not come into this exquisite world to hold ourselves hostage from love.

Hafiz

Let me not dawdle, not waste any time…mines and yours

Let me get to the point, be straight forward, stop beating around the bush

let me stop dilly and dallying, dally and dillying

Cut the crap Ernest say it already; why is it so hard to say?

Why is it even harder to do?

Because *it is* harder to do

Maybe, maybe it's just harder to be

But no matter which way I slice it, dice it or it entices

Owning it without stoning it

It is harder to be in one, good one, happy one, sad one, bad one, with anyone, everyone, no one.

There is a problem here Houston

I AM the problem Houston

Here on earth, in the dirt and girth for all its gritty worth

Wish I could go to…trip to the moon real soon, maybe noon

Still need a spoon to be fed in bed

It is not the end, not the beginning, but the long long long pause in between

That is what gets me, got me, won't let me go, got me by the toe of life

Wrangling strangling, cutting of, cutting off; getting on the tree of life

It is not light, Dark; stark; feeling it; now; courage to finally; fi—na—lly

It ain't that bad, been around since the beginning of time, my time, your time, ancient time,

future time, all the time

You understand what I am trying to say, but you want me to say it anyway

OK

Relationships are Hard.

Harder.

Relationships with women, the Hardest thing there is, in the world to do, to be, end of story

That ain't true just as sure I am a Jew

This is only the start, you know it two

Whoever you are waiting for me

I wait for you

* * *

In 2004 as the High Holy days of Rosh Hashanah and Yom Kippur headed toward the New Year, I was launched into one of the themes of the holidays, renewal. It is a time to recast one's ideals, goals, behaviors and at age fifty-eight and still single, the need for an intimate marital relationship was ever present, with vigor. "I'm going to get into a relationship this year. I am going to find someone," I declared. Having previously made such statements, this time I knew it would happen, because it came from the deepest part of my desire, and from the place of my biggest fear of intimacy, to simply trust another person: the terror of overcoming my terror to trust another with my love, to render myself vulnerable to being hurt in loving relationship of the deepest commitment—to get married.

While attending the Martin Luther King Jr. birthday celebration at the Jewish Community Center (JCC) in Manhattan, I saw an attractive woman with an intense look that made me take notice. As she attended to the people who arrived, I realized she was an employee. I wondered who she was, but did not think about her beyond the delight she provided to my eyes.

One evening, riding home on the Broadway bus, I looked up from my newspaper, and she entered and sat directly in front of me. I gathered myself, "Excuse me, don't you work for the JCC?"

She turned and faced me, "Yes, I do."

"My name is Ernest, what's your name?"

A protective cover gripped her face, and she turned away without answering. Assuming she was being cautious, I continued, "I study Hebrew at the JCC and I have seen you there."

Resuming eye contact, she inquired without registering surprise, "Why are you studying Hebrew."

"I'm studying Hebrew because I want to be able to understand the Torah in its original language, and be able to speak in the native tongue."

Her countenance began to thaw, and sensing her defenses lowering, I asked, "What's your name?"

"Karen." And a smile burst forth from the face of her soul and washed over me like a waterfall of orange blossoms and warmed me all over. Brushed back by the unexpected rush of sensual energy that radiated from her, the moment captivated me and I thought, "I want to know this woman."

We met for coffee and during the conversation Karen asked, "How old are you?"

"I'm fifty-eight." Karen's head spun right, jolted, I assumed, because I was twenty-one years her senior. Seamlessly I continued, "I exercise five to six days a week. I eat at the healthy end of the scale…" and as I prattled on, Karen looked at me and I could see that she was still interested in what I had to say. My relatively youthful appearance and slim muscular physique mitigated potential rejection, so I thought.

The descent into intimacy began, and I began free falling, falling free, freely, without an emotional parachute, and kept falling and falling in love with Karen Ruth Sander, like never before, until Love blossomed for me.

In December 2004, I had experienced enough of Karen to say, "I love you." Her eyes widened in disbelief and fear; she looked like she was ready to bolt, and she would have, except there were neither horses to hop-on nor a taxi to hop-in, because we were sitting on her couch.

She asked, "How do you know that?"

"You are Special. You are cut from a different cloth."

"But you have not known me long enough," she replied.

"I have known you three months and I see what you can't see about yourself. You are kind, gentle, a good soul, and it runs deep within you, a core component of your nature. I haven't known you a long time, but I have known you long enough to fall in love with you; this is only the beginning, and my love will grow. I know you don't feel the same way now. But if I'm lucky, you will feel the same way later; and if I'm luckiest, we will know each other a very long time."

Two months later she confessed her love for me. I proposed in December 2005. She accepted and we agreed to marry in April 2006.

I was the first black man Karen dated, and she expressed concern that her mother may not find me acceptable: "because you are black." My age was secondary. Arnold, Karen's father, died in 1997. I met her brother Ron and his then Israeli girlfriend Dania, when we spent New Year's Eve together. My being black was not an issue for Ron or Dania. Karen and I discussed when and where I should meet her mother. Ron offered his support in whatever way that Karen needed. Karen sought counsel from her boss, Rabbi Joy Levitt.

Joy was unsure what Karen, a youthful and attractive thirty-seven, would see in a man twenty-one years her senior. When I met Joy she greeted me warmly, and later said to Karen, "I get it now." Joy also provided Karen with practical advice on how to introduce me to her mother.

The first thing she said, "Present all the good things about Ernest, and how happy and excited you are to share this news with her." That

Karen should talk forthrightly about the "challenges" that exist because I am twenty-one years her senior, and African American. Joy waxed with rabbinic wisdom: "Don't de-emphasize the challenges, show her that you have thought about them and their implications; that you are not twenty years old and naïve, but you are realistic and have considered if you can overcome them; that all relationships have challenges, and you never know how things are going to turn out, even when on the surface all the major variables are aligned. Ask your mother what she thinks of the challenges, and tell her she is free to ask you any questions about her concerns, thoughts and feelings. Then let her meet Ernest as soon as possible, so he is not some big mystery."

Karen took her mother to brunch and told of our meeting and what a wonderful person I am, and that we had been seeing each other exclusively. Karen's mother was happy and surprised that she was dating someone. Overjoyed that Karen was confiding in her, few questions were raised about the potential challenges of me being an African American and the age difference.

Given my prior experience with two white women who said they loved me, I was concerned about being rejected again. I raised the issue with Karen and she said, "Don't worry, whatever my mother says after she meets you won't effect my feelings about you."

"I'm not concerned about *your feelings* changing, but the trajectory of our relationship," I said.

Karen immediately followed up, "No matter what my mother says our relationship will remain viable." Feeling relatively safe, we took the Long Island Railroad to her mother's home. I grew more anxious the closer we got. Karen's mother met us at the railroad station. "Ernest, this is my mother, Ilse."

"It's nice meeting you, Mrs. Sander."

"My name is Ilse, call me Ilse," she countered, annoyed I thought.

We arrived at her home and as I hung-up my coat, Ilse looked at me and said with a smile and lilt in her voice, "You are so tall." I knew then the evening was going to go well. Ilse, Karen, and I, sat in the living room making who-is-this-black-Jewish-man-my-daughter-is-in-love-with conversation. As Ilse and I measured each other, unexpectedly, our souls touched and we introduced ourselves beneath the layer of polite conversation, and began to know each other as an aura of orange blossoms radiated from her. Ilse's soul was palpable, and when she was out of earshot, I said, "You got your soul from your mother." It was love at first sight. When we left I told Karen, "I am in love with two Sander women."

Then I wondered why Karen was unnecessarily concerned about me meeting her mother. Ilse accepted me without reservations. Why the need to seek advice from Rabbi Joy Levitt? I concluded that Karen, single woman and never married or engaged, masked her fears about relationships and her concerns about me being black.

When I challenged Karen with this hypothesis, she said nothing. I later discovered that her brother Ron, and his now fiancé Dania, both had the same concern about Ilse, and neither had an issue with my being black. Being a descendant of Africa, the black man labeled as inferior species, is such an all powerful specter, pervasive, and insidious, that the reality of its effect on one's psyche is not likely to be evidenced until one is personally challenged, where one's core values lie—in the protected sanctuary of one's uncensored thoughts, uncensored feelings—which may lie shrouded in one's consciousness, or lay dormant in the unconscious, until prodded into the repertoire of human behavior.

I had no concern about Karen meeting my family because my mom and both sisters are not racially vexed; all went well when both families got together.

One year after meeting Karen, I was at her mom's home celebrating Rosh Hashanah and bringing in the New Year. Ilse said, "I want to talk to you." We sat down and spoke about a range of topics, including what it means to be Jewish. I said there must be a commitment to Judaism and teaching children the Jewish tradition otherwise they are not likely to remain connected to the Jewish faith. Ilse readily concurred and said she wanted her grandchildren to be raised as Jews.

I said, "Well, it is lucky for you I am Jewish. Karen said she would have gone out with me even if I was not Jewish."

Sitting with her back against the chair, Ilse blanched and sat up. Speaking with unnecessary fear she said, "No." as if that corrected what she heard. "She said that?"

Nodding slowly, I said, "Yes. I asked her because I wanted to know."

Shaking her head, Ilse waved her hand in disgust, "I could not deal with that. I could not deal with you. I want the Jewish Tradition to be passed down to my grandchildren; I want them to be Jewish."

"Why is that important to you?"

"Why? Why I want the Tradition handed down? I thought you would understand."

"I do understand for me, but I want to hear it from you, and not make assumptions about your thoughts and feelings."

"I see in my synagogue that some have married non-Jews and they are involved, and that is really okay, for them; but for me: mixed marriages, they just don't work."

As the new melody of "mixed marriage" played between the lines, I said, "I agree. You lived in Germany, experienced the gradual erosion of Jewish prerogative, escaped Hitler, and have used that life experience as a teaching tool to pass down the Jewish heritage. But what can Karen and I give our children? Karen can't, in the twenty-first century, give them your firsthand experience in Germany. We only have the Jewish Tradition: holidays, rituals, synagogues, and Torah to pass down, the Eternal of Judaism. That's why I feel it is necessary to incorporate as much Jewish observance into our life together.

Karen and I had what seemed on its face, irreconcilable differences. I had a kosher kitchen, she did not. I did not travel on Shabbat, talk on the phone or watch television, and attended synagogue weekly. Karen traveled on Shabbat, talked on the phone, watched television, and she did not belong to a synagogue. Still, I remained madly in love with Karen as we tried to broker a life style that would be acceptable to both of us—that is, create a space for the two of us to be happy, individually, as a couple, and as a Jewish family with children.

A philosophy and pragmatism I embrace wholeheartedly and dub, The Integrity of Compromise, which is intrinsic to a happy marriage, tested the limits of my capacity to walk my talk, as Karen and I attempted to build a loving foundation that would lead to a Jewish life style that we both stated we wanted. What exactly would be the "style" in the Jewish life that we could both live with and be able to live with each other, without anger or regret, or left feeling coerced or unduly compromised as we duly compromised?

It was the weekly Shabbat experience that created our greatest challenge to stay a couple. I wanted to light candles, have Shabbat meals, and attend services regularly. Karen came to appreciate lighting candles, having Shabbat meals, and said she would attend synagogue when we had a family.

Karen chose the Water's Edge restaurant as the venue for our ceremony. The wedding day arrived and it was a morning of glorious sunshine, with bursting yellow blossoms radiating against the canvas of an impeccable blue sky that painted our spirits blemish free, and hugged us brightly. Ron Sander picked me up from my apartment in his car and drove me to the Water's Edge.

We emerged from the car and were standing a few feet from the Water's Edge dock, which tethered a white yacht, still, in the calm waters, and paradise gained was apparent. I looked across the shimmering river and the Manhattan skyline revealed a montage of buildings of varied glass and stone, color, texture, height, width, singularly stellar and each building exuded a deceptive quiet pride in its exquisite architectural radiance. I sauntered into the front door as the beautiful scene, serving as backdrop, shown through the glass enclosed panels.

My first task was to tie Ron's tie into a Windsor knot as I did for him in Tel Aviv when he married Dania four months earlier. The men gathered for the Tish. The room was festive as fifty men, with Rabbis Weinstock and Meir Fund leading the singing of songs and nigguns, rhythmically banged on the table and all clapped hands as the voices soared. Then it was time to go. Rabbi Fund said, "Who will walk with you?"

I shrugged and said, "No one in particular."

Rabbi Fund took his arm and wrapped it around mine and said, "I will walk you out." A visceral tinge caressed: I felt honored to have my teacher of Torah bless me with his caring. Surrounded on all sides by men singing and dancing in charismatic harmony with the drummer and guitar player, I was in a state of ecstasy living my fantasy, as my entourage accompanied me to Karen, who awaited me to confirm in the bedeken, that she was the woman I intended to marry. I arrived and lifted Karen's veil, thereby confirming she was the bride that I wanted to marry.

The ceremony began. I walked up the aisle holding the hands of my mom and my cousin Stephen. Beyond an excitement I could not anticipate, I was unaware I was smiling with the force of a deep and unrelenting animation until I saw the photographs that captured how wondrously happy I was to be getting married. After my four year old niece Jordyn, the flower girl, drew adoring oozes and ahs dropping rose pedals on the aisle, everyone rose to their feet when Karen and Ilse stood at the room's entrance.

Karen, in her ivory colored dress, and Ilse were poised and beautiful, exquisite, pristine living sculptures, as they waited for the wedding march to begin. When the music began Karen smiled a radiant smile that propelled a magnetic energy that galvanized the spirit of the day. Momentarily stunned at the Great Happiness Karen radiated because she was about to marry me, a wave of electrical charges streaked through my body. Everyone in the room was mesmerized and absorbed Karen's Great Happiness, then released it back into the ether of our ceremony creating a cocoon of ever expanding exuberance and, plain ole fun. Rabbi Fund charismatically engaged the guests in a Chasidic niggun, gently urging their participation as he wandered down the aisle. Rabbi Lee Friedlander gave a beautiful speech, and then Rabbi Weinstock performed the wedding ceremony with a grace that warmed my soul. We exchanged vows and then Rabbi Weinstock said, "Break the glass." I crushed the glass and the room erupted in shouts of "mazal tov" as Karen jumped joyously into my arms and our future. After our private time together, we joined our guests and reveled in celebrating as the band sent everyone into rapturous delight; a delight we both longed for, and hoped for; relishing the portraiture covered in sunlight and grace, the portraiture of our love.

*   *   *

On December 24, 2007 at 9:21 AM, Eliot Akiva Adams aka Elie Akiva was born. He weighed 5 lbs. 14oz. And Karen and I weighed in with maximum joy at the birth of our son. Ilse was present and basked in the miracle of life, her first grandchild at age eighty. The biggest miracle was that I fathered Eliot—the old fashioned way—because I was diagnosed with prostate cancer in December 1994. I was warned that if I did not have a medically sanctioned treatment, metastasis loomed and death would follow shortly. I did not succumb to the fear engendered by the diagnosis and prognosis. Instead, I chose to go against the medical advice. If not, Karen and I would not exist; Eliot would not exist; and Ilse would not have had a grandchild. Fortunately, I found and followed the nutritional advice of Dr. Jack O. Taylor.

Thank God!

Addendum: Karen attends synagogue with Elie Akiva.

Dr. Jack O. Taylor holds a Master of Science Degree in Biology/

Human Nutrition from Bridgeport University in Connecticut in addition to his Doctor's degree from Logan College in St. Louis, Missouri. He is licensed by the State of New York as a Certified Dietitian-Nutritionist. He holds Diplomate Status with the American Clinical Board of Nutrition and is a member of the examining board. The ACBN is composed of board certified primary care physicians of all disciplines—including MD, DO, DC—who have gone further than the doctorate degree to become board certified in nutrition.

Epilogue

Out of the huts of history's shame,
I rise
Up from a past rooted in pain
I rise
I'm a black ocean, leaping and wide
Welling and swelling I bear in the tide
Leaving behind nights of terror and fear
I rise
Into a daybreak that's wondrously clear
I rise
Bringing the gifts that my ancestors gave
I am the dream and the hope of the slave
I rise
I rise
I rise

Maya Angelou

Human liberty is not about holy people doing holy things; it is, rather, about unholy people doing holy things

Rabbi Yosef Y. Jacobson

Change is the most reliable parameter in life, and one must change with the times, or, the times will not change: time changes; times change. The America I was born into is not the America I live in now; it is a better America; it is also an America that needs to be better. Black youth in the Sixties challenged America and demanded Perfection: we sought higher education, higher level of respect and treatment, full equality, and even higher level of Self-respect and Dignity. We wanted it all and all wanted it, but we did not know we were flying in the ether, that our righteous and morally deserved ambitions would crash land, due to the gravity of human limitation, exposed in the inherent slow pace of people's capacity to change—both black and white—their ideas, values, beliefs, and behavior.

Maturing while transitioning from Negro, colored, to black to Black, was a search for self-recognition with human qualities draped in an unspoken but implied African motif; Afro American to African American was the step by step explicit embrace of Africa as our black, Black, progenitor, while simultaneously proclaiming our American identity: African American, not just another hyphenated American, but a psychological necessity, socially essential, and at this time in American history, indispensable. With Negro, colored, black and Black jettisoned as inadequate identifiers and qualifiers, to the historical winds of change, it is now time, the right time, to consider a more calculated, deliberate gust of wind that will *gracefully discard blackness* to a respectful grave—times change.

That there is a black culture that has been forged by the humanity and creative talents of African descendants does not discount my argument: even as I fervently say that I felt wholesome and whole, felt the connection, a trembling sensation, between my African heritage and my humanity, when I listened to Alex Haley describe his historical and biological links to Africa. When cultural paradigms, blackness in this instance, are used as refuge, to descend and seek cover, and not as steps on the universal ladder of achievement, then one is doomed to the narrow platform that *being black through blackness* is the only valid expression, which masks the fear of looking up, then climbing up, to obtain a more comprehensive and inclusive view of life.

Listening to a New York City high school black girl from Guyana on WNYC National Public Radio one morning, she described how black classmates and peers chastised her for being able to speak Dutch because it was a white language and she was black. Sounding exasperated, she both defended herself and enlightened her classmate's narrow view: "There is no state called Black." I was thunderstruck by her cogent response, how insightful and accurate it was, yet, how not quite accurate. There is no geographic body of land called Black, but there is a body of matter that may accurately be called Black, a physiological state known as: the State of Mind. This circumscribed view of the world, the Black State of Mind, literally living from the locus of one's head, and not what is actual before you, predicated on irrational fear, triggered by rational circumspection, is the single best reason to calibrate a wind that deletes blackness as defensive moat and conscripted place to live. However, an essential corollary to comprehend: one may identify being black with vigorous pride, without having blackness as stultifying impediment.

All African Americans have been exposed to blackness, many influenced by blackness, ipso facto, merely growing up black in the American culture. Given the congenital origin of the United States, with African and African American slaves defined by the Founding Fathers as intellectually and morally inferior in the Constitution, and embedded in the mental and physical constitutions of the Founding Fathers and American culture, it may credibly be put forth that blackness was the offspring of the rapacious and unholy union of black hopelessness and the propounding of the Founding Fathers racist ideology and practices.

After the legal demise of Jim Crow, the inferiority complex refused to die a natural death—likely due to its lengthy history, socially acceptable bashing of black Americans, and failure to significantly change the feelings and thinking in both black and white Americans. The most insidious aspect of the inferiority complex is its repressive nature, the way it skulks around and insinuates itself into one's character without warning or notice—infecting choices and decisions. The hidden infections, disguised medicinally, as free choice, poisoned my mom, dad, sisters Florita and Audrey, Uncle Charlie, childhood friends and numerous others known and unknown to me, compromising the lives they lived. Notwithstanding the notable success of many African Americans, the perception and internalization of blacks as inferior remain, treacherously alive, subtle, and well camouflaged among both blacks and whites, in the reservoir of fears we harbor about the other, the history in our voices, and the rock hard myths that refuse to dissolve.

Blackness manifests uniquely and in multiple ways for each individual. It is engaging for many, less for others, tangential for some. It may not be in conscious awareness or felt as detrimental to self-interest even when it is "in motion." In the spring of 2000 I attended an award ceremony in Washington D.C., sponsored by The Foundation for Ethnic Understanding, dedicated to promoting racial harmony, improving understanding and reducing bigotry between ethnic communities, an organization headed by Marc Schneier, an Orthodox rabbi and co-founded in 1989 with the late Joseph Papp. The current president of the board is Russell Simmons, black Hip-Hop mogul and entrepreneur. The event was to honor black and Jewish members of Congress for mutual cooperation. Awards were received by Congresspersons Shelia Jackson and Nita Lowy. Attendees included Representatives Charles Rangel, Jerrold Nadler, Gary Ackerman, John Lewis, Ed Towns, Elliot Engel, Benjamin Gilman, Bob Filner and members of the NAACP.

The ceremony was held in a small room in the Capitol. Charles Rangel, distinguished Congressman from New York, stood on the podium opposite Bob Filner, a Jewish Congressman from California, and addressed him. Representative Rangel began his remarks, accurately, with firm conviction, but categorically, "I am black, and you are Jewish…" The history in his voice, the racial history of America, determined the impossibility of a black man and a Jew being housed in one body and one soul. Inside my head I screamed, "Look, look, I am black and I am Jewish." I was stunned because no one seemed to notice that I sat with a yarmulke on my head, three steps from the podium, and none of the Jews present disabused the false suggestion.

The most enduring characteristic of my blackness was and is my induced American inferiority complex and its complexity: silent but deadly, it plagued me unconsciously for the first thirty years of my life, infecting my thinking, goals, and the steps and slow pace of the steps I took to look up, then climb up, from the refuge and shelter of the Basement. Extreme anxiety, signature piece of my inferiority, manifested when I had taken law school exams, which at times did not feel like extreme anxiety, like the time I decided not to take the bar exam upon graduation from law school; it certainly did not feel like an inferiority complex—even though I flagellated myself as "a dumb and stupid nigger," and sometimes worse—until I entered psychotherapy when the Whispers War was consciously unleashed, initially ravaging me viciously, until I was able to sort out and sort through my troubled self from my true self—the mythological from the biological. I then learned to cope with the specific pain of inferiority's complexity, then "manage" it. My career trajectory was altered and I will always wonder if, I would have practiced law, if, but for, feeling the complexity and complexion of inferiority? How much would my grades have been altered if I had not been self-terrorized? My confidence severely depleted? Would the drive to be a psychologist have been the same?

My feelings of inferiority and the accompanying shame of my failures or perceived underachievement have abated significantly but have not been permanently deleted: When the Whispers War and anxiety, rarely extreme these days, make an appearance, as usual always uninvited, I struggle less intensely and for shorter periods; it was my good fortune to be able to recognize, own, and struggle with my demons despite the pain. It is my fervent hope, and fear, that I don't pass the baton of inferiority to the next generation.

In 1976 I was in group psychotherapy—with eight whites and three blacks—and naturally got to know and share intimacies with the group members. I became friends with Ben, a white Jewish man. One day right before the session was to begin, we sat lounging in the therapist's office and talking on the couch, and with great affection and sincerity, he waxed, "You are different," smiling a clever smile as the words rolled slowly out of his mouth. Where he was rolling to, I had no idea. "You are like one of us." His sincerity dispelled and warmed my uncertainty. "You are one of us."

I assumed he meant an accepted member of the group. Damn, I felt good.

"You are not black," said with respectful conviction.

"No, no, no, no, no," I raised up in alarm. Ben was looking through me and not at me. He was on the right train but the wrong track. "I'm a Black Man," I said with full force and convocation of my African heritage, indispensable. I had felt invisible and rejected and insulted trying to buy a hamburger as a Negro boy in the South; now I felt invisible and rejected and insulted as a Black Man in the North while experiencing trust, acceptance and intimacy with the very same white man. Upset beyond measure, when the group began I told of Ben's de-appellation of my identity, stripping away my "brotherhood," my blackness. Like the red white and blue plaid patched soft quilt-like blanket that granted me a sense of safety, and that I used to comfort myself when a young child, blackness had become my trusty "blanket." Even though we shared the deepest of intimate and painful details of our lives, I did not trust Ben or any of the other whites as white, to be supportive of me in the trenches of battle as a Black man.

I was upset, embarrassed, and insulted because I felt naked, stripped of a significant aspect of my identity, the most independent, and most notorious of the white American culture. My blackness, raw, immature, "genetically" distended, doomed to exist in the nighttime of my fears and hopes, was integral to my integrity and self-image: for without blackness, I was invisible to myself, amorphous, existing only as a wisp of a man. I was not able to look up from the shelter of blackness, thus, unable to understand that even though Ben did not look at me, his personal affection, his de-appellation, did look through me, but looked straight to and directly at my humanity. Today I would say to Ben, "I am black, and I am like you; you are white, and you are like me. You are one of us."

Hence, I did not take umbrage when Rabbi Woznica, during one of our conversations said, "I forgot you were black." Neither his memory nor his vision were impaired as Rabbi Woznica found black and human me, in good standing, and, acceptable to be a Jew.

Seemingly, I was capable and open to veritable friendships with whites by my membership in the psychotherapy group, and I was, but I did not develop a genuine, down-home, intimate relationship until Meyer Goldstein blossomed in my life. Living in the same building and having frequent close contact allowed me to see that Meyer, with an honest smile and sincere laughter, was guileless, who genuinely liked me, came to trust me, and his assumption about me and the human species was: "I believe what people tell me until proven otherwise."

My modus operandi, in my damn near paranoid mode was, "No one is trusted until proven otherwise."

He was the first person I met who appeared with no "agenda," and the first person I let into the inner sanctum of my Trust, of my soul. Our association led me to his father, Rabbi Baruch Goldstein, and uncle, Rabbi Noah Golinkin and his family, and their invitation to enter their lives was accepted because they proved, over time, they were truly worthy of my Trust. Being welcomed by both families to experience their religious tradition began to dispel my anti-white and anti-Semitic notions. There was a noticeable absence of concern about my being black, and for the first time in my black life, it felt good to be "invisible" as *they* looked right through me, embraced my character and touched my soul.

It took me twenty years to trust the Goldsteins perennial stellar treatment, even as they accepted me unconditionally, creating a place for me in their family. When Riva Goldstein died in 2001, funeral services were held at Beth Israel Synagogue, Baruch's former pulpit. All the Goldsteins, Baruch, Meyer, Sue-Rita, Jonah, Liza, Sarah, and Daniel formed a line as people queued up to pay their respects. As the congregants and the Goldsteins were exchanging greetings and condolences, I was sitting down observing how enthusiastically Baruch was being received, admiring the love and respect paid to him and Riva; it was amazing to witness. Baruch saw me sitting down, popped out of the line and came over to me. "What are you doing sitting here?"

Unsure of the import of his question, I said, "I'm just taking in what's going on, they really love Riva and you."

"So why are you sitting here? Come," he grabbed my arm and pulled me up, "come with me, join us, you should be up here, you are part of the family."

I felt a little embarrassed, and conspicuously black, as I joined the line with *my* family, and the congregants greeted and treated me like the family member that I was.

As the Goldsteins love watered my rock-hard racial posture, my blackness, ever so slowly, disintegrated and dissolved, no longer integral to my existence; it took two decades for my blackness to reconstitute itself, to return to its origin, to the soul given to me by God, to my humanity; no longer camouflaged, a "New World" was revealed, an expanse of new people and new opportunities, with new paths to choose, if I only so desired. I capitalized. I freely chose to walk through this new found corridor, and became a Jew. Then I wondered: has American Jewry always been open to welcoming black people into the tribe? Or did it become, like many American institutions, more open during the turmoil of the Sixties? What is most germane in the twenty-first century is that any black person, who so desires, may explore Judaism with an open mind, an open heart, and be accepted as a black person, accepted as a Jew, without fear of rejection.

I was shocked when Rabbi Woznica said that some white Jews "... will want to be your friend because you are black," but I was also surprised when Rabbi Matalon asked how I would handle racist Jews. Different mindsets for sure, and both contained truths that should be acknowledged. There were no other issues of race discussed or even alluded to by either rabbi, and none were needed, for me. Most black Americans enter predominantly white environments, no matter how collegial, with caution, and are prepared, at minimum, for "friendly fire"—but know that it is not likely to be "deadly fire" in the Jewish community. Like the time the Jewish man asked me in a synagogue, with a yarmulke on my head, "Are you a black Jew?" In actuality, it is more accurate to say it is ignorance and lack of sensitivity that lead to such exchanges. I characterize such an exchange as "friendly fire" because it burns, feels caustic, and potentially lethal; the only way it could have become "deadly fire" was if I succumbed to the "false" positive of my pain—"false" because it was only one individual and not representative of my experiences as a Jew.

At this juncture in American social life, white Jews are naturally curious as to how a black person arrived to be sitting next to them in synagogue—ninety-nine percent of the time there is no malice aforethought. One black Jewish friend bristles and feels insulted when asked his status as a Jew. Given my individual personality, I am flattered that white Jews have enough interest to ask me the typical question: "How did you become a Jew?" Even when asked, "Are you a Jew?"—though the official protocol states one Jew is not supposed to ask another Jew how they came to be Jewish.

White Jews that are born and raised in America are white, and like all white Americans, have been subject to whiteness: from the cultural drumbeat orchestrated by the Constitution defining black people as "three fifths of a man," "race science" theory, and biblical Providence of the superiority of whites over blacks. White Americans don't think about *being* white on a daily basis, because America was founded as a nation of white presumption, priority, and privilege; these white "rights" are embedded in every fragment of American life, and continue to impact today. Like blackness, whiteness manifests uniquely and in multiple ways for each individual; it is engaging for many, less for others, tangential for some. Whiteness may not be in conscious awareness, and/or a white person may not feel that he has insulted, disregarded, or degraded black Americans, even when the behavior is "in motion." For example, when my synagogue mates thought I was too fragile and not capable of summarizing my Bar Mitzvah dvar Torah. Moreover, in the wicked world of oppression and its corrupt hierarchy, African Americans are also vulnerable to whiteness, as propagated by the American culture, as well as blackness, as "auto-immune" cultural disorder. This "twofer," has been a deadly duo to African American psychological health.

I was flummoxed and flabbergasted when told by white non-Orthodox Jews that I should not associate with white Orthodox Jews because they are racist. The common cliché came to mind: "It takes one to know one." Choosing wisely, but out of fear and ignorance, I voided the Orthodox and avoided their synagogues. I assumed that the people who loved me would not steer me wrong, thus I did not challenge their notion, and their judgment overruled Rabbi Woznica's recommendation. Living as a Jew and among Jews revealed this was an example, not uncommon, of the intramural competition between the differing Jewish denominations.

There is a segment of the Orthodox Jewish community that believe, sincerely, that all non-Orthodox Jews are *not real Jews*; the non-Orthodox Jews in contrast consider the Orthodox as primitive, self-righteous, and archaic. Some Jews consider marriage between the Orthodox and non-Orthodox an abomination and at best a "mixed marriage." In Israel there is "Civil War" animosity between religious and secular Jews, and the Orthodox and non-Orthodox rabbinate. Orthodoxy is the only legitimate branch of Judaism officially recognized in Israel—non-Orthodox rabbis are not permitted to perform legally recognized marriages or conversions. The imagined unity of Jews and Israel that I admired and envied from afar all my life, shattered into shards of disappointing reality. In my humble opinion, I believe the Orthodox deserve holy credit for adhering to the traditional Tradition; a healthy tension between non-Orthodox and Orthodox serves Jews and Judaism well.

Being African American and Jewish is a lot easier than most black people may imagine, and for sure, a lot of other people. One caveat: do not expect Perfection. There will be disagreements about politics and racial issues, seemingly on racial grounds, but there will be a lot more common ground, if we keep our heads above ground. That is, all of us in our humanity, having grown up in the American racial culture, are capable of misunderstanding or misstatements that are insensitive and offensive; the key to getting past the perceived offense, as in a successful marriage or any long term relationship, don't presume the worst based on the fears engendered, negative thoughts, and emotions aroused within oneself. If you feel that you have been attacked or devalued, accompanied by the resulting anger, anxiety, or unsafe feelings that emerge from within, try and "absorb" the "blow" of the words found demeaning, but do not be politely enraged, while hiding your true feelings, then permanently disregarding the other person without a conversation.

As an alternative, you may allow your thoughts to unfold in private, consult others to get their understanding, then return to discuss what angered you in an air of conciliation. Obviously, such an endeavor is not easy, and *I am not very good at it*, but I do struggle in trying to give the *other* person the presumption of innocence. In the law of human interaction, in trying to be in a relationship, when an error occurs the capacity for forgiveness must be greater than the ability to err, and even greater than the negative emotions aroused, no matter how inappropriate or egregious.

Affirmative Action, overwhelmingly supported by African Americans—because it provides entrée to our wishes and dreams—will remain a hot-button issue for many reasons in the larger American culture and the same can be expected in the American Jewish community. I don't dare make any guess about the numbers of American Jews who are pro and con Affirmative Action, but I have met many on both sides of the issue. From personal experience, I can say that whatever position taken, no one presented as a die-hard racist, and it did not negatively influence my interpersonal relationships. That is, there were honest disagreements—admittedly, when opposition was voiced, I felt a visceral response that left me feeling uneasy—and since I am an Affirmative Action baby, proudly so, I always convey my personal story as example qua example—I would not have become a Jew without it—and then move on.

Whether I was a student, tourist, or visiting Israel for personal reasons, I have always been welcomed by Israeli citizens. I fell deeply in love with Israel, and Israel, requited my love. Being in Israel makes me feel refreshed and is a place that feels like home, and if I can ever afford it, I will purchase a home there. Given the ongoing security issues, all Americans, especially black Americans, need to know that close scrutiny is absolutely necessary to maximize safety as one enters and leaves the country. One may feel profiled, and to a certain extent you will be, especially if you are a black man traveling alone. But do not forget, and remember, Israel is also concerned about your safety and well-being in its rigorous efforts to thwart the irrational mindsets of its foes.

In 1999 Judy Reid called me because her nephew Shawn Davis was scheduled to go to Israel as an exchange student for two weeks. "How do you think he will be treated?" She asked. Her second question, "Will he be safe?" Her voice was heavy with concern, and I decided to answer the easier question first.

"Shawn will be chaperoned and the necessary security precautions will be taken to insure his wellbeing." As I answered, I understood that Shawn's safety in Israel was not her primary concern: I assumed she and all the parents had received assurances from the Israeli sponsors of the trip. I knew that both her questions were really one question. I heard the history in her voice and began thinking of the best way to answer her unspoken primary worry. I put a frame on the picture that she had in her mind: "Will my nephew be rejected and mistreated because he is black? Will he be accepted and treated well by the Jews?" I recounted my two earlier visits to Israel and the favorable treatment I received, but sensing I had not fully won her over, I said, "Shawn will not be discriminated against, nor suffer any disrespect or abuse in Israel because he is a black adolescent male. Israel does not have the same racial culture and history as we have here in America. *The Jewish people will welcome your nephew* and he will be treated well."

A soft sigh, suggesting resolution, told me I allayed her anxiety. I later learned that Shawn had a memorable time.

I wrote this book because I was inspired by Sandee Brawarsky and my own latent ambitions. When you write a book exploring your life, you venture down unforeseen emotional roadways and psychological alleys; that harbor rich insights and "new" experiences. You discover knowledge and understanding not previously known about yourself, your family, friends, and culture. I confess there was an absence of noble reason when I first began to write and desired to publish my story, but as I wrote and learned and re-learned about all aspects of the largeness and complexity of life and my life, I realized on the journey that there was something worth saying and saying honestly, something worth spending time on besides the gratification you receive exploring yourself for weeks, months and years, seemingly without end. Beside my personal gain of alleviating the shame of my failures and the centuries of inferiority I had ingested and believed, I have come to understand that my failures and struggles came to define a core part of my character and a strength I had not fully recognized; that life has not been easy, but it has been easier because of the fierce battles I have waged, even when the blows were of knockout proportion and pain.

As many people that read this book, there will be many more varied interpretations and understandings. I won't predict how I think they will chart on the opinion polls, but it is my sincere hope that all Americans, especially African Americans, given the ongoing amorphous legacy of American slavery, will see my humanity, and my Holiness, in my shame, inferiority, failures, efforts, tears, fears, successes and joys, and may they please, God willing, and, with God's help, may they see their own.

Acknowledgments

I have had the idea of being an author since college days, wishing and wanting, but not having a topic to write about. Becoming a Jew provided the motivation and satisfied my long held thirst. However, writing this book took an effort and fortitude that I did not anticipate. With no formal training my initial efforts were met with criticism that made me numb: I was told I needed a ghostwriter. Rejecting that idea, I attended the Ernest Adams School of Writing, learning the craft by reading classic works and popular authors. Writing is a task done alone, seemingly, but communication of your creation requires intimate and honest feedback. I was fortunate to have proven authors read my second attempt, encourage and guide me. Ari Goldman and Sam Freedman, Columbia University Journalism professors said, "You are a writer. This is what you should be doing." Sam provided guidance in how to write the prologue and other writing tips. In addition, Sam let me audit his renowned non-fiction writing class which further enhanced my writing knowledge. Allan Kozinn, New York Times music critic, provided melodious advice on writing the epilogue and astute criticism on other chapters. Grace Edwards was the editor who made my story flow more smoothly. Gregg Linn and Rabbi Mark Cohen provided guidance for the glossary. There were countless others who read and gave me feedback, not always pleasant, and not always accepted, but always appreciated.

The idea for writing this book came from Sandee Brawarsky. She planted the idea, watered it and encouraged me throughout the entire process. I am forever grateful. Florita and Audrey's memories filled in a lot of gaps. My dad encouraged me when I began the writing process. My mom provided details of her life, our life, which made my story, our story. To my beautiful wife Karen, who provided sage advice, supported and tolerated me and: I adore you.

I alone am responsible for all the shortcomings.

Glossary

Aliyah: being called to recite the blessings before and after the Torah portion is read.

Ashkenazi: Jews with ancestry from Central and Eastern Europe and Russia are Ashkenazim

Aufruf: the custom of calling up the groom for an aliyah on the Shabbat before his wedding.

Bar Mitzvah: ceremony for a boy at age thirteen marking assumption of adult religious obligations.

Bat Mitzvah: ceremony for a girl at age twelve or thirteen marking assumption of adult religious obligations.

Bedeken: a ceremony at a wedding where the groom inspects the bride to make sure she is the one he intends to marry.

Beit Din: a religious court of law that adjudicate matters of a religious nature in a dispute between parties.

Bema: pulpit

Ben: son

Beshert: in a marital context it means the 'intended one', the person whom the bride or groom was fated to marry.

Door of No Return: located on Goree Island, it is the last portal passed through by Africans being shipped to the New World for slavery.

Dvar Torah: a sermon intended to explain the meaning of a passage of the Torah; it is given during the Torah service

Divrei Torah: plural of dvar Torah.

Gabai: the person who reminds everyone who has an aliya when it is their time to ascend the bema.

Goy: a non-Jew.

Goyim: plural of goy.

Haftorah: a selection from the writings of the Prophets read after the Torah is read on Shabbat.

Haftorah trop: cantillation marks that indicate how the reader of the Haftorah chants each word.

Halacha: refers to Jewish law; coming from the Biblical injunction to 'walk in His ways'

Havdalah: a ceremony marking the end of Shabbat or religious holiday and the beginning of the new week.

Heimish: Yiddish…means warm or friendly.

Ketubah: wedding contract where a man agrees to provide for his wife.

Kiddush: ceremonial blessing over wine; and the subsequent meal after the Shabbat service is therefore called the Kiddush.

Kiddush cup: goblet used at religious ceremonies in which wine is blessed.

Kol Nidre: "all vows." Refers to the first service of Yom Kippur, in which congregants ask G-d to release them from all vows that they might make from one Yom Kippur until the next.

Leyne: The reading of the Torah portion either on Shabbat or during the weekday reading.

Lynch law: the lynching of African Americans by mobs of whites; a carnival atmosphere sometimes occurred as people took pictures and later sold them.

Maariv: the evening service. See Shacharit.

Mechitza: a partition separating men from women during Orthodox religious services.

Matzah: unleavened bread used by the Israelites during their escape from Egypt and eaten in place of bread during the Passover holiday.

Mikvah: is a ritual bath used to cleanse or purify for religious purposes and before resuming sexual relations following a woman's menstrual period.

Mincha: the afternoon service. See Shacharit

Minyan: a quorum of ten Jewish adults needed to conduct a religious service.

Mossad: Israeli spy agency.

Neshama: soul; the very essence of being.

Nigguns: religious wordless melodies.

Parasha: division of the biblical text into weekly sections which are read at the Torah service.

Ruach: spirit; literally means "wind."

Sephardim: those with Spanish/Portuguese ancestry are Sephardim, and those from the Middle East (including Syrians, Moroccans, Egyptians, etc.) are also called "Sephardim."

Shabbat: the Sabbath; the seventh day of the week, starting at sundown on Friday and ending 25 hours later. Following the example set in the Creation Story, in which God completed the creation on the 7th day, no work is permitted on Shabbat.

Shabbos Goy: a non-Jew who performs those tasks prohibited by Jewish law on the Sabbath.

Shacharit: the morning prayer service; one of three prayer services mandated by the Talmud; the others, Mincha and Maariv.

Shiur: a class where a religious topic is taught.

Simchat Torah: Holiday celebrating the completion of the reading of the Torah and the beginning of the cycle again.

Talis: prayer shawl worn by men on Shabbat morning

Talis bag: to hold the talis

Tashlich: the custom of symbolically casting away one's sins during Rosh Hashanah (Jewish New Year) when bread crumbs are thrown into a body of water.

Tiferet: beauty and truth

Tikkum Olam: repairing the world; commonly used to justify social action as a way of "perfecting the world."

Tish: a table; a wedding ceremony when men gather to sing songs and sign the ketubah.

Torah: The Five Books of Moses. It's the history of the Jewish people from the creation of the world until their travel into the Promised Land. It is also the source of laws that govern Jewish life, and is supplemented by the laws of the Talmud.

Torah service: the part of the Shabbat or weekday service when the Torah is read.

Torah trop: cantillation marks indicating how the Torah reader chants each word.

Yad: a pointer with a closed hand at the top having its forefinger outstretched. Used by Torah readers to follow the text, and to prevent the hand from touching the parchment which may be damaged by oils on the hand.

Ulpan: a class for intensive Hebrew study, often meeting several hours a day.